PRAISE OR PERFORMANCE?

Praise or Performance?

A Short Theological Introduction to the Psalter

MICHAEL S. MOORE

WIPF & STOCK · Eugene, Oregon

PRAISE OR PERFORMANCE?
A Short Theological Introduction to the Psalter

Copyright © 2025 Michael S. Moore. All rights reserved. Except for brief quotations in critical publications or reviews, no part of this book may be reproduced in any manner without prior written permission from the publisher. Write: Permissions, Wipf and Stock Publishers, 199 W. 8th Ave., Suite 3, Eugene, OR 97401.

Wipf & Stock
An Imprint of Wipf and Stock Publishers
199 W. 8th Ave., Suite 3
Eugene, OR 97401

www.wipfandstock.com

PAPERBACK ISBN: 979-8-3852-2193-6
HARDCOVER ISBN: 979-8-3852-2194-3
EBOOK ISBN: 979-8-3852-2195-0

VERSION NUMBER 03/20/25

Contents

Abbreviations | vii

Introductory Remarks | 1

1 Why Lament? | 16
2 Why Praise? | 52
3 Primary Theological Motifs in the Psalter | 77
4 What is Sung About Today in Congregational Worship? | 94
5 Concluding Remarks | 105

Bibliography | 107
Name Index | 127
Scripture Index | 133

Abbreviations

The abbreviations below complement those listed in the SBL Book of Style

*	hypothetical emendation
ʹ	indicates reverse side of a cuneiform tablet
//	in parallel with
1QH	The *Hodayot* scroll from Qumran Cave 1
AcBib	Academia Biblica
AfO	*Archiv für Orientforschung*
AG	Analecta Gregoriana
AGH	*Die akkadische Gebetsserie "Handerhebung"* (Ebeling)
AIL	Ancient Israel and Its Literature
AJEC	Ancient Judaism and Early Christianity
ANE	Ancient Near East
ANEM	Ancient Near Eastern Monographs
AOAT	Alter Orient und Altes Testament
Arab	Arabic
ATR	*Australasian Theological Review*
AYBC	Anchor Yale Bible Commentaries
AYBD	*Anchor Yale Bible Dictionary*. Edited by D. N. Freedman. 6 Vols. 1992. Reprint. New Haven: Yale University Press, 2008.
AYBRL	Anchor Yale Bible Research Library
b.	*Talmud Bavli*

BBR	*Bulletin of Biblical Research*
BCE	"before the common era"
BCOT	Baker Commentary on the Old Testament
BCP	Book of Common Prayer
BI	*Biblical Interpretation*
Bib	*Biblica*
BibInt	Biblical Interpretation Series
BJSUCSD	Biblical and Judaic Studies at the University of California, San Diego
BN	*Biblische Notizen*
BT	*The Babylonian Theodicy*
BTB	*Biblical Theology Bulletin*
BTS	Biblisch-Theologische Studien
BZ	*Biblische Zeitschrift*
BZABR	Beihefte zur Zeitschrift für Altorientische und Biblische Rechtsgeschichte
CAD	*Chicago Assyrian Dictionary*
CAI	*A Corpus of Ammonite Inscriptions*, 2nd Ed. Edited by W. E. Aufrecht. University Park, PA: Eisenbrauns, 2019.
CANE	*Civilizations of the Ancient Near East*, 1995. Edited by J. Sasson. Peabody, MA; Hendrickson, 2000.
CAT	*The Cuneiform Alphabetic Texts from Ugarit, Ras Ibn Hani, and Other Places*, edited by M. Dietrich *et al.* Münster: Ugarit-Verlag, 1995.
CBD	*Catholic Bible Dictionary*
CBQ	*Catholic Biblical Quarterly*
CBQMS	Catholic Biblical Quarterly Monograph Series
CCLI	Christian Copyright Licensing International
CCM	Contemporary Christian Music
CD	Cairo Damascus Document
CE	common era
CMHE	*Canaanite Myth and Hebrew Epic: Essays in the History of the Religion of Israel*, by Frank Moore Cross. Cambridge: Harvard University Press, 1973.
COS	*Context of Scripture*, 3 Vols., edited by W. W. Hallo and K. L. Younger. Leiden: Brill, 1997–2002.

CRB	Cahiers de la *Revue Biblique*
CSEL	*Corpus Scriptorum Ecclesiasticorum Latinorum*
CT	*Christianity Today*
CTQ	*Concordia Theological Quarterly*
CWM	Christian Worship Music
D	intensive form of the Semitic verb
DAT	*Deir ʿAllā Texts*
DBWE	*Dietrich Bonhoeffer Works English*. Edited by H. G. Barker and M. S. Brocker. Translated by D. W. Stott. Minneapolis: Augsburg Fortress, 2013.
DDD	*Dictionary of Deities and Demons*, 2nd Ed. Edited by K. van der Toorn *et al*. Leiden, Brill, 1999.
DH	Deuteronomistic Historian (Joshua-Kings)
DILA	*The Dialogue of Ipu-Wer with the Lord of All*
DJD	*Discoveries in the Judean Desert*
DN	divine name
DOTPr	*Dictionary of Old Testament Prophets*. Edited by M. J. Boda & J. G. McConville. Downers Grove: InterVarsity Press, 2012.
DOTW	*Dictionary of Old Testament Wisdom, Poetry and Writings*. Edited by T. Longman & P. Enns. Downers Grove: InterVarsity Press, 2008.
DSS	Dead Sea Scrolls
DSSSE	*The Dead Sea Scrolls Study Edition*, edited by F. G. Martínez and J. C. Tigchelaar. 2 Vols. Leiden: Brill, 1997.
DTTM	*Dictionary of Targumim, Talmud, and Midrashic Literature*. Edited by M. Jastrow. London, Luzac, 1903.
EA	*Die El Amarna Tafeln*, edited by J. A. Knudtzon, 1915. Reprint. Aalen: Zeller, 1964.
EDSS	*Encyclopedia of the Dead Sea Scrolls*. Edited by L. H. Schiffman and J. C. VanderKam. Oxford: Oxford University Press, 2000.
Ee	*Enūma eliš*
Eg	Egyptian
EHJ	*Encyclopedia of the Historical Jesus*. Edited by C. A. Evans. New York: Routledge, 2008.
EJ	*Encyclopedia Judaica*. 22 Vols. Edited by M. Berenbaum and F. Skolnick. Detroit: MacMillan Reference, 2007.

EPRO	Etudes préliminaires aux religions orientales dans l'empire romain
ER	*Encyclopedia of Religion.* Edited by L. Jones. New York: MacMillan Reference, 2005.
Erra	*The Erra Epic*
et alia	"and others" (Lat)
ETL	*Ephemerides Theologicae Lovanienses*
et passim	"and throughout" (Lat)
ExpTim	*Expository Times*
FAT	Forschungen zum Alten Testament
FB	Forschung zur Bibel
FH	*Fides et Historia*
FRLANT	Forschungen zur Religion und Literatur des Alten und Neuen Testaments
G	simple form of the semitic verb
GE	*Gilgamesh Epic*
Gk	Greek
GKC	*Gesenius' Hebrew Grammar.* Edited by E. Kautzsch. Trans. by A. E. Cowley. Oxford: Oxford University Press, 1910.
GN	geographic name
GNT	Greek New Testament
HAL	*Hebraisches und aramaisches Lexicon zum Alten Testament.* Edited by L. Koehler, W. Baumgartner and J. Stamm. 3rd Ed. Leiden: Brill, 1967, 1995, 2004.
HAT	*Handkommentar zum Alten Testament*
HBS	*Herders Biblische Studien*
HBT	*Horizons in Biblical Theology*
HeBAI	*Hebrew Bible and Ancient Israel*
HS	*Hebrew Studies*
HSM	Harvard Semitic Monographs
HTR	*Harvard Theological Review*
HTS	Harvard Theological Studies
HUCA	*Hebrew Union College Annual*
HUCASup	*Hebrew Union College Annual* Supplement
ICC	International Critical Commentary
IDB	*Interpreter's Dictionary of the Bible*

IJST	*International Journal of Systematic Theology*
Int	*Interpretation*
JAOS	*Journal of the American Oriental Society*
JBQ	*Jewish Bible Quarterly*
JEHS	*Journal of the Evangelical Homiletics Society*
JESOT	*Journal for the Evangelical Study of the Old Testament*
JETS	*Journal of the Evangelical Theological Society*
JJS	*Journal of Jewish Studies*
JNES	*Journal of Near Eastern Studies*
JPT	*Journal of Psychology and Theology*
JQR	*Jewish Quarterly Review*
JR	*Journal of Religion*
JRE	*Journal of Religious Ethics*
JSFSC	*Journal of Spiritual Formation and Soul Care*
JSOT	*Journal for the Study of the Old Testament*
JSOTSup	Journal for the Study of the Old Testament Supplement Series
JSS	*Journal of Semitic Studies*
JTI	*Journal of Theological Interpretation*
JTISup	Journal of Theological Interpretation Supplements
JTS	*Journal of Theological Studies*
KAI	*Kanaanäische und aramäischen Inschriften*, 5th Ed. Edited by H. Donner and W. Röllig. Wiesbaden, Harrassowitz, 2002.
KBo	*Keilschrifttexte aus Boghazköi*
KJV	King James Version
KHAT	Kurzer Handkommentar zum Alten Testament
Lane	*An Arabic-English Lexicon*, by Edward W. Lane. London: Williams and Norgate, 1863.
Lat	Latin
LCBI	Literary Currents in Biblical Interpretation
LGRB	Lives of Great Religious Books
LHBOTS	Library of Hebrew Bible/Old Testament Studies
Lud	*Ludlul bēl nēmeqi*
LW	*Luther's Works*. Translated by F. C. Ahrens. Minneapolis: Fortress, 1960.
m.	masculine

m.	*Mishnah*
Maq	*Die assyrische Beschwörungssammlung Maqlû*. Translated by G. Meier. Horn: Berger, 1937.
MC	Mesopotamian Civilizations
MIO	*Mitteilungen des Instituts für Orientforschung*
Miss	*Missiology*
MJTM	*McMaster Journal of Theology and Ministry*
MT	Masoretic Text
NA	Neo-Assyrian
NAS	New American Standard Version
NCBC	New Century Bible Commentary
NIBC	New International Biblical Commentary
NIV	New International Version
NKJV	New King James Version
NRSV	New Revised Standard Version
OB	Old Babylonian
OBC	The Oxford Bible Commentary
OBO	Orbis Biblicus et Orientalis
OBT	Overtures to Biblical Theology
OG	Old Greek (Septuagint, LXX)
OT	Old Testament
OTE	*Old Testament Essays*
OTL	Old Testament Library
OTP	*Old Testament Pseudepigrapha*, 2 Vols. Edited by J. Charlesworth. Garden City, NY: Doubleday, 1985.
OTR	Old Testament Readings
OtSt	Oudtestamentische Studiën
OWC	Oxford World's Classics
OWN	*Oudtestamentlich Werkgezelschap in Nederland*
pace	"with all due respect" (Lat)
passim	"elsewhere" (Lat)
PBM	Paternoster Biblical Monographs
PH	Primeval History (Gen 1–11)
Ph	Phoenician
pl.	plural

PN	proper name
PresG	*Presbyterian Guardian*
ProEccl	*Pro Ecclesia*
PRSt	*Perspectives in Religious Studies*
PRU	*Le Palais Royale d'Ougarit*
PSB	*Princeton Seminary Bulletin*
PSSD	*Payne Smith Syriac Dictionary*. Oxford: Clarendon Press, 1903.
ptc.	participle
PTMS	Princeton Theological Monograph Series
Q	Qur'an
R.	Rabbi
Rab.	Rabbah (as in *Gen. Rab.* or *Lam. Rab.*)
RB	*Revue biblique*
RBL	*Review of Biblical Literature*
RBS	Resources for Biblical Study
REC	Reformed Expository Commentary
RelEd	*Religious Education*
RelS	*Religious Studies*
ResQ	*Restoration Quarterly*
RevExp	*Review and Expositor*
RHR	*Revue de l'histoire des religions*
R&T	*Religion and Theology*
RTU	*Religious Texts from Ugarit* (Wyatt)
Š	causative form of the semitic verb
SAA	State Archives of Assyria
SAALT	State Archives of Assyria Literary Texts
SAAS	State Archives of Assyria Studies
Sam	Samaritan Pentateuch
SANE	Sources of the Ancient Near East
SANT	Studien zum Alten und Neuen Testaments
SB	Standard Babylonian
SBL	Society of Biblical Literature
SBLDS	Society of Biblical Literature Dissertation Series
SBLGPBS	Society of Biblical Literature Global Perspectives on Biblical Scholarship

SBLRBS	Society of Biblical Literature Resources for Biblical Study
SBLSymS	Society of Biblical Literature Symposium Series
SBS	Stuttgarter Bibelstudien
SBT	Studies in Biblical Theology
SBTS	Sources for Biblical and Theological Study
SCJ	*Stone-Campbell Journal*
SBAnt	*Studies in the Bible and Antiquity*
sg.	singular
SHANE	Studies in the History and Culture of the Ancient Near East
SID	*Studies in Interreligious Dialogue*
SocR	*Sociology of Religion*
SOTSMS	Society for Old Testament Studies Monograph Series
SSJS	Shofar Supplements in Jewish Studies
Sum	Sumerian
Šur	*Šurpu: A Collection of Sumerian and Akkadian I Incantations*, 1958. Translated by E. Reiner. *AfO* 11. Osnabrück: Biblio-Verlag, 1970.
t.	*Tosefta*
TBl	*Theologische Blätter*
TDOT	*Theological Dictionary of the Old Testament*
TEP	*Tale of the Eloquent Peasant* (Parkinson)
TgJ	Targum Jonathan
TgN	Targum Neofiti
TgO	Targum Onkelos
Th	*Theology*
TLZ	*Theologische Literaturzeitung*
TZ	*Theologische Zeitschrift*
UBCS	Understanding the Bible Commentary Series
Ug	Ugaritic
UNP	*Ugaritic Narrative Poetry*, edited by S. B. Parker. WAW 9. Atlanta: Society of Biblical Literature, 1997
UT	*Ugaritic Textbook*, by Cyrus H. Gordon. AnOr 38. Rome: Pontifical Biblical Institute, 1965
VT	*Vetus Testamentum*
VTSup	Supplements to *Vetus Testamentum*

WAW	Writings from the Ancient World
WBC	Word Biblical Commentary
Wehr	Wehr, Hans. *A Dictionary of Modern Written Arabic*, edited by J. Milton Cowan. Ithaca, NY: Cornell University Press, 1966.
WGRW	Writings from the Greco-Roman World
WOC	*An Introduction to Biblical Hebrew Syntax*, by B. K. Waltke and M. O'Connor. Winona Lake: Eisenbrauns, 1990.
WTJ	*Westminster Theological Journal*
WUNT	Wissenschaftliche Untersuchungen zum Neuen Testament
WW	*Word & World*
ZA	*Zeitschrift für Assyriologie und vorderasiatische Archäologie*
ZAR	*Zeitschrift für Altorientalische und Biblische Rechtsgeschichte*
ZAW	*Zeitschrift für die alttestamentliche Wissenschaft*
ZDMG	*Zeitschrift der deutschen morgenländischen Gesellschaft*
ZThK	*Zeitschrift für Theologie und Kirche*

Introductory Remarks

AFTER RELOCATING THE FAMILY to Phoenix in the summertime, the decision is quickly made to take a day trip north to Sedona, a touristy village known for its ruddy red peaks, modern jazz festivals, Pink Jeep Tours... and cooler temperatures. Drawing closer to the city a road sign suddenly pops into view which reads, "We use the 1662 Book of Common Prayer." Researching what this might mean, it soon becomes clear that the 1662 Book of Common Prayer is as sacred to many Anglicans as the 1611 King James Bible is to many fundamentalists.[1] Both retain the Elizabethan language of their day ("thee," "thou," "thine"), and just as the KJV has gone through several accommodations,[2] so has the BCP.[3] The purpose of the sign is to alert passersby to the fact that the worship protocols of *this* congregation go all the way back to what they believe to be the BCP's "authorized" version.

The pages below post another, similar sign: "We use the Bible's Book of Common Prayer,"[4] a phrase drafted by Dietrich Bonhoeffer (and others)

---

1. White (*Controversy*, 13–29) details the convoluted history of the KJV Only movement.

2. Cf. e.g., the ET known as the NKJV (Naudé and Miller-Naudé, "Revisions").

3. Jacobs (*Prayer*) details the history of these accommodations.

4. The original title of the Psalter is תהלים ("praises"). OG translates this as Ψάλμοι ("Psalms"), and eventually it comes to be known in Christian circles as the βίβλος ψαλμῶν ("Book of Psalms," Luke 20:42; Acts 1:20). Westermann (*Psalms*, 20) prefers to call it an anthology of "hymns," while Barton ("Willows," 84) designates it "the hymnbook of God's people." Kselman ("Psalms," 775) depicts the Psalter as "a collection of sung poetic prayers," while Harrichand ("Lament," 102) dubs it a "prayer manual." Haberman (*Psalms*, xv) calls it "the world's first prayer book," but of course this is

1

to describe the book of Psalms.[5] The goal is simple: to help contemporary worshipers (re)discover the spiritual power embedded in their prayer book. Granted, contemporary interest in this subject ranges somewhere between active disinterest and passive indifference,[6] but to worshipers concerned about the health and welfare of their congregations the concern is quite real.[7] The pages below are hardly the first to address it because, as Gary Anderson points out, "The book of Psalms is a staple for prayer for both Jews and Christians."[8] Alan Ross agrees, noting that worshipers "have for centuries sung, prayed, and expounded" the Psalter.[9] As early as the 4th century, for example, Athanasius of Alexandria (d. 373) depicts it as a mirror reflecting "all of human life," for "no matter what you seek—whether it be repentance or confession or relief from trouble—each of these things the Psalter shows you how to do, and in each case the words you want are written down for you, enabling you to say them as your own."[10] Impressed by its breadth *as well as* its depth, Ambrose of Milan (d. 397) hails the way it provides "instruction from history, teaching from the law, prediction from prophecy, and chastisement from denunciation," suggesting that "anyone with eyes to see may discover in it a complete gymnasium for the soul."[11]

---

inaccurate. The Sumerian prayers to Dumuzi uncovered at Nippur (Radau, *Prayers*), the Hittite prayers of Mursili II (Gurney, *Prayers*), and the Assyrian prayers in *AGH* all predate תהלים.

5. Cf. Bonhoeffer, *Prayerbook*; Holladay, *Prayerbook*. Limburg ("Psalms," 524) prefers to call the Psalter a "worship book." Schaper ("Psalter," 173) points out that an "extraordinary number of textual witnesses" testifies to the fact that the Psalter, "both in its Hebrew original and its Greek version, as well as its Old Latin and Vulgate renderings, is a pillar, probably the main pillar, of the Jewish and Christian liturgical traditions." Janowski (*Arguing*, xvi) observes that one of the Psalter's main attractions is that it is simultaneously both "strange and familiar."

6. Phillips (*Hymnal*, 1) asks, "Who reads a hymnal? Hardly anyone today, and that has been the case for at least a century of English-language religious practice. Even singing from hymnals is now on the decline, as congregations increasingly move to projecting the lyrics of hymns and praise songs onto large screens."

7. Woods et al. ("Kerygma," 92) lament the fact that "church musicians, worship leaders, songwriters, not to mention average worshipers, do not know philosophically and theologically what they are all about when it comes to worship," and that "without a biblically-informed model we run the risk of producing and performing worship music that is inarticulate and driven by cultural trends."

8. Anderson, "Imprecation," 267. Thomas (*Acts*, 22) points out that "today's Church may be unfamiliar with the Psalms, but NT Christians knew them well and cited them often."

9. Ross, *Psalms*, 11. Atwood ("Poetry," 1) recognizes that "the Psalms have been central to the life of the church since its earliest days."

10. Athanasius, "Letter to Marcellinus," 116.

11. Ambrose, *Explanatio Psalmorum* 1.4, 8. N. T. Wright (*Psalms*, 2) finds in the

Augustine of Hippo (d. 430) credits it for "rekindling" in his spirit a passionate desire "to recite them, if I could, all over the world against the *typhus* of the human race."[12]

Medieval reformer Martin Luther (d. 1546) describes the Psalter as "a little Bible . . . so that anyone who cannot read the whole Bible has almost an entire summary of it here, comprised in one little book."[13] John Calvin (d. 1564) calls it "an anatomy for all parts of the soul,"[14] and John Donne (d. 1631) calls it "the manna of the church," for just "as manna tastes to every man like that which he most desires, so does the Psalter minister instruction and satisfaction to every man in every emergency."[15] Switching to a gardening metaphor, Eugene Peterson (d. 2018) compares the Psalter to a rake or hoe, hailing it as "the best tool available for working the faith."[16] Worshipers can "choose to ignore the Psalms," he warns, "but by so doing they are not thereby excluded from praying, but will have to hack their way through formidable territory by trial and error and with inferior tools."[17] Literary critic Robert Alter calls the Psalter "the most urgently, personally present of all the books of the Bible,"[18] philosopher Emmanuel Lévinas (d. 1995) calls it "a book of pure spirituality,"[19] and poet Rainer Maria Rilke (d. 1926) calls it "one of the few books in which one can bring every bit of oneself under shelter, however distraught."[20]

To be sure, readers from very different backgrounds admire different aspects of the Psalter,[21] but for those committed to "working the faith" it's

---

Psalter a judicious balance of "power and passion, horrendous misery and unrestrained jubilation, tender sensitivity and powerful hope."

12. Augustine, *Confessions* 9.4. Lat *typhus* is a transliteration of Gk τῦφος, a medical term meaning "debilitating fever" (Hippocrates, *Epid.* 4.2) and later, "vanity, arrogance, delusion" (Polybius, *Hist.* 3.81.9).

13. Luther, "Preface." Robinson (*Inspiration*, 269) insists that "the Book of Psalms is not only the living and passionate utterance of Israel's piety at its highest, but also supplies the data for an epitome of Old Testament theology," and Anderson ("Creed," 284) notes that the Psalter includes most of the major themes of the OT: "Election and covenant, rejection and restoration, *Heilsgeschichte*, creation, and providence, the way of life and the way of death".

14. Calvin, *Psalms* 1.xxxvii. The term נפש ("soul") plays a substantive role in the Psalter (e.g., Pss 6:3; 7:5; 13:2; 16:9; 19:7; 22:20; 23:3; 25:1; 30:3, 12 *et passim*).

15. Donne, "Sermon," 150.

16. Peterson, *Psalms*, 2.

17. Peterson, *Psalms*, 4. Cf. Tucker, "Psalms," 578–93.

18. Alter, *Psalms*, xiii.

19. Lévinas, *Outside*, 121.

20. Rilke, *Letters*, 126.

21. Proposing that the term עלמות ("young women") in the superscription to Psalm

commonly understood that prayer is one of the most difficult of all spiritual disciplines.[22] Richard Foster believes this is because prayer is the discipline best able to "catapult" worshipers "onto the frontier of spiritual life."[23] Standing in the shadow of these testimonials, Thomas Merton (d. 1968) raises several questions:

> "Why has the Church always considered the Psalms to be her most perfect book of prayer? Does she love the Psalms merely because they are ancient, venerable religious poems? Merely out of conservative refusal to change? Or does she use them because she has been commanded to do so by God? Does she sing them merely because they are the inspired word of God?" No, he replies, for "the Church likes what is old not because it is old, but because it is *young*."

For Merton the Psalter, though chronologically old, is a living wellspring from which worshipers "drink divine praise at its pure and stainless source."[24] Engaging these questions from another angle altogether, C. S. Lewis imagines a dialogue between an older demon (Screwtape) and his young protégé (Wormwood) over how to sabotage the prayer-life of his human "client": (a) "The best thing," he suggests, "is to keep him from the serious intention of praying altogether," but if this fails, then (b) persuade him "to produce in himself a vaguely devotional mood in which real concentration of will and intelligence have no part." But if this fails as well, then (c) "teach him to estimate the value of each prayer by its success in producing the desired feeling."[25] *Summary:* In light of these testimonials is it appropriate to ask

---

46 "is a technical term referring to women's voices and that this heading suggests that this song should be sung by women," Farmer ("Psalms," 146) argues that the psalmist's reference to the "God of Jacob" in 46:7 does not "prevent women from claiming the God of that tradition as their own."

22. Foster (*Celebration*) lists the spiritual disciplines as meditation, fasting, study, simplicity, solitude, submission, service, confession, worship, guidance, celebration, and prayer.

23. Foster, *Celebration*, 33. Gerstenberger (*Petition*, 1) contends that prayer is "a common experience for all humanity because, inherently, humans cannot avoid relating themselves to the outside world nor searching for place and meaning in the theater in which they find themselves." Bonhoeffer (*Prayerbook*, 27) adds that "when read only occasionally," the Psalms "are too overwhelming in design and power," but when prayed "seriously and regularly they soon invite other, little devotional prayers to take a vacation."

24. Merton, *Psalms*, 7. Jeremiah uses similar language: "My people have committed two evils: they have forsaken me, the fountain of living water, and dug out cisterns for themselves, cracked cisterns which can hold no water" (Jer 2:13).

25. Lewis's *Screwtape Letters* (here letter #4) is widely hailed as a keenly insightful

whether or to what degree the Psalter is still considered to be strong enough to protect Wormwood's "clients" from his demonic designs?[26]

From a literary-historical perspective the Psalter stands alongside many other "great texts" from the ancient world, a literary masterpiece fully comparable to anything written by Homer or Vergil, Sîn-lēqi-unnini, or Ilimilku.[27] The superscriptional headings[28] framing many of these compositions identify several things, not least the "genre/type" of each psalm[29] via deceptively simple terms like שיר,[30] מזמור,[31] תפלה,[32] משכיל,[33] שגיון,[34] מכתם,[35] and תהלה.[36] Yet some of these terms remain lexicographically obscure[37] and

---

examination of prayer. Goldingay (*Psalms*, 448) observes a recurring pattern in the Psalms where a suppliant recalls a past answer to prayer, then reengages that answer with another prayer.

26. Pemberton addresses the lament-praise polarity in two volumes: the first (*Hurting with God*) helps worshipers learn how to pray honestly and holistically, while the second (*After Lament*) helps them learn how to praise God unpretentiously.

27. These are the authors/editors of the Iliad and Odyssey, the Aeneid, the Gilgamesh Epic, and the Ba'al Epic. Reiner ("Literatur," 210) delimits "great texts" to myths, epics, autobiographies, propaganda literature, poetry (including hymns and prayers), love lyrics, laments, elegies, wisdom literature (both philosophical and didactic), humorous literature, and elevated prose. Foster (*Muses*, 13–18) basically agrees with this taxonomy.

28. 116 of the 150 canonical psalms (77%) have superscriptions.

29. Responding to Kynes (*Obituary*, 2), Fox ("Theses," 75) argues that "genre" is not an illegitimate term, but following Frow (*Genre*, 63–67) Sneed ("Methods," 30) suggests that "genre" is better replaced by the term "mode." Ferris (*Lament*, 153, 63) argues (a) that the constituents of a given genre need not be completely uniform, and (b) that they need not be understood as originally functioning in only one *Sitz im Leben*. Much more may be said, but Millar (*Calling*, 137) is probably right to regret how much contemporary Psalms research focuses on "genre wars."

30. "Song." Cf. Pss 30, 45, 46, *et alia*. Of interest also is the fact that, in spite of a few passages like Ps 81:2–3, very little direction is given toward matters of instrumentation (cf. discussion in Anderson, *Depths*, 8–9).

31. "Song." Cf. Pss 3, 4, 5, 6 *et alia*.

32. "Prayer, praise." Cf. Pss 17, 42, 86, 142 *et alia*.

33. "Wisdom song." Cf. Pss 32, 41, 42, 78 *et alia*.

34. Unknown. Cf. Ps 7:1. OG ψαλμός ("psalm"); Vg *psalmus* ("psalm"); Syr omits. Hab 3:1 reads, "A prayer (תפלה) of the prophet Habakkuk according to שגינות."

35. Unknown. Cf. Pss 16:1 and the first verses of 56–60. OG reads στηλογραφία ("stele-inscription"); Vg. *tituli inscriptio* ("inscription title"); Syr omits.

36. "Praise." Cf. Ps 145:1. OG αἴνεσις ("praise"); Vg *laudatio* ("praise"). Syr omits.

37. One of the least understood terms is סלה ("Selah"), a word mentioned over 70 times in the Psalter (cf. *CBD* 822), translated in OG as διάψαλμα ("musical interlude?"); Vg *diapsalma*; Syr and Tg omit. Smith ("Inspiration," 253–59) freely acknowledges the difficulties involved in defining these terms.

this invites contemporary interpreters to bypass them,[38] choosing instead to classify the Psalms within "modern" categories; i.e., in terms of their *macro-structure* and/or *micro-structure*.[39] Working within the *first* of these rubrics, students like Gerald Wilson,[40] Jerome Creach,[41] Erhard Gerstenberger,[42] Clinton McCann,[43] Patrick Ho,[44] Jean-Marie Auwers,[45] Nancy DeClaissé-Walford,[46] Joseph Brennan,[47] and David Howard (among others) justifiably protest the fact that most contemporary studies of the Psalms focus predominantly upon micro-structural concerns,[48] discounting its identity as a carefully structured literary text.[49] Yet with regard to the *second* rubric it's

---

38. Yet Gerstenberger (*Petition*, 2) cautions that even though "we have to use our own modes of thinking and rubrics," we should "always be mindful of their inadequacy over against ancient models."

39. Janowski (*Arguing*, xiii) labels these approaches *Psalter*exegese (macrostructural) and *Psalmen*exegese (microstructural). Anderson ("Imprecatory," 279) argues that "if the life of prayer is not merely that of learning words but knowing the occasions on which they are to be used, then the historical critical method will be of limited value." Millar (*Calling*, 137) contends that "those longing to harness the power of the Psalms for personal or community devotion stand side by side with those whose primary interest is uncovering the practice and development of the Israelite cult," and Bellinger ("Psalms," 33) argues that the Psalter's theological value comes not so much from its literary-historical origins as the fact that it is "sung by a worshiping community."

40. Wilson, *Psalter*, 1–11.

41. Creach, *Refuge*, 122–26.

42. Gerstenberger, "Psalter," 3–13.

43. McCann, *Psalms*, 25–50.

44. Ho, *Design*. McCann (*Design*) claims that "Ho's work is the most comprehensive attempt to date to explore the shape and shaping of the Book of Psalms."

45. Auwers, *Psautier*, 27–29.

46. DeClaissé-Walford, *Psalter*, 31–35.

47. Brennan ("Harmonies," 26–27) insists that "the Psalter has not developed in a haphazard and arbitrary way, but has been carefully woven together so that previously independent compositions, or smaller collections of such compositions, now comment on or respond to one another. Hence, for a proper understanding of the Psalter it is not enough to study each of its 150 components in the historical context from which it originally springs. They must all be studied in their relationship to each other, since all of them together convey more than they do if looked at separately."

48. Howard (*Structure*, 20). Abernethy ("Psalms," 659–80) examines the macro-structure of the Psalter over against the book of Isaiah, pointing out that both have dual introductions, central hinges, and corollary emphases on Torah observance, the nations, divine kingship in Zion, and worship.

49. This directly challenges Driver's (*Introduction*, 351) remark that "the order of the individual psalms appears often to have been determined by accidental causes," not to mention Augustine's ("Psalm 150," 449) remark that "the arrangement of the Psalms . . . contains the secret of a mighty mystery." More recently Boyle ("Psalms," 194) claims that "the Psalter has so far resisted any consensus in structural logic." Macrostructural

impossible to chronicle the history of Psalms research without mentioning the work of Hermann Gunkel (d. 1932), the exegete responsible for identifying within the Psalter a variegated collection of several *types*:[50] lament psalms (individual[51] and communal[52]), *thanksgiving* psalms (communal[53] and individual[54]), *praise* psalms,[55] *royal* psalms,[56] *Zion* psalms,[57] *wisdom* psalms,[58] *alphabetic* psalms,[59] *historical* psalms,[60] *pilgrimage* psalms,[61] *reprisal* psalms,[62] and *hybrid* psalms.[63] Prior to Gunkel most interpreters read

---

concerns are of great interest today, in part, because it is now known that the canonical Psalter is not the only Jewish prayerbook of the Second Temple period. OG includes an "extra psalm" (Ps 151), the Syriac Psalter includes several more, and the Qumran caves yield a number of psalmic compositions inspired, if not actually composed by a figure simply known as מורה הצדק ("Teacher of Righteousness,"; 1QpHab 2.2; 5.10; 7.4). Cf. Sanders (*Psalms Scroll*); Flint (*Psalters*); Davage ("Psalms"); Swanson ("Qumran," 247–62); and Moore (*Babbler*, 94–121).

50. Gunkel (*Psalmen*) uses the term *Gattungen*, which translates into English as "genres/types," recognizing that within each type there are various *degrees* of overlap because (a) so many psalms fit into more than one type (e.g., the mention of Zion in a lament psalm or the mention of reprisal in a psalm of thanksgiving); and (b) "*Gattungen* are theoretical constructions since practically no instances of a pure *Gattung* exist" (Prinsloo, "Psalms," 364).

51. Pss 13, 22, 25, 26, 28, 31, 35, 42–43, 51, 52, 54, 71, 77, 86, 88, 102, 120, 130, 142.

52. Pss 12, 44, 60, 74, 79, 80, 83, 85, 94, 123.

53. Pss 67, 75, 107, 136.

54. Pss 30, 32, 33, 66, 118:19–29, 138. Muck ("Psalm," 8) holds every psalm to be "personal in form even when they appear in communal or hymnodic voice."

55. Pss 8, 19:1–6, 29, 34, 40, 65, 93, 97, 98. Foster prefers to call Ps 29 a "call to praise" ("Praise," 76–77).

56. Pss 47, 93, 95, 96, 97, 98, 99, 100.

57. Pss 2, 9, 20, 48, 50, 65, 84, 87.

58. Pss 1, 14, 19:7–14; 53, 119. Shying away from the classification "wisdom," Mays ("Torah-Psalms," 12) argues that the focus on Torah in Pss 1, 19, and 119 is designed to "provide an introduction to and a perspective" on the Psalter as a whole.

59. Each line of Pss 9–10, 25, 34, 37, 111, 112, 119, and 145 begins with a successive letter of the Hebrew alphabet; i.e., an acrostic.

60. Pss 74, 78, 95:7–11, 105, 106.

61. Pss 120–34 each begin with the phrase שיר המעלות ("a song of ascents").

62. Pss 57–59, 69, 109, 137, 139, and 149 are sometimes called "imprecatory" or "vengeful" psalms. Lewis (*Psalms*, 27) calls them "maledictory psalms."

63. Murphy ("Wisdom," 163), e.g., thinks that Ps 32 contains characteristics of the "thanksgiving psalm" as well as a measurable amount of "didactic influence," arguing that its "wisdom elements (vv. 1, 2; 8–11) serve as a wrapper for a thanksgiving testimony (vv. 3–7) addressed to God directly." Similarly, Perdue (*Wisdom*, 312) sees in Ps 119 "a didactic poem borrowing heavily from the form of lament," while Brettler ("Psalm," 373–95) interprets Ps 136 as an example of *inner-biblical exegesis* of a Torah text (Deut 10:17—11:5).

the Psalter as a random collection of privately composed religious poems.[64] Gunkel rejects this approach as "romantic" and "naive,"[65] but one of his students, Sigmund Mowinckel (d. 1965), takes a very different tack, proposing a "one-size-fits-all"[66] hypothesis that the Psalter is the product of just one major source—the priestly cult.[67] Intrigued by the way the royal psalms celebrate the enthronement of Yhwh (and his vicar the king),[68] as well as the priestly rituals used by neighboring cultures to celebrate the enthronements of *their* deities (e.g., the crowning of Marduk in the Babylonian Creation Epic),[69] Mowinckel argues that the Hebrew royal psalms must serve a similar function in an *Israelite* enthronement ritual.[70]

Most of his colleagues, however, reject this proposal on two counts: (1) the bulk of the Hebrew Psalter overwhelmingly focuses on lament, not enthronement,[71] and (2) nowhere does Tanak even mention an "Israelite enthronement ritual."[72] In one particularly pointed response Heidelberg

---

64. Two proponents of this view today are Young (*Introduction*, 309) and Futato (*Psalms*, 68–69).

65. Muilenberg ("Form Criticism," 7), however, refuses to let Gunkel's identification of different types inordinately dismiss the artistry of individual poets, and Foster ("Praise," 75) insists that "Gunkel's view of genre constitutes only one particular view." Meanwhile, Brueggemann (*Message*, 169) proposes that "theodicy is a characteristically Jewish concern that may correct or discipline a Christian restriction of the Psalms to privatistic, romantic spirituality."

66. Weiser (*Psalms*, 62–63, 378, 617) and Dahood (*Psalms*) also gravitate to the "one-size-fits-all" approach, the first by tracing everything in the Psalter to the "covenant renewal ceremony" (Josh 24:1–26), and the second by reading it predominantly through lenses shaped almost exclusively by Canaanite mythic texts (cf. Moore, "Dahood," 35–38).

67. Mowinckel (*Psalms*, 109–39). Westermann ("Klage," 44) points out that Gunkel already recognizes the temple cult as *one* of the Psalter's *Sitze im Leben*, but that Mowinckel "radicalizes this thesis."

68. N.B. the phrase יהוה מלך ("Yhwh is king") in Pss 93:1; 96:10; 98:1; and 99:1. Futato (*Psalms*, 165) calls these "divine kingship psalms."

69. *Ee* 5.79 reads, "Anšar (embraced) him and published abroad his title, 'Victorious King.'" Cf. Lambert, *Creation*, 3–144.

70. Without engaging Mowinckel directly Howard ("Kingship," 204–5) observes that (a) several of the "seam psalms" linking several of the Psalter's "books" highlight royal motifs; and (b) that this suggests an intentional "pattern of royal psalms."

71. Cf. Moore, *Babbler*, 49–52. Kaiser ("Lamentations" 127–33) finds that 41% of the Psalter alludes in some way to lament (62 of 150 psalms), but Charlesworth (*Hymnbook*, xvii) notices that the *Odes of Solomon*, a pseudepigraphal collection structurally influenced by the Psalter, "includes no lament."

72. Gruenwald (*Rituals*, 1–39) insists that there can be no mythical meaning apart from ritual "activity" (תעשה), and that the latter always precedes the former. Mowinckel's response in his *Vorwort* to the 1966 edition of *Psalmenstudien* (cited in Roberts, "Mowinckel," 105) is (a) the Babylonian *akītu* (New Year) festival celebrates Marduk's

professor Claus Westermann (d. 2000) challenges Mowinckel's presumption that there exists in Israel an "absolute timeless entity called *cult*," presuming instead that in Israelite worship there is an "indissolvable connection with regard to the history of God's dealings with his people," one which "develops gradually in all its various associations; viz., those of time, place, instrumentality, and personnel."[73] Whatever its implications, Jim Roberts wonders whether this dispute has as much to do with the text of the Psalter as it does with a brilliant student's desire to challenge the thinking of his equally brilliant teacher; i.e., that "in contrast to Gunkel, who still holds to the primarily Protestant view of classical liberalism that true piety is individual piety and thus tends to be dismissive of communal expressions of piety, Mowinckel, influenced by the new interest in primitive religion and the stirrings of the liturgical renewal movement, is far more open to the genuineness and importance of communal piety."[74]

Contemporary Psalms research thus stands on a rather dynamic continuum. At one end of this continuum Gunkel's disciples stress the historical desirability of tracing each psalm back to its original *Sitz im Leben* ("situation in life"),[75] while at the other end Wilson and his colleagues emphasize the need to read the Psalter as "great literature"[76] arranged into five scrolls,[77]

---

kingship, so the repeated phrase יהוה מלך ("Yhwh reigns," Ps 94:1; 96:10; 97:1 *et passim*) most likely celebrates Yhwh's kingship at a similar *type* of festival (cf. Bidmead, *Akītu*, 29–41; Roberts, "Mowinckel," 97–115; Moore, *Babbler*, 45–57); and (b) that rather than imagining this festival as something borrowed, it's more likely that it contains components preceding "the well known and well attested autumn and New Year's festival, the feast of tabernacles."

73. Westermann (*Psalms*, 20, 24) goes on to say that "the observation that the life situation of the Psalms is the cult cannot really be right, for that which really, in the last analysis, occurs in the Psalms is prayer." Brueggemann (*Message*, 18) thinks (a) that Westermann "follows the form-critical analysis of Gunkel and rejects the liturgical analysis of Mowinckel," and (b) he urges that "lament is the basic form of psalmic expression, and that most other psalm forms are derived from or responses to the lament."

74. Roberts, "Mowinckel," 97.

75. Creach contends that many "higher critics" tend to "deny Davidic authorship" in order to "determine that the contents of the book come from a variety of religious traditions" (*Refuge*, 12).

76. Anderson (*Depths*, 18–19) states the point quite clearly: "The most important question has to do with the psalms as literature, or better, as poetry. These poems 'create a world,' to use the language of contemporary interpreters of literature . . . The psalms bring us into God's world, which often clashes with the marketing, militaristic world in which, most of the time, we have our being."

77. Book 1 (Pss 1–41), Book 2 (42–72), Book 3 (73–89), Book 4 (90–106), and Book 5 (107–50). Unlike Brueggemann's (*Message*, 11) division of the Psalter into three categories (orientation, disorientation, and reorientation, broadly paralleling Genesis'

probably to mirror the five scrolls of Torah.[78] Without minimizing the significance of this debate or the importance of Psalms research generally,[79] the pages below go on to focus on yet another continuum, one in which the Psalter stands at one end while something else stands at the other. Sociologist Neil Postman explains:

> Television is our culture's principle mode of knowing about itself. Therefore—and this is the critical point—how television stages the world becomes the model for how the world is properly to be staged.... As typography once dictates the style of conducting politics, religion, business, education, law, and other important social matters, television now takes command.[80] In courtrooms, classrooms, operating rooms, board rooms, churches, and even airplanes Americans no longer talk to each other; they entertain each other. They do not exchange ideas; they exchange images. They do not argue with propositions; they argue with good looks, celebrities, and commercials.[81]

---

sequence of creation, un-creation, and re-creation), Foster ("Praise," 75) argues (from a Hellenistic rhetorical perspective) that the Psalter consists of just two categories: *proclamation* and *prayer*, the first to persuade human audiences (including the self), and the second to persuade the deity. Not to be overlooked is Davis's ("Psalm 22," 93) observation that "the *Formgeschichte* project of Hermann Gunkel and his followers establishes the distance between traditional and modern understandings of the historical circumstances in which the Psalms originate. In a deeper sense, however, historical scholarship has confirmed the essential insight that underlies their devotional use: namely, that these songs are the common property of all who worship the God of Israel. Like a blues song, they speak a vividly metaphorical language that is intensely personal and yet not private. It is because of their repeatability as responses of faith to ordinary human experience that the Psalms continue to serve as the single most important resource for both Jewish and Christian prayer, thus exercising profound influence on the practical theologies of those communities."

78. So Collins ("Alleluia," 21). Where things get interesting are the various literary, sociological, and theological rationales put forward to explain the Psalter's macro-structure, yet Nasuti's ("Psalms," 311) summary remains sound: "Whereas most of the 20th century is devoted to refining and developing the form-critical insights of Hermann Gunkel and Sigmund Mowinckel, recent attention focuses on the literary shape and theological orientation of the book of Psalms as a whole." Creach (*Refuge*, 13) adds that "this paradigmatic shift is due (a) "to the fact that atomistic methods like form criticism have begun to diminish," and (b) "that the Qumran Psalm manuscripts provide new data on the editorial history of the Psalter." Cf. Gerstenberger ("Torah") and the volume of next-generation essays published by Barbiero et al. (*Psalter*).

79. Cf. Wray Beal, "Psalms," 605–13.

80. *Illustration:* Near the beginning of Rob Reiner's film *The Princess Bride* (1987) an exasperated grandfather (Peter Falk) says to his reluctant-to-read grandson (Fred Savage), "When I was your age, television was called books."

81. Postman, *Amusing*, 92–93.

However this analysis is generally perceived, Postman's colleagues hold it to be as prescient as it is precise. Lee Barron, for example, agrees that "many celebrities possess talent and unique skills or looks," but that "talent and achievement are no longer mandatory" because "image is now everything."[82] Robin Barnes acknowledges that while "*fame* is traditionally associated with individual demonstrations of superior skill," *celebrity* depends upon "marketing, timing, and instant appeal."[83] Karen Sternheimer recognizes that "celebrity and fame are not simply distractions, but unique manifestations of . . . American social mobility" because they so mindlessly promote the politically correct "illusion that material wealth is possible for everyone."[84] Ellis Cashmore observes that while the Western reading public once panned "stories about the so-called private lives of the rich and famous," it now "spends more time following the lives of celebrities than . . . 'legitimate' news." The reason for this sea change, he suggests, is that the advertising industry has been remarkably successful in "whetting our appetites and cultivating our tastes" to accept whatever product it wants consumers to "need."[85] To the basic question, "How does celebrity occur?" Sharon Marcus spotlights three factors: (a) the performances of aspiring artists; (b) the public's power to determine who does or does not "deserve" fame; and (c) the power of electronic media.[86] Of these three factors—personal effort, public perception, and the media—Chris Rojek finds the most influential to be public perception.[87]

The point here, of course, is that contemporary Western worshipers are hardly immune to the celebrity culture virus. In fact, in some ways they are more vulnerable to it now than ever before because, as the Kreiders point out, "legal compulsions to attend church have disappeared and social compulsions are withering," the result being that "consumer values are pervasive (and) people attend worship services because they want to receive something." But if "they find that it does not make them feel better . . .

---

82. Barron, *Celebrity*, 2.

83. Barnes, *Outrageous*, 19. Habermas (*Glauben*, 23) contends that "the language of the market today enters into every pore, forcing interpersonal relationships into a schema of self-centered orientation based upon individual preferences."

84. Sternheimer, *Celebrity*, xiii. On the "wealth" motif, cf. below.

85. Cashmore, *Celebrity/Culture*, 1. Cf. Stearns (*Consumerism*); Thompson (*Advertising*); Clark (*Want Makers*); and Rutherford (*Dilemma*).

86. Marcus, *Celebrity*, 1.

87. Rojek (*Celebrity*, 9). Pointing out that the English term "celebrity" derives from Lat *celeber* ("crowded, frequented, populous, prevalent, widespread, noted, famous"), Rojek goes on to suggest that "the increasing focus of the public face in everyday life is a consequence of the rise of public society, a society which cultivates personal style as the antidote to formal democratic equality."

they simply do not return."[88] Long aware of the correlation between "societal consumerism" and "idolatries in churches," Marva Dawn contends that most churchgoers today attend "simply to be entertained," always with the expectation that "the worship leaders or preacher will give a good performance."[89] Pointing to parallels between 21st century televangelists and the traveling medicine shows of the 19th century, Quentin Schultze points out that one of the greatest similarities between the two is that each "offers free entertainment in exchange for an opportunity" to sell "medicines" to "troubled people."[90] Alongside these sociological critiques, Douglas Bond laments the fact that "people used to turn to poetry to express their deepest feeling, their highest joys and their darkest grief." But now, "anesthetized as our culture is by amusement technology, our sorrows and our joys are so benumbed, so diluted by virtual distractions, there is little or no need for such outdated things as poetry."[91] Along this line Patrick Reardon worries that contemporary worship leaders "are far too disposed to establish their personal sentiments and spontaneous feelings as the standard for prayer. So, if the words of a particular prayer (even a psalm inspired by the Holy Spirit) express emotions and responses with which people do not 'feel comfortable,' the tendency is to think that it is impossible to pray them without being insincere."[92]

---

88. Eleanor and Alan Kreider (*Worship*, 26). Tanner ("Suffer," 144) points out that the rise of contemporary "praise music" coupled with the widespread elimination of liturgies like the "prayer of confession" combine to create "a sense of 'false happiness' as the main purpose and normal state of the Christian Church and of individual Christian lives. In short, to be a Christian in 20th century America means to be 'happy.'" Conversely, worshipers who are not always "happy" are not "faithful Christians."

89. Dawn, *Worship*, 53–54 (cf. Amos 6:1–6; Moore, *WealthWarn*, 103–7). Lash ("Performing," 37–46) outlines several ways and means by which the "performance" of Scripture can be a legitimate theological activity, but "performance" designed to feed the celebrity virus is a completely different matter. Lepojärvi's ("Worship," 543–62) interpretation of C. S. Lewis's *The Four Loves* is one of the more insightful attempts to identify the distinction.

90. Schultze, *Televangelism*, 128. Unwilling to "dismiss the importance of therapeutic culture making the world a better place," Gabriel ("Damage," 25) nevertheless worries that "this framework has a tendency to foreclose other possible responses to the troubles of the world" (cf. Klunzinger and Moore, "Codependency," 159–74).

91. Bond, "Postpoetry," 66. This is to say nothing about the potential long-term impact of AI technology on the creation of future poetry and prose (cf. Katz and Morgenthau, *Code*; Charaoui et al., *Literature*; Bringsjord and Ferucci, *Creativity*). Wells ("Conclusion," 203–4) recognizes that "the language of poetry doesn't easily connect in a sound-byte culture" because "the Psalms call for *time*.... not *tweets*."

92. Reardon, *Psalms*, 215. Witvliet ("Words," 10) suggests that "the Psalms function as a kind of language school," i.e., as "texts that can help us practice ways of speaking that form in us dispositions that correspond to the words themselves." Platt (*Radical*,

In short, the celebrity culture virus affects everything it touches in Western religious culture, from how leaders are trained,[93] to how the young are educated,[94] to how mission is managed,[95] to how campuses are designed (both physical and electronic),[96] and yes, to how congregational worship is conducted. To be sure, the last of these is not the only aspect of Western religious culture to experience the effects of the celebrity virus, but given its high visibility it tends to cast the longest shadow over the tectonics segregating the postmodern present from the premodern past.[97] Compare, for example, the apostle Paul's admonition to the Ephesian church:

καὶ μὴ μεθύσκεσθε οἴνῳ	Do not get drunk with wine[98]
ἐν ᾧ ἐστιν ἀσωτία	Which leads to self-indulgence[99]
ἀλλὰ πληροῦσθε ἐν πνεύματι	But be filled with the Spirit,
λαλοῦντες ἑαυτοῖς	Speaking to one another[100]

---

3) worries that congregations unwilling to learn from this "language school" stand in danger of "embracing values that are not only unbiblical, but that actually contradict the Gospel we claim to believe."

93. DeGroat (*Narcissism*, 67–86) wonders how and why so many Jacob-like "tricksters" wind up becoming American megachurch leaders (cf. also Vaters, *De-Sizing*, and Camenga, *Unearth*).

94. See Beaty, *Celebrities*, 63–136; Moore, *Babbler*, 156–65.

95. Cf. Nascimento, *Evangelization*, 5–22; Hof, "Missiology," 321–38; Moore, "Profile," 461–70.

96. See Plekon, "Building," 6–10; Moore, *Faith*, 198–203.

97. Webber (*Worship*, 20) recommends attending to the "biblical, ancient roots together with insights and practices from Christian history to constitute the foundation for addressing the third issue faced by today's Church: How do you deliver the authentic faith and great wisdom of the past into the new cultural situation of the twenty-first century? The way into the future," he suggests, "is not an innovative new start for the Church," but that "the road to the future runs through the past."

98. Cumont (*Religions*, 70) documents from multiple ecclesiastical sources that wine is a predominant element in Mithraic feasts like the *taurobolium*. In Canaanite myth, moreover, the deity El gets so drunk he loses control of both bladder and rectum, then collapses before his guests "like a dead man" (*km mt*, CAT 1.114.21).

99. Eph 5:18. This Gk term (ἀσωτία) consists of an alpha privitive prefixed to the root *σωτια, which though unattested, likely derives from the verb σῴζω, "to save." With the vss (Vg *luxuria*, "luxury, debauchery"; Syr ܐܠܐܣܘܛܐ, transliteration of ἀσωτία) most ETs translate "excess" (KJV) or "debauchery" (NIV, NRSV), or "dissipation" (NAS, NKJV), but the opposite of "saved" is "lost" or, as Paul puts it, "dead in your trespasses" (Eph 2:1).

100. In the epistle to the Colossians Paul goes deeper, urging them to "teach (διδάσκοντες) and admonish (νουθετοῦντες) one another" (Col 3:16) with psalms.

ψαλμοῖς καὶ ὕμνοις καὶ ᾠδαῖς   With psalms and hymns and spiri-
πνευματικαῖς   tual songs,
ᾄδοντες καὶ ψάλλοντες   Singing and chanting psalms[101]
τῇ καρδίᾳ ὑμῶν τῷ κυρίῳ   In your heart to the Lord.[102]

This admonition is designed to sensitize Ephesian worshipers to two concerns: (a) that worship stands upon a *praise-performance* continuum habitually exposed to attractive counterfeits[103] and (b) that these counterfeits must be abandoned when they threaten to marginalize or displace the teaching ministry of psalmody.[104]

Given these preliminaries, the pages below pursue three goals:

- (1) To examine several representative Psalms from a holistic theological perspective, attending carefully to the ANE contexts out of which they originate as well as the early contexts within which they thrive;[105]

- (2) To show how the "inferior tools" utilized by many celebrity culture advocates stack up against the "superior tools" of the Psalter;[106] and

---

Listening to a rock-and-roll band perform on a brightly lit stage is not "speaking to one another," nor does it enhance the ministry of "teaching and admonishing one another."

101. Eph 5:19 (lit., "singing and psalming"). The phrase ᾄδοντες καὶ ψάλλοντες may here be a participial echo of ᾄσομαι καὶ ψαλῶ in Ps 27:6, but even if not, the translations "make melody" (NRSV) and "make music" (NIV) are obscurantist because ἀείδω often refers to "chanting" and ψάλλω to "recitation." In other words, Paul's focus is on *theological substance*, not *musical format*.

102. Eph 5:18–19.

103. Peterson, *Psalms*, 2. Ephesus was traditionally influenced by the worship of Artemis, a Greek fertility goddess associated by the Romans with Diana (Acts 19:24–28; cf. Fleischer, *Artemis*; Hoenn, *Artemis*; Moore, *WealthWarn*, 190–93). Corinthian worshipers face a different, but similar set of apostolic admonitions in 1 Cor 10–14. The classic study of ancient Mediterranean religions in the Hellenistic period is Cumont, *Religions* (esp. pp. 46–72).

104. Cf. Dawn (*Wars*, ix–xv); Byars (*Wars*, 1–20); Pinson (*Worship*, 1–17); and Moore (*Babbler*, 162). Unlike many Puritan interpreters of Ephesians (cf. examples in McMahon, *Psalmody*, 6–11), Paul's recommendation is not for "psalms, psalms, and more psalms." Still, Coverdale's lament rings uncomfortably true: "Wolde God that oure mynstrels had none other thynge to playe vpon . . . saue Psalmes, hymnes, and soch godly songes as Dauid is occupied with all" (*Psalmes*, iv, cited in Duguid, *Psalmody*, 1).

105. This will occasionally include intertextual analyses of Hebrew words and phrases alongside those found in other, esp. poetic texts. Comparisons between Qur'an and the Psalter have a long history on several levels (cf. Ho, "Successful," 203–20), but the comparisons below tend to focus predominantly on theological concerns.

106. This contrast came into sharp focus for me when a young worship-leader tearfully lamented her dismissal from her church's worship-team because "You don't have

- (3) To suggest a few ways in which the biblical prayer book can help guide contemporary worshipers toward a deeper, healthier, and more transcendent awareness of the divine presence.[107]

---

the image we're looking for."

107. Cf. Moore, "Presence," 166–70. In addition to a healthy theology of worship the Psalter also contributes to the formulation of healthy theologies of pastoral care (cf. Klunzinger and Moore, "Codependency," 159–74). Praising Pemberton's book, *Hurting with God: Learning to Lament with the Psalms*, Hardin (*Psalms*, 288) remarks that while "books on prayer are plentiful, less common are those which approach the study of prayer from a deep inquiry into the historical and linguistic realities of the biblical text. Rarer still are those which digest this information into something palatable to the average reader, making real-world connections to the realities of everyday life. A pearl of great price is that book on prayer that brings all of the aforementioned qualities to the table—historical investigation, textual analysis, readability, and real-world application—from deep, personal experience with the subject matter."

1

Why Lament?

On May 7, 1945, officials of the German Third Reich surrendered to officials of the Allied Supreme Command, signaling thereby the end of World War II in Europe, arguably the most savage war in history. Soon afterwards Heidelberg Prof. Claus Westermann published an essay on the phenomenon of lament, noting its centrality to the Israelite story:[1]

	Deuteronomy	Exodus
Prehistory	26:5	1:1
Distress	26:6	1:6–22
Cry for help (**lament**)	26:7a	3:7–9
Divine response	26:7b-9	3:10-Num 36:13
Human response	26:10–15	15:1–21

Pondering this centrality he then asks, "If lament is so central to Israel's story, then why is it so conspicuously absent from contemporary congregational worship?"[2] In many ways this question has yet to be seriously addressed by contemporary Western worshipers. Aware of the postwar problems plaguing

---

1. Westermann, *Psalms*, 21 (cf. Moore, *Chaos*, 1–12). Seerveld ("Church," 140) defines "lament" in no uncertain terms: "A biblical psalm of lament is not just a sad lyrical monologue bewailing your forlorn and outcast state, but instead is an intense emergency-room cry to the Lord whom you trust to hurry and come through with life-or-death help."

2. Westermann, "Klage," 44–80.

many of his readers,[3] particularly (a) the crippling effects of PTSD on the lives of surviving soldiers and their families,[4] as well as (b) the lingering toxic effects of forcibly imposed Nazi political theatre as a substitute for authentic worship,[5] he nevertheless comes to a stark realization; viz., that the factors responsible for lament's eclipse originate not so much from immediate postwar aftereffects as from the cultural values organically embedded within Enlightenment culture itself:[6]

- *First*, Western Enlightenment culture tends to objectify anything and everything having to do with God and/or God's creatures,[7] particularly

---

3. Mahlendorf (*Shame*, 1) admits that several things kept her from writing down her story as a young German survivor of Nazism, "but not that I feared running into feelings or remembering traumatic experiences that might surprise me. Rather, I was afraid of discovering who I might have become had the Nazi regime lasted."

4. Jefferis (*Hamas*, 143–47) argues that the world is still paying for the rash decisions made in the aftermath of World War II; e.g., the Balfour Declaration's impact on the conflict between Israel and its neighbors (cf. Hass, *Holocaust*, 1–22).

5. The overwhelming majority of German Evangelical Church pastors support Hitler's vision of what he envisions to be a "patriotic" church (i.e., one fully dominated by the Nazi masquerade), while only a tiny minority (led by Martin Niemöller, Paul Schneider, Dietrich Bonhoeffer, and Karl Barth) create a resistance movement, the German Confessing Church (cf. Busch, "Barmen," 25–38). Campbell (*Leviathan*) recognizes the strikingly similar situation in 21st century American churches in response to the rise of "patriotic Christian Nationalism."

6. Explanations of the Enlightenment are vast and varied. Pagden (*Enlightenment*, 17) defines it as "a new understanding of the place of humanity in nature, and in a nature conceived as independent of any divine regulator." For Zafirovsky (*Enlightenment*, 1) "the values and institutions of universal liberty, equality and justice, democracy, science and technology, progress, individualism, optimism, happiness, human life, economic prosperity, market freedom and the like . . . can be considered primarily the ideals and legacies of the Enlightenment as their main foundation and point of origin." But for Smith (*Irrationality*, 5), "any utopian effort to set things in order permanently, to banish extremism, and to secure comfortably quiet lives for all within a society constructed on rational principles, is doomed from the start."

7. The objectification process begins the moment the Hebrew Bible (an Oriental text) is translated into Greek (an Occidental text), as Schorch ("Hebrew," 44) explains: "A Hebrew text, when translated, has less effect on the reader than the original. The reason is that the ideal union between form and content which characterizes the original has been destroyed." Many worshipers, moreover, are unable or unwilling to distinguish literal from symbolic language, as Janowski (*Arguing*, 22, citing Burke, "Literal-Mindedness," 110) observes: "Since the reformation . . . literal-mindedness has replaced traditional symbolic thinking," for "while the latter creates a 'system of correspondences' that is thought to be inscribed by the hand of God, literal-mindedness is characterized by a sophisticated . . . incapacity to understand symbolism," a problem which becomes acute when attempting to understand "premodern religious symbol systems" because of the way such systems force us to "enter a world of meaning that is opposed to literal-mindedness," that is, "a world of meaning not unlike that of the Psalms."

- in scholastic settings like high schools, colleges, universities, seminaries, divinity schools, and the like.[8]
- *Second*, this objectification mentality stands in sharp contrast to what philosopher Martin Buber calls "dialogical speech";[9] i.e., the symbol-laden discourse shaping poetic texts like the Psalms for the express purpose of nurturing greater intimacy between creature and creator.[10]
- *Third*, it should therefore come as no surprise that worshipers unacquainted with this "dialogical speech" often fail to appreciate the essentiality of lament.

Westermann's analysis spotlights one of the Psalter's greatest gifts; viz., that its "dialogical speech" quietly protects worshipers from the temptation to engage in the idolatrous activity of worshiping a foreign god in a foreign language.[11] Whenever worshipers (for whatever reason) jettison the "superior tools" of the Psalter for the inferior tools of the celebrity culture,[12] this

---

8. Cf. Bloom (*Closing*); Washburn (*University*); and Buckley ("Amerika"). Not all Europeans inevitably fall prey to the effects of objectification. Dietrich Bonhoeffer, e.g., demonstrates his resistance to it when he decides to leave a comfortable teaching career in America and England to return to direct the Confessional seminary at Finkelwalde in war-torn Germany. Bultmann ("Welchen," 129–30, cited in Hege, *Myth*, 56) insists that "any attempt to speak *about* God inevitably leads to sin because to speak *about* God requires both the objectification of God and also my detachment or distance from the claim of God on me and my life."

9. Buber's book *I and Thou* observes that many, if not most people speak of God not in terms of "I and Thou," but in terms of "I and It"; i.e., objectively, not relationally. Basking in Buber's shadow, Janowski (*Arguing*, 29) sharply contrasts "the information-oriented language of daily life and the concept-oriented language of commerce" with "the image-oriented language of the Psalms."

10. Balentine (*Prayer*) prefers to call this discourse "divine-human dialogue," and insofar as this applies to *parallelismus membrorum* in semitic poetry, Landsberger ("Eigenbegrifflichkeit," 355–72) coins the term *Eigenbegrifflichkeit* to describe it, a term Janowski (*Arguing*, 14) translates as "stereometric thought."

11. John Calvin (*Psalms*, xxxvii) writes about the Psalms: "Here the prophets themselves, seeing they are exhibited to us as speaking to God, and laying open all their inmost thoughts and affections, call, or rather draw, each of us to the examination of himself in particular, in order that none of the many infirmities to which we are subject, and of the many vices to which we are bound, may remain concealed." Habermas (*Glauben*, 23) argues that the problem facing postmodern worshipers today is that "the language of the market enters into every pore" of contemporary life, "forcing interpersonal relationships into schemas of self-centered orientation."

12. Peterson, *Psalms*, 2. Hitler was one of the first successful promoters of Western celebrity culture (cf. Munn, *Hitler*, 1–11).

inevitably encourages them to *mask* their sins, not *confess* them.[13] Thus James Leonard, in his review of *The Psalms as Christian Lament*,[14] observes that

> the authors justify their commentary on the lament psalms by noting that the intense and almost violent kinds of lamentation found in Psalms are hardly practiced in Christian worship today," even in the face of "pervasive increasing and deepening causes for lament" within contemporary culture.[15]

Agreeing with Westermann's diagnosis, Walter Brueggemann projects its implications onto a broader plane by asking, "What happens when appreciation of the lament as a form of speech and faith is lost?"[16] The answer, he suggests, is the inevitable development of a "theological monopoly" fundamentally designed to reward "docility and submissiveness," which in turn transforms churches and synagogues into sociopolitical kindergartens determined to "reinforce and consolidate the political economic monopoly of the *status quo*."[17] Lament's eclipse, in other words, opens wide the door to "psychological inauthenticity and social immobility,"[18] a grim forecast which affects not only congregational worship but also the professional

13. Europe's large empty churches are often compared with America's large churches of empty people. Moreover, a common pretension today is that digital conversations on social media platforms can somehow create genuine community, even though (a) the U. S. Surgeon General prescribes cigarette-type warning labels on these platforms to protect children and adolescents from online predators and bullies; and (b) some governments have begun to appoint cabinet-level ministers to address the growing effects of social isolation. *Examples:* Japan's Minister of Loneliness and Isolation Ayuko Kato and the UK's Minister of Loneliness Stuart Andrew (cf. Dumm, *Loneliness*; Mettes, *Loneliness*; DuChene and Sundby, *Loneliness*).

14. Waltke et al.

15. Leonard, *Lament*.

16. Brueggemann ("Lament," 59) reframes Buber's *I-Thou* polarity via the question, "What difference does it make to have faith that permits and requires this form of prayer (i.e., lament)? My answer is that it shifts the calculus and redresses the redistribution of power between the two parties, so that the petitionary party is taken seriously and the God who is addressed is newly engaged in the crisis in a way that puts God at risk. As the lesser petitionary party (the psalm speaker) is legitimated, so the unmitigated supremacy of the greater party (God) is questioned, and God is made available to the petitioner. The basis for the conclusion that the petitioner is taken seriously and legitimately granted power in the relation is that the speech of the petitioner is heard, valued, and transmitted as serious speech."

17. This is precisely what happens in 1930s Germany.

18. Brueggemann, "Lament," 59–60, 67. Beckett ("Lament," 207–8) makes sociopolitical application: "Lament is an essential practice for peacemakers and justice advocates: simultaneously directing their pain to God and expanding their imagination for the tasks ahead. Indeed, without lament they are stripped of a potent resource for rightly orienting themselves to the world and inviting transformative divine action."

guild of biblical scholars where, according to Samuel Balentine, "the Enlightenment's emphasis on rational, objective inquiry informs a period of biblical scholarship which accentuates the autonomy of both the Bible and the scholar," thereby creating a culture in which "the Bible is no longer exclusively the sacred text of the Church."[19]

The Psalter is designed to protect worshipers from such idolatry. The lament psalms in particular are an effective resource proven to be able to stop the relentless gravitational pull of what can only be described as an insatiable black hole.[20] In fact, as Michael Spencer sees it, "the psalms of lament" powerfully "speak to the abandonment of survivors, providing a theological, trauma-informed framework to engage traumatic experiences and hold this devastating pain against the backdrop of praise for God's 'steadfast love' (*ḥesed*)."[21] Basking in the testimonials listed above, he argues that the Psalter's impact derives not merely from its *function* but also from its *form*.[22] Indeed, at the risk of sounding simplistic, the template behind this form is readily summed up by a single word: **balance**. To explain, every lament psalm tends to contain five structural components: (1) divine address, (2) statement of faith, (3) lament, (4) supplication, and (5) vow of praise.[23] What this immediately means is that *the lament psalms never focus solely upon lament*. Their genius, rather, is (a) to re-situate it within a colloidal framework designed to keep worshipers from straying off into activities focused upon anything and everything except confession and repentance;[24]

---

19. Balentine, *Prayer*, 249. Suriano ("Foreword," xii) is quick to insist that the "historico-critical method" is not entirely "devoid of theological concerns."

20. Gillingham (*Psalms*) carefully details this protection-history.

21. Spencer, "Lament," 307. On *ḥesed*, cf. below.

22. Cf. Wilson, "Structure," 229–46. Cf. Murphy, "Reflections," 21–28. Newmeyer (*Language*, 6) explains the polarity as follows: "Formalists are absolutely correct in their commitment to characterizing form independently of meaning and function. But at the same time functionalists are right that meaning and function can help to shape form."

23. Westermann, "Klage," 48. Not all lament-psalms always contain every one of these components, nor do they always appear in the same order, but enough do to prove the existence of this template.

24. The membrane separating education from entertainment does not need to be made of concrete. In the words of Charlie Starr ("English," 78), "Great literature, if it entertains well, will also educate without falling into the trap of being merely educational." Yet Wolff (*Anthropology*, 1–2) observes that for atheists "objectification presents an insoluble problem. Just as it is impossible for a man to confront himself and see himself from all sides or for a person who is still developing to know of himself whose child he is, just so certainly does man fundamentally need the meeting with another, who investigates and explains him. But where is the other to whom the creature man could just put the question: 'Who am I?'"

and (b) to see to it in the process that each lament ends on a note of hope.[25] To anticipate our conclusions, *nothing challenges the ideological legitimacy of the celebrity culture more than the Psalter's awareness, affirmation, and preoccupation with the phenomenon of lament.*

INDIVIDUAL LAMENT

Following Gunkel and Westermann,[26] contemporary students of the Psalter subdivide the lament psalms into two subcategories: *individual* and *communal.*

Psalm 13

One of the most concise examples of an individual lament is Ps 13:[27]

עד ענה יהוה	How long, Yhwh?	*(divine address)*
תשכחני נצח	Will you forget me forever?[28]	*(lament)*
עד אנה תסתיר את פניך ממני	How long will you hide your face from me?[29]	
עד אנה אשית עצות בנפשי	How long must I suffer anxiety in my soul?[30]	

---

25. Psalm 88 seems to be the only exception to this general rule. Begrich ("Tora," 81–92) argues that what empowers the inclusion of praise in the lament psalms is the off-stage impact of (presumed) priestly salvation oracles. Following Westermann (*Psalms*, 27–35), Brueggemann ("Lament," 57) contends that "thanksgiving is in fact the lament restated after the crisis has been dealt with." For Simmons (*Talking*, 200) the Psalms go out of their way to include all "forms of praise, even the third of them which are complaints."

26. Gunkel, *Introduction*, 1–21; Westermann, "Klage," 44–80.

27. Human ("Suffering," 270) describes this poem as "a wrestling with God that is arguably the most concise articulation of a crisis experience in the Old Testament."

28. Ps 13:1. That Yhwh might actually "forget" is unthinkable, of course, as Qur'an emphasizes in its retelling of the Moses story. Explaining monotheism to Pharaoh, Moses says لا يضل ربى ولا ينسى, "My lord (lit., "my rabbi") neither errs nor forgets" (Q 20.52).

29. Ps 13:1. That this is no shallow complaint is clarified by Yhwh's final message to Moses: "Soon you will lie down with your ancestors. Then this people will begin to prostitute themselves to the foreign gods in their midst, the gods of the land into which they are going; they will forsake me, breaking my covenant that I have made with them. My anger will be kindled against them in that day. I will forsake them and hide my face from them; they will become easy prey, and many terrible troubles will come upon them. In that day they will say, 'Have not these troubles come upon us because our God is not in our midst?' On that day I will surely hide my face on account of all the evil they have done by turning to other gods" (Deut 31:16–18). Ross ("Laments," 136–41) discusses God's "hiddenness" at length.

30. Ps 13:2; lit., "put counsels in my soul"; cf. OG θήσομαι βουλὰς ἐν ψυχῇ μου, "put counsels in my soul"; Vg *ponam consilia in animam mea*, "lay plans in my soul";

יגון בלבבי יומם   The pain daily pillaging my heart?[31]
עד אנה ירום איבי עלי   How long shall my enemy gloat over me?[32]
הביטה ענני יהוה אלהי   Consider and answer me, O Yhwh, my God   (*supplication*)
האירה עיני פן אישן המות   Enlighten my eyes lest I fall into death's sleep[33]
פן יאמר איבי יכלתיו   Lest my enemy says, "I have prevailed"[34]
צרי יגילו כי אמוט   And my opponents rejoice over my ordeal[35]
ואני בחסדך בטחתי   I put my trust in your *ḥesed*[36]   (*statement of faith*)
יגל לבי בישועתך   My heart rejoices in your deliverance[37]
אשירה ליהוה כי גמל עלי   I will sing[38] to Yhwh for he has ransomed me.[39]   (*vow of praise*)

Syr ܐܬܒܐ ܐܬܗܘܐ ܐܒܐܬ, "put sorrow in my soul"; Tg אשוי מליכה בנפשי, "take counsel with my soul." Rejecting Porteous' ("Soul," *IDB* 4.428) claim that "the Hebrew cannot conceive of a disembodied *nefesh* ('soul')," Steiner (*Disembodied*, 21) argues, on the basis of evidence from the Katamuwa inscription, that "belief in the existence—and afterlife—of disembodied souls is extremely widespread in the ancient Near East" (cf. Moore, *Disembodied*).

31. Syr ܐܘܡܪܐ ܒܠܒܝ, "misery in my heart."

32. Ps 13:2. Lamenting the scorn and contempt of enemies is a common motif in the Psalter (see, e.g., Pss 7:5; 8:2; 13:2, 4; 18:17; 3:8; 41:11; 42:9; 43:2; 44:16; 55:3; 61:3; 64:1; 74:3, 10, 18; 89:22; 106:10; 143:3). In Qur'an Moses discovers Aaron's involvement in the golden calf incident, after which Aaron begs him تشمي بي الاعداء ("not to let my enemies gloat over me," Q 7.150).

33. Ps 13:3. In *CAT* 1.19.3.44–45 King Danel equates the "grave of my son" (*qbr bny*) with "his sleep" (*šnth*; cf. *RTU* 306–7; McAlpine, *Sleep*, 139). Sleep motifs and death motifs sometimes blur together in Near Eastern texts; e.g., "God 'redeems' (يوفى) the souls of people at their 'death' (موتها) as well as the souls of the living when they 'sleep'" (منامها, Q 39.42).

34. Ps 13:4 (lit., "I have [dis]abled him"); OG ἴσχυσα πρὸς αὐτόν ("I am stronger than him"); Syr ܘܙܟܝܬܗ ("I have conquered him").

35. Ps 13:4. Cf. parallel line in v. 2.

36. Ps 13:5. MT חסד, when paralleled by רחם ("mercy," as in Ps 51:1), tends to denote "mercifulness," but otherwise its primary meaning is "(covenant) loyalty." Zobel ("חסד," 53) explains that even though "*ḥesed* is not the content of the *berît* ("covenant"), both *ḥesed* and *berît* are based on friendship. For while *berît* emphasizes the intensity and permanence of this friendship, *ḥesed* expresses its inherent kindness" (cf. discussion below on חסד).

37. Heiler (*Prayer*, 259–60) and Kraus (*Psalms 1–59*, 142) suggest that the (often abrupt) transition from lament to praise in the lament psalms is due to a change in the psalmist's mood, but Cartledge ("Lament," 86) suggests rather that it is a rhetorical device designed to motivate the deity into action (a common technique in ANE incantation texts).

38. Ps 13:6. MT אשירה ליהוה ("I will sing to Yhwh") is the opening line to one of Tanak's greatest songs, the song of victory at the Red Sea (Exod 15:1).

39. Ps 13:6 MT גמל, "to requite, ransom"; OG ᾄσω τῷ κυρίῳ τῷ εὐεργετήσαντί με καὶ ψαλῶ τῷ ὀνόματι κυρίου τοῦ ὑψίστου, "I will sing to the Lord who has treated me

Psalm 22

Psalm 22 expands these five components into a prayer designed to help worshipers focus more clearly and intentionally upon the character of the covenant-making God to whom they have allegedly pledged their allegiance, beginning with its achingly familiar *divine address*:[40]

אלי אלי למה עזבתני   My God, my God, why have you forsaken me?[41]
רחוק מישועני   Why are you so far from saving me?[42]
דברי שאגתי   So far removed from the words of my groaning?[43]
אלהי אקרא יומם ולא תענה   I call out by day, O God, but you do not answer
ולילה ולא דומיה לי   And by night, but find no relief[44]

Next comes a *statement of faith* housed within an historical *précis*:

ואתה קדוש   But you are holy[45]
יושב תהלות ישראל   Enthroned upon the prayers of Israel[46]

---

kindly and I will psalm the Name of the Lord Most High" (OG apparently reads עלי as an abbreviation of עליון).

40. As is well-known, Christ recites this psalm on the cross (Matt 27:46), but as Menn ("Lament," 317–27) observes, it is also midrashically applied to the character of Queen Esther in the *Psalms Midrash*; i.e., that she prays this psalm in her hour of distress (e.g., *Midr. Teh.* 22.1). Dahlke ("Passion," 199–237) chronicles its usage in the early church.

41. Ps 22:1. The interrogative למה, though not overtly repeated, covertly initiates the following line (*GKC* 150a). Qur'an repeatedly addresses the fear of abandonment; e.g., "Your Lord has not abandoned you, nor does he hate you" (Q 93.3); and "Do not set up another deity alongside Alla, lest you be 'disgraced and abandoned'" (مذموما مخزولا, Q 17.22). Cf. footnote on Ps 30:7.

42. Ps 22:1. N.B. the synonyms in this psalm for "salvation": ישע ("to save," v. 1); פלט ("to be safe," v. 4); מלט ("to escape," vv. 5, 8); צלח ("to deliver," vv. 8, 20). Whereas the biblical psalmist asks for divine deliverance, a Qumran psalmist exhorts worshipers to deliver themselves: "May your hand deliver you" (תושיע ידך, 4Q380 1.2.4).

43. Ps 22:1. Cf. OG παραπτωμάτων, "my transgressions"; Vg *delictorum meorum*, "my transgressions"; Syr ܚܛܗܝ, "my transgressions." Tg אכילותי ("my cries") best parallels MT שאגה, and N.B. that שאג describes the "roaring" of lions in v. 13 and *ṯgt* the "bellowing" of bulls in Canaanite myth (*CAT* 1.14.3.16).

44. Ps 22:2. Cf. Syr ܘܠܐ ܫܠܝܬ ܠܝ, "but you do not tarry with me."

45. Ps 22:3. Qur'an sometimes uses the Arab cognate to describe Alla as القدوس (*al-Qadosh*, "the Holy One," Q 62.1), but this title appears much more often in biblical descriptions of the deity (cf. below and Moore, *Chaos*, 67–75).

46. Ps 22:3. Cf. OG σὺ δὲ ἐν ἁγίοις κατοικεῖς ὁ ἔπαινος Ισραηλ, "but you dwell among saints (pl.), the praise (sg.) of Israel"; Vg *tu autem in sancto habitas Laus Israhel*, "but you dwell in a holy place (sg.), the praise (sg.) of Israel"; Syr ܐܢܬ ܩܕܝܫܐ ܝܬܒ ܒܬܫܒܘܚܬܐ ܕܐܝܣܪܐܝܠ, "you are holy, seated upon Israel's praise (sg.) for you"; Tg ואנת קדיש דמיתב עלמא על תושבחן ישראל, "but you are holy, seated forever upon the praises (pl.) of Israel." Sensitive to the versions, many ETs translate תהלות as "praises," not "prayers."

בך בטחו אבותינו   In you our ancestors trusted
בטחו ותפלטמו   They trusted, and you delivered them
אליך זעקו ונמלטו   Unto you they cried and were delivered
בך בטחו ולא בושו   In you they unashamedly invested their trust[47]

Next comes the *lament* proper:

ואנכי תולעת ולא איש   But me? I am a worm,[48] not a man,
חרפת אדם ובזוי עם   Scorned by men and despised[49] by people
כל ראי ילעגו לי   All who look at me mock me
יפטירו בשפה יניעו רוש   They curl up their lips and shake their heads, sneering,
גל אל יהוה יפלטיהו   "He hoped in Yhwh; let *him* rescue him,[50]
יצילהו כי חפץ בו   Let *him* deliver him, for this one is his 'darling.'"[51]
כי אתה גחי מבטן   Indeed, you took me from the womb[52]
מבטיחו על שדי אמי   And nurtured me to faith[53] at my mother's breast
עליך השלכתי מרחם   I was dependent upon you from conception
מבטן אמי אלי אתה   You have been my God since my mother bore me[54]

Next comes the *supplication*:[55]

---

47. Ps 22:4–5. N.B. that בטח ("to trust") repeats three times in these two verses, a positive historical emphasis much like that framing Ps 105 vis-à-vis Ps 106 (cf. Brueggemann, *Astonishment*, 15–20). ANE worship conducted out of shame is usually taboo; e.g., "Ba`al hates ... shame-driven sacrifice" (*šna b`l ... dbḥ bṯt*, CAT 1.4.3.17–19).

48. Ps 22:6. In Isa 41:14 the prophet calls Jacob (Israel) a תולעת ("worm").

49. Ps 22:6. Whereas men vengefully "despise" (בזה, 22:6), God does not (22:24). Qur'an teaches that "whatever new reminder comes to them from the Most Compassionate, they always turn away from it" and that soon "they will hurry toward the consequences of their scorn" (يستوزعون, Q 26.5–6).

50. Ps 22:8 MT גלל, lit., "to roll toward"; OG ἤλπισεν, "he hoped"; Vg *speravit*, "he hoped"; Syr ܐܬܬܟܠ ܥܠ ܡܪܝܐ, "he put his confidence in the Lord."

51. Ps 22:8, lit., "for he delights in him." Cf. the similar taunt aimed at the suffering Christ: "Look, he's calling for Elijah ... let's see if Elijah will come take him down" (Mark 15:35–36). Interpreting אלי אלי as a reference to אליהו (Elijah) is a telling display of biblical illiteracy.

52. Ps 22:9. A song in a Qumran hymnal reads: "You (God) take him (i.e., the צדיק, "just man") from the womb (מרחם) for a season of goodwill to keep your covenant" (1QH 7.18).

53. Lit., "caused me to trust."

54. Ps 22:10; lit., "from the belly of my mother." Cf. the similarly visceral maternal imagery in Job 3:1–3, 10–12, 16.

55. Gerstenberger (*Petition*, 7) contends that "ancient Israel ... is a late heir of the millennial tradition of supplication, drawing into her treasure of sacred poetry some thirty to forty specimens of individual complaint and petition that originate in pre-Yahwistic curing ceremonies of old."

אל תרחק ממני	Do not withdraw from me[56]
כי צרה קרובה	For distress is near[57]
כי אין עוזר	And there is no one to help[58]
סבבוני פרים רבים	Many bulls surround me
אבירי בשן כתרוני	Bashan's bulls encircle me[59]
פצו עלי פיהם	Opening wide their mouths
אריה טורף ושאג	Like hungry, roaring lions.[60]
כמים נשפכתי	I am poured out like water[61]
והתפרדו כל עצמותי	My bones are all disjointed
היה לבי כדונג	My heart is like wax[62]
נמס בתוך מעי	Melting inside my chest[63]
יבש כחרש כחי	My energy evaporates into a dry piece of pottery[64]
ולשוני מדבק מלקחי	My tongue sticks to my jaw[65]
ולעפר מות תשפתני	You drag me down into the dust of death[66]

56. Ps 22:11. Cf. רחק ("to be distant") in v. 1.

57. Job laments the proximity of "distress" (עמל, 3:10; רגז, 3:17, 26) in his opening lament, and the psalmists often warn about the יום־צרה ("day of distress," Ps 20:1; 50:15; 77:3; 86:7) as well as the יום־רעה ("day of evil," Ps 27:5; 41:14).

58. Ps 22:11. In 30:11 the psalmist begs Yhwh to "be my helper" (עזר לי היה), and Qur'an insists that God is the خير الناصرين ("best of helpers," Q 3.150).

59. Ps 22:12. Located in northern Transjordan southeast of the Sea of Galilee, Bashan is known for its cattle and other livestock (Amos 4:1–3). Dell ("Animal," 275–91) discusses the Psalter's fondness for animal imagery in descriptions of human behavior, and Ulmer ("Psalm 22," 109–11) traces the appearance of animal metaphors found in Ps 22 into several rabbinic texts.

60. Seerveld ("Church," 147) suggests that Ps 22 is about "the terror of facing ravenous lions and wild dogs—the haughty pious, the faith establishment, the 'Barabbas' rabble crowd, and the gambling Roman mercenaries. These act demonically toward the Lamenter, like wild animals who kill and cannot be touched by human norms of just-doing and mercy."

61. Ps 22:14. Justin Martyr (*Dial.* 103.7–8) takes this to refer to the drops of sweat falling from Christ's forehead in Gethsemane (cf. Lieu, "Justin," 206).

62. Ps 22:14. Cf. 68:2: "As wax melts before the fire, so let the wicked perish before God."

63. Ps 22:14. Van Wolde ("Psalm 22," 665) suggests that the "molten wax" metaphor is based on the conceptual metaphor "Yhwh is fire" and as such "demands that the addressee switch from the perspective of the enemies to Yhwh," underlining the truth that "human enemies are not the criterion for behavior or emotion, but the suzerain."

64. Ps 22:15. Job scrapes himself with a חרש ("piece of broken pottery," Job 2:8).

65. Ps 22:15. To a demon-possessed man a Canaanite exorcist says, "Let your tongue no longer stutter, and stop your incessant drooling" (Ug *al t'lg lsnk al tpq apq*, CAT 1.169.11–12).

66. Ps 22:16. OG κατήγαγές με, "you bring me down"; Syr ܫܕܝܬܢܝ "you fling me"; Tg לבית קבורתא אמטיתני, "you lay me down into the house of burial."

כי סבבוני כלבים	As the dogs surround me[67]
עדת מרעים הקיפוני	As gangs of wicked men badger me
כארי ידי ורגלי	My hands and feet are bound
אספר כל עצמותי	I can count all my bones[68]
המה יביטו יראו בי	They stare at me and gloat
יחלקו בגדי להם	Dividing my garments among themselves
ועל לבושי יפלו גורל	And casting lots for my clothing[69]
ואתה יהוה אל תרחק	But you, Yhwh, do not withdraw
אילותי לעזרתי חושה	Rush to my aid, O my Helper
הצילה החרב נפשי	Deliver my soul from the sword
מיד כלב יחידתי	My life from the claws of the dogs[70]
הושיעני מפי אריה	Save me from the mouth of the lion
ומקרני רמים עניתני	And rescue me from the horns of the wild ox[71]

Finally, this great text ends with an extended *vow of praise*:

אספרה שמך לאחי	I will recount to my family your Name[72]
בתוך קהל אהללך	In the midst of the assembly I will praise you[73]
יראי יהוה הללוהו	Let those who fear Yhwh praise him
כל זרע יעקב כבדוהו	Let all Jacob's descendants glorify him
וגורו ממנו כל זרע ישראל	Let all Israel's descendants fear him
כי לא בזה ולא שקץ ענות עני	For the needy he does not detest or despise[74]

67. Ps 22:16. N.B. that the Phoenician queen Jezebel is surrounded and devoured by actual dogs (2 Kgs 9:35–37).

68. Ps 22:17. In Qur'an the deity asks, "Does anyone think we cannot 'reassemble his bones?'" (نجمع عظامه, Q 75.3).

69. Ps 22:18. To someone suffering from a demonically induced stutter, a Canaanite exorcist says, "May El put some clothing over your nakedness" (Ug *lbš il yštk ʿrm*, CAT 1.169.12–13), the opposite of the sentiment here.

70. Ps 22:20. In 35:17 יחידה again stands in parallel to נפש ("soul, life"); Tg reads רוחא דגושמי, "from the breath in my body."

71. Ps 22:21. Craigie (*Psalms* 1.201) begins the vow of praise here, but Kibbe ("Answered," 43–53) postpones its beginning to the next verse.

72. Ps 22:22. One of the Amarna letters presumes that a monarch's "name" can be considered "established" in an earthly place. Speaking to the Egyptian pharaoh, the mayor of Jerusalem (ʿAbdi-ḫeba) says, "See, the king has 'established his name' (Akk *ša-ka-an šum-šu*) in the land of Jerusalem forever, 'and cannot abandon it'" (*ù la-a i-li-iḫ-e e-za-bi ša*, EA 287.60–63; also 288.5–6). Yhwh does something similar when he establishes his name in the Jerusalem Temple (Deut 12:5; cf. Pss 5:11; 7:17; 8:1, 9; 9:2, 10; 18:49; 20:1, 5, 7, *et passim*; cf. Moore, *Chaos*, 122). On השם (Ha-Shem, "the Name") cf. below.

73. Ps 22:23. The ("great") "assembly" appears four times in the Psalter, three times in the vows of praise concluding three lament psalms (Pss 22:23, 26; 35:18) and once near the end of a thanksgiving psalm (107:32).

74. Ps 22:24 (lit., "the needs of the needy"). N.B. the alliteration of ענות עני and ענה in v. 21 (discussed in Moore, *Anomalies*," 235–38).

ולא הסתיר פניו ממנו	Nor does he hide his face from them[75]
ובשועו אליו שמע	He rather listens when they cry out to him[76]
מאתך תהלתי בקהל רב	My prayer ascends to you in the great assembly[77]
נדרי אשלם נגד יראיו	My vows I pay to those who revere him[78]
יאכלו ענוים וישבעו	The needy shall eat and be satisfied[79]
יהללו יהוה דרשיו	The seekers for Yhwh will praise him
יזכרו וישבו אל יהוה	They will remember and return to Yhwh[80]
כל אפסי ארץ	All the ends of the earth
וישתחוו לפניך	Will bow before you
כל משפחות גוים	All the families of the Gentiles
כי ליהוה המלוכה	For the kingship belongs to Yhwh
ומשל בגוים	As ruler of the Gentiles[81]

75. Ps 22:24. Tob 13:6 reads, "If you turn to him with all your heart and with all your soul, to do what is true before him, then he will turn to you and will not 'hide his face' (יסתר אנפוהי) from you" (4Q196.17.2).

76. Ps 22:24. King Kirta is chided by his son Prince Yaṣṣib for *not* listening to the cries of the "poor" (Ug *dl*), choosing instead to let them suffer oppression (*CAT* 1.16.6.48).

77. Ps 22:26. MT מאתך ("from you"); OG παρὰ σοῦ ("before you"); Vg *apud te* ("before you"); Syr ܡܢ ܨܐܕܝܟ ("in your presence"). Not only do the vss. support this translation, but the parallel preposition נגד ("before, in front of") does as well, not to mention לפניך ("before you") in v. 27. Whether this "great assembly" refers to the "Great Assembly" of later rabbinic tradition (כנסת הגולה, *m. 'Abot* 1.1) is unlikely.

78. Ps 22:25. Syr ܕܟܝܐ, "those cleansed by him." A Qumran psalmist imagines "vows" as valid only when "there is no Belial in your midst" (אין בקרבך בליעל, 4Q88 10.9–10). Qur'an teaches that "'the just (الأبرار) . . . are those who 'pay their vows' (يوفون) because '"they fear' (يخافون) the Day of sweeping horror" (Q 76.5, 7).

79. Ps 22:26. Hosea warns that every arrogant Israelite who refuses to "know" Yhwh "shall eat, but not be satisfied; they shall prostitute themselves, but not multiply" (Hos 4:10; cf. Moore, *WealthWarn*, 89–97).

80. Ps 22:27. Duhm (*Psalmen*, 74) argues that the modal shift beginning in v. 22 "has nothing whatsoever to do" with the individual lament in vv. 1–21, but Kraus (*Psalms 1–59*, 298) reads vv. 22–31 as a response to a salvation oracle likely delivered by a cultic official. Lyons ("Psalm," 641) interprets this shift as a rhetorical reflection on the "suffering-vindication-global-recognition-of-Yhwh" sequence laid out in passages like Isa 54, 56–66, but Charney ("Innocence," 33) sees the shift purely as rhetorical in that it "can be seen as parts of a connected line of argument aimed at persuading God to uphold cultural values and intervene in the life of the speaker." In other words, "Ps 22 makes an elaborate case to re-establish innocence and become God's public champion."

81. Ps 22:27–28. Cf. the anthropological shift in 1QM 7.6: "The kingship belongs to the God of Israel *and the holy ones of his people*" (ובקדושי) והיתה לאל ישראל המלוכה ובקדושי עמו). Perrin (*Kingdom*, 51) observes that "too often when people hear the phrase 'the kingdom of God' their thinking goes back to the preaching of Jesus—and then stops." But the fact remains that "the kingdom is already operational through the process of creation." Moreover, "there has never been, nor will there ever be, a tribe, a race, a sub-culture, or any other segment of society that falls outside the purview of the kingdom."

אכלו וישתחוו כל דשני ארץ   All who sleep in the earth will eat and worship[82]
לפניו יכרעו כל ירדי עפר   Everyone cast down into the dust will worship him
ונפשו לא חיה   Even those souls no longer breathing[83]
זרע יעבדנו   Posterity will serve him
יספר לאדני לדור   They will speak of the Lord to the next generation.
יבאו ויגידו צדקתו   They will come and tell of his justice
לעם נולד כי עשה   To a people yet unborn that he is their Maker![84]

Psalm 86

Stylistically no two laments look exactly the same. Some, for example, begin with a string of questions (like Psalm 13), while others begin with a string of imperatives, like Psalm 86:

הטה יהוה אזנך   Incline your ear, O Yhwh[85]
ענני כי עני ואביון אני   Answer me, for I am poor and needy[86]
שמרה נפשי כי חסיד אני   Protect my soul,[87] for I am *ḥasid*[88]

---

82. Ps 22:29. MT (lit., "fat of the land"); OG πίονες ("rich, wealthy"); Vg *pingues* ("greasy"); Syr ܓܐܒܢܐ ("hungry of the land"); Tg סיפי ארעא ("warriors of the land"). In light of the versional ambiguity Dahood (*Psalms* 1.143) proposes that דשני be read ד (rel. pronoun) + שני ("sleep"); i.e., "those who sleep," thereby preserving the parallel with ירדי עפר ("those descending to the dust") and ונפשו לא חיה ("his soul is not alive"). Whether ארץ refers to the netherworld here seems likely (cf. 1 Sam 28:13), even though this connotation is not as prevalent in Tanak as it is in Canaanite myth.

83. Cf. Steiner (*Souls*, 66–100), and footnote on Ps 13:2.

84. Ps 22:31; cf. OG ἐποίησεν ὁ κύριος, "the Lord has made"; Syr ܥܒܕ ܡܪܝܐ, "the Lord has made"; Vg *nascetur quem fecit Dominus*, "let him be born whom the Lord has made"; Tg פרישן דעבד, "what he has done is wonderful." Cf. the similar use of עשה in Ps 86:8–10.

85. Ps 86:1. Not only is Yhwh depicted with humanoid "ears," he is asked to "incline" one here and in v. 6 (cf. Wolff, *Anthropology*, 7–9). Wagner (*Body*, 87–144) discusses why some body parts are deemed more acceptable than others in OT depictions of divine activity.

86. N.B. the alliteration shaping this line.

87. Ps 86:2. Cf. v. 4 below and the phrase *tǵrn npš* ("protect the soul") in CAT 2.23.22–23.

88. Ps 86:2. OG ὅσιός εἰμι ("I am pious"); Vg *sanctus sum* ("I am holy"); Syr ܛܒܐ ܐܢܐ ("for I am good"); Tg ארום חסידא אנא ("for I am *ḥasid*"). Technically the *ḥasid* is someone who models faithfully the divine *ḥesed* eternally embedded in Yhwh (see below). From a sociohistorical perspective Puuko ("Feind," 47–65) argues that the *ḥasidim* in the Maccabbean period are a strict religious party diametrically opposed to the Hellenists, but Morgenstern ("*Ḥᵃsîdîm*," 59–73) demurs, limiting this designation to the post-exilic psalms because the pre-exilic psalms, in his opinion, tend to focus on the *ṣedaqim* (צדקים, "righteous ones"). Contemporary ultra-Orthodox Jews try to lay

הושע עבדך הבוטח אליך	Save your servant who trusts in you[89]
אתה אלהי	For you are my God[90]
חנני אדני	Be gracious to me, Lord
כי אליך קרה כל היום	For I cry out to you every day
שמח נפש עבדך	Cheer up the soul of your servant
כי אליך אדני נפשי אשא	For I lift up my soul to you
כי אתה אדני טוב וסלח	Because you, O Lord, are good and forgiving[91]
ורב חסד לכל קראיך	Altogether merciful[92] to all who call upon you[93]
האזינה יהוה תפלתי	Give ear[94] to my prayer, O Yhwh
והקשיבה בכל תחנונותי	Attend to each one of my pleas
ביום צרתי אקראך	When I am in distress I call upon you[95]
כי תענני	Because you answer me[96]
אין כמוך באלהים אדני	Lord, there is no one like you among the gods[97]

exclusive claim to the term *ḥasidîm* (חסידים; lit., "pious ones"), but originally the term simply denotes "those mobilized by (covenant) loyalty" (1 Macc 2:24; 7:13; cf. Zobel, חסד, 53; Ringgren, "חסיד" 78; cf. below). In Qur'an the Arab cognate حشد ("to mobilize") occurs in texts (a) where Pharaoh sends "mobilizers" (حشدين) to gather forces against Moses (Q 26.53) and (b) where Solomon "mobilizes" (وحشد) his armies against Israel's enemies (Q 27.17).

89. Ps 86:4. Dahood (*Psalms* 2.292) notes that the title "your servant" often occurs in vassals' letters to their masters (e.g., EA 55.5; CAT 2.12.5; 19.11; 81.5).

90. Ps 86:2. None of the versions support it, but many ETs (KJV, NIV, NRSV) recognize that the phrase הבוטח אליך ("the one who trusts in you") makes better syntactic sense coming after הושע עבדך ("save your servant") than after אתה אלהי ("you are my God").

91. Ps 86:5. A Qumran psalmist conditions this as follows: "You forgive those who turn away from transgression" (הסולח לשבי פשע, 1QH 6.24), but the Nazarene conditions it sociologically: "Forgive our sins as we forgive those who sin against us" (Matt 6:12).

92. Ps 86:5. OG πολυέλεος (lit., "poly-merciful").

93. Ps 86:5. MT לקרא ("to call upon") appears twice in this psalm (vv. 5 and 7). Wary of most form-critical analyses, Millar (*Calling*, 137–66) equates "calling on the Name" with "praying."

94. Ps 86:6 (cf. 86:1). This Š ipv. (האזינה) recurs several times in the Psalter, sometimes (a) at the beginning of a psalm, and (b) in parallel with שמע ("Listen!" cf. Pss 55:1; 49:1; 39:12).

95. Ps 86:7 (lit., "on the day of my distress"). Searching for her father Kirta, Thitmanat wails at the gate "like someone distressed" (*km nkyt*, CAT 1.16.2.28).

96. Ps 86:7. As a polysemantic term, ענה can mean "answer," "testify," "afflict," and/or "humble," depending on the context in which it appears (cf. Moore, "Anomalies," 235–38).

97. Ps 86:8. Cf. "Who is like you, Lord, among 'the gods?'" (אלים, 1QH 15.28). Rigid monotheists balk at henotheistic statements like this, but then find it impossible to explain the phrase "other gods" (אלהים אחרים) in passages like the Decalogue (Exod 20:3). To recognize the fact that Israel's neighbors worship multiple divine beings does not automatically posit the existence of such beings.

ואין כמעשיך   Nor are there any accomplishments like yours[98]
כל גוים אשר עשית   Let all the nations you have made[99]
יבואו וישתחוו לפניך אדני   Come worship you, Lord,
ויכבדו לשמך   And glorify your Name[100]
כי גדול אתה ועשה נפלאות   Because you are great and do wonders[101]
אתה אלהים לבדך   You alone are God
הורני יהוה דרכך   Guide me onto *your* path,[102] O Yhwh
אהלך באמתך יחד לבבי   Permit me to walk singlemindedly[103] in *your* truth
ליראה שמך   And fear your Name
אודך אדני אלהי   Allow me to give you thanks, O Lord my God
בכל לבבי   With all my heart[104]
ואכבדה שמך לעולם Let me glorify your Name forever
כי חסדך גדול עלי For great is your *ḥesed* to me[105]
והצלת נפשי משאל תחתיה   When you deliver my soul from Sheol below[106]
אלהים זדים קמו עלי   O God, impudent men rise up against me
ועדת עריצים בקשו נפשי   Bands of bullies seek my life
ולא שמוך לנגדם   They do not acknowledge you[107]

---

98. Ps 86:8. One would be hard-pressed, for example, to find anything even *approximating* the Exodus in, say, the myths about Marduk or Osiris or Baʿal.

99. Ps 86:9. Cf. the similar use of עשׂה ("to make") in 22:31.

100. Ps 86:9. Cf. footnote on Ps 22:23 and N.B. that Qur'an repeats the phrase فسبح باسم ربك ("Glorify the Name of your Lord") like a chorus (Q 56.74, 96; 69.52; and 87.1).

101. Ps 86:9. Yhwh promises Moses at the burning bush that he will "strike" (נכה) Egypt "with all my wonders" (בכל נפלאתי, Exod 3:20). N.B. that נפלאת ("wonders") appears in all four choruses of Ps 107 (vv. 8, 15, 21, and 31).

102. Ps 86:11. N.B. that ירה ("to teach, guide, coach") is the verbal root of תורה ("torah"), and that in 1QH 10.9–10 another psalmist prays, "You have set me up . . . as a foundation of truth and of knowledge for those 'on the upright path' (לישרי דרך)."

103. Ps 86:11 (lit., "my heart united"); OG εὐφρανθήτω ἡ καρδία μου τοῦ φοβεῖσθαι τὸ ὄνομά σου ("let my heart rejoice in fearing your Name"); Syr ܚܕܝ ܠܒܝ ܒܕܚܠܬܐ ܕܫܡܟ ("my heart rejoices in fearing your Name among the gods"). Lasater ("Heart," 652–68) argues that the "divided heart" is an ethical and theological problem solvable only by instruction from Yhwh, the only Unifier of divided hearts.

104. Ps 86:12. Markter (*Ezechiel*, 67) documents the prevalence of the "heart" motif in ANE texts, calling it a *Zentralbegriff* ("central idea").

105. Ps 86:13. On *ḥesed*, cf. below.

106. Ps 86:13; cf. 49:14–15. Whereas some derive "Sheol" from the verb שׁאל ("to inquire") or the verb שׁאה ("to be desolate"), Wächter ("Unterweltsvorstellungen," 335) derives it from a contraction of אל + שׁ (i.e., "that which is not"). Whatever its etymology, Sheol is a place of "entangling cords" (Ps 18:5) where souls descend (30:3), where the wicked are put to shame (31:17), where the foolhardy are "home" (49:14), and a place of "power" (49:15; 89:48) responsible for inflicting "pangs of distress" (116:3).

107. Ps 86:14 (lit., "they do not put you before them"). Syr ܠܐ ܐܬܕܟܪܘܟ ("they do not mention you").

ואתה אדני אל רחום	But you, Lord, are a God of mercy[108]
וחנון ארך אפים	Gracious and slow to anger[109]
ורב חסד ואמת	Abounding in *ḥesed* and faithfulness
פנה אלי וחנני	Turn to me and be gracious to me
תנה עזך לעבדך	Pass your strength on to your servant
והושיעה לבן אמתך	And save the son of your handmaid[110]
עשה עמי אות לטובה	Make me into a sign of your favor
ויראו שנאי ויבשו	So that those who spitefully stare me down may be ashamed[111]
כי אתה יהוה עזרתני ונחמתני	For you, Yhwh, are my help and my comfort.

Psalm 51

One of the Psalter's most gut-wrenching laments is David's very personal, very gritty confession of his adulterous affair with Bathsheba and murder of her Hittite husband to cover it up.[112] Like Ps 86, Ps 51 begins with a string of imperatives:

חנני אלהים כחסדיך	Be gracious to me, O God, according to your *ḥesed*[113]

---

108. Ps 86:15. In Qur'an Moses prays in the wake of the "golden calf" incident, "My Lord! Forgive me and my brother, and admit us into Your mercy," for "you are the most merciful of the merciful" (وأنت ورحم الرحمن, Q 7.151; lit., "you are the mercy of the mercies"; cf. שיר השרים, "the song of songs" = "The Greatest Song").

109. Ps 86:15. A sectarian psalmist from Qumran twice calls the deity "slow of anger" (ארוך אפים) in the same prayer (1QH 9.24; 10.6).

110. Ps 86:16. "Son of your handmaid" (בן אמתכה) also occurs in 1QS 11.16 (with *plene* spelling).

111. Ps 86:17. Contrasts like this one are, if anything, even more anthropocentric in *Hodayot*, the non-canonical songbook from Qumran Cave 1. The song in 1QH 10.20–30, e.g., is a chiastic poem contrasting the behavior of the wicked with the deity's empowerment "through me" (i.e., through the poet himself). The sentiment in Ps 69:6: "Let not those who hope in you be put to shame because of me" is not so anthropocentric.

112. Cf. Moore, *Reconciliation*, 123–37; *Babbler*, 247–48. Vishanoff ("David," 273–98) points out that many Arabic "translations" of the Psalter are in fact targum-like commentaries written by Muslim authors using a wide range of strategies designed to turn David into an "appropriately Islamic" figure. In order to accomplish this, David's role as "king" is often trumped by his role as "prophet" (cf. Acts 2:30). Adultery and murder are problems handled differently by each interpreter. Some turn him into a model of repentance, while others, following mainstream Muslim scholarship, hagiographically ignore or mitigate his sin, much like the chronicler does with the Davidic tradition (cf. Wellhausen, *Prolegomena*, 182; Moore, *Faith*, 17–18).

113. Ps 51:1. On חסד cf. below. It's no accident that the first thing for which David pleads is *ḥesed*.

כרב רחמיך מחה פשעי	According to your great compassion blot out my sin[114]
הרב כבסני מעוני	Cleanse me thoroughly from my iniquity[115]
ומחטאתי טהרני	And purify me from my sin[116]
כי פשעי אני אדע	For I know my crimes[117]
וחטאתי נגדי תמיד	And my sin haunts me continually[118]
לך לבדך חטאתי	Against you alone have I sinned[119]
והרע בעיניך עשיתי	And done what is evil in your sight[120]
למען תצדק בדבריך	Therefore you are justified in your verdict
תזכה בשפטיך	And faultless in your judgment[121]
הן בעוון הוללתי	Indeed, I was born in wickedness
ובחטא יחמתני אמי	And in sin did my mother conceive me[122]
הן אמת חפצת בטחות ובסתם	Knowing that you desire clarity over concealment[123]

114. Ps 51:1. Not surprisingly, Ps 51 begins with three parallel terms for "mercy": חסד, חנה, and רחם, the last one recurring often in the Arabic title الرحيم, Al-Raḥīm ("The Merciful One," Q 1.3 *et passim*).

115. Ps 51:2. MT כבס designates the kneading and squeezing undertaken by a "fuller" ("launderer") to wash clothes (cf. كبس, "to squeeze, knead"); cf. the verb חטא ("to scrub, purge" in the D form) in v. 7. At Ugarit it can be designated by the syllables $^{LÚ}ka_4$-bi-sú (PRU 6.136.8).

116. Ps 51:2–3 includes three synonyms for "purification": כבס, מחה, and טהר.

117. Ps 51:3 (lit., "transgression"). David knows he is guilty of murder, a very serious crime. Deutschmann ("Bloodguilt," 55–69) shows how the Tekoan woman's story (2 Sam 14:1–24) alerts the king to its seriousness (cf. Moore, *Babbler*, 261–65; *Faith*, 59–64).

118. Ps 51:3 (lit., "is before me continually").

119. Ps 51:4. Tg קדמך בלחודך חבית ודביש קדמך עבדית ("Before you alone have I done and hidden what is bad").

120. Ps 51:2–5 uses two words for "sin" (חטא, פשע) and two words for "evil" (עון, רעה). Other terms for "evil" occur in Pss 7:4; 53:2; 82:2 (עול); and 6:8; 7:14; 28:3; 36:4; 59:3, 6 (און).

121. Ps 51:4. The generic term דברים ("words,") stands in plural parallel with שפטים ("judgments"), though some ETs translate "sentence" (NRSV) and "verdict" (NIV) in the singular. Paul cites this verse in Rom 3:4 (cf. Krašovic, "Justification," 416–33), and the Qumran Scroll of the Rule uses it to describe a hypocrite: "May God's anger and the wrath of his 'judgments' (משפטי) consume him" (1QS 2.15). On משפט ("justice"), cf. below.

122. Ps 51:5. Often cited as "proof" for "original sin," this line exemplifies poetic hyperbole, not historical report. Another example of metaphorical hyperbole about birth occurs in 1QH 11.8, באו בנים עד משברי מות ("children come through the breakers of death"). Finstuen (*Sin*, 189) attributes the 20th century resurgence of belief in original sin to "the advent of the Age of Anxiety and the personal popularity of its chief expositors, Reinhold Niebuhr, Billy Graham, and Paul Tillich."

123. Ps 51:6. OG ἰδοὺ γὰρ ἀλήθειαν ἠγάπησας τὰ ἄδηλα καὶ τὰ κρύφια, "for you love truth, (not) hidden secrets." Following Pope's (*Job*, 302) interpretation of טחות in Job 38:36, Dahood (*Psalms* 2.4) suggests that it may here reflect an awareness of the

חכמה תודיעני	Teach me what wisdom is[124]
תחטאני באזור ואטהר	Scrub me with hyssop so that I may be cleansed
תכבסני ומשלג אלבין	Wash me so that I may be whiter than snow
תשמיעני ששון ושמחה	Let me again experience joy and gladness[125]
תגלנה עצמות דכית	Let the bones you have crushed rejoice
הסתר פניך מחטאי	Shield your face from my sins[126]
וכל עונתי מחה	And wipe away all my iniquity
לב טהור ברא לי	Create in me a clean heart[127]
ורוח נכון חדש בקרבי	And establish within me a new spirit[128]
אל תשליכני מלפניך	Cast me not from your presence
ורוח קדשך אל תקח ממני	Nor take your holy spirit away from me[129]
השיבה לי ששון ישעך	Restore to me the joy of your salvation
ורוח נדיבה תסמכני	And foster within me a compliant spirit[130]
אלמדה פשעים דרכיך	So that I may teach transgressors your ways[131]

Egyptian deity Thoth (Eg *ḏḥwty*), known colloquially as "the clever-minded one" (Vos, "Thoth," 862), and that סתם may here obliquely refer to the "secret lore" of the Canaanites because the Daniel in Ezek 28:3 refers not to the hero of the biblical book of Daniel, but to the Canaanite king Danel in the Aqhat myth (*CAT* 1.17-19).

124. Ps 51:6 (lit., "cause me to know wisdom"; OG reads δηλόω, "to clarify, reveal"). At Ugarit the goddess Athirat praises her husband: *thmk il ḥkm ḥkmk ʿm ʿlm ḥyt ḥẓt thmk* ("Your decree, O El, is wise / Your wisdom eternal / Your decree creates a life of good fortune").

125. Ps 51:10 MT שמע (lit., "to hear"); OG ἀκουτιεῖς ("to hear"); Vg *auditui* ("to hear"); Syr ܐܫܡܥܝܢܝ ܒܒܣܝܡܘܬܟ ܘܒܚܕܘܬܟ, "fill me with your sweetness and your gladness."

126. Ps 51:10. In one Canaanite myth empowerment is described as uninterrupted exposure to *pʿn bʿl* ("the face of Baʿal," *CAT* 1.12.1-33).

127. Ps 51:10. In 4Q542 1.9-10 Kohath son of Levi contrasts a "duplicitous heart" (לבב ולבב) with a "pure heart" (לבב דכא). Cf. Markter, "Herz," 67.

128. Ps 51:10. Blenkinsopp (*Creation*, 176-90) observes that biblical creation theology involves three stages: *creation, un-creation,* and *re-creation* (cf. Moore, *Chaos*, 13-26).

129. Ps 51:11. Whether רוח קדש refers to a "holy spirit" or "the Holy Spirit" is unclear, but N.B. (a) the poetic parallel with רוח נדיב ("willing spirit") in v. 12, and (b) the literary-historical problems created by the presumption that the psalmist here intentionally introduces the third person of the trinity. The Qumran Scroll of the Rule insists that the "the 'holy spirit of the community' (רוח קדושה ליחד) cleanses a man of all his iniquities" (1QS 3.7-8; cf. Price, *Secrets*, 205-8), and van Wolde ("Purification," 340-60) interprets this to mean that "purity is the *sine qua non* for God's holy spirit to stay and keep active in the midst of the Israelites. In this view, the impure world of words and deeds is the total from which the pure ones are to be separated." On קדש ("to be holy"), cf. below.

130. Ps 51:12. MT נדיב ("willing, compliant, volunteer"); OG πνεύματι ἡγεμονικῷ ("capable, teachable"). N.B. the phrase לב נדיב ("willing heart") in Exod 35:5, 22, a passage clearly echoed in 2 Cor 8–9.

131. Ps 51:13. MT למד, "to teach, cause to learn"; OG διδάξω ἀνόμους τὰς ὁδούς σου, "I will teach the lawless your ways." N.B. the parallel with "cause me to know wisdom"

הצילני מדמים אלהים	Deliver me from bloodguilt,[132] O God
אלהי תשועתי	O God of my salvation
לשוני צדקתיך תרנן	Let my tongue sing of your justice[133]
אדני שפתי תפתח	Open my lips, O Lord
ופי יגיד תהלתך	Let my mouth declare your praise[134]
כי לא תחפץ זבח	For you take no delight in sacrifice *per se*
ואתנה עולה לא תרצה	Sacrificial offering *per se* does not please you
זבחי אלהים רוח נשברה	For godly sacrifice requires a broken spirit[135]
לב נשבר ונדכה אלהים	A broken and contrite heart,[136] O God,
לא תבזה	You do not despise
היטיבה ברצונך את ציון	Shower on Zion as many benefits as you desire,[137]
תבנה חומות ירשלם	Rebuild Jerusalem's walls
אז תחפץ זבחי צדק	So that you may once again take delight in just sacrifice,
עולה וכליל	Burnt offerings and holocaust offerings
אז יעלו על מזבחך פרים	And bulls again sacrificed on your altar![138]

---

in v. 6.

132. Ps 51:14 (lit., "bloods"); Syr ܕܡܐ ("the blood"). In 1 Sam 25:31 Abigail warns David about the consequences of "shedding blood for no reason" (לשפך דם חנם), a warning he ignores with the murder of Uriah. Interestingly, the Damascus Document notes that "David's accomplishments are effective, except for Uriah's blood" (CD 5.5; cf. Shepherd, *Bloodguilt*, 236–53; Moore, *Babbler*, 245–55).

133. Ps 51:15. N.B. the (re)appearance of the silence-sound polarity in Ps 39:1–2, 9. On צדק ("justice"), cf. below.

134. Ps 51:14–15. Cf. the psalmist's unsuccessful attempt to stay silent in 39:2.

135. Ps 51:17.

136. Ps 51:17 (lit., "broken and crushed heart"). The opposite of a "broken heart" is a "foolish heart" (אוילי לב; lit., "inexperienced heart"), one eventually judged at Qumran by "the truthseekers" (דורשי אמת, 4Q418 69.2.4–8). Isaiah 66:2 champions the "contrite spirit" (נכה רוח). Markter (*"Herz,"* 57–58) investigates Ezekiel to determine "whether and under what circumstances a renewing of the heart is possible."

137. The conclusions to several psalms reference Zion and/or Jerusalem (e.g., Ps 2:6; 14:7; 51:18; 78:68; 102:21; 128:5; 129:5; 132:13; 135:21; 146:10). Contra Roberts ("Zion," 332) and Laato (*Zion*, 100–102) Wanke (*Zionstheologie*, 23–31) dates the Kohathite Zion psalms to the post-exilic period.

138. Ps 51:19. N.B. the inclusion of אז ("then") for emphasis. Haggai tells returning exiles that the reason for their economic woes is because even though they have rebuilt the temple and its altar, they have not purified it "properly" (Hag 2:10–14; cf. Moore, *WealthWarn*, 113–17).

Psalm 55

Psalms 41 and 55 deal with the painful problem of personal betrayal.[139] Psalm 41:9 reads:

גם איש שלומי אשר בטחתי בו   Even my dear friend[140] in whom I trust,
אוכל לחמי   The one who shares my bread,
הגדיל עלי עקב   Even *he* betrays me[141]

Psalm 55 expounds this motif considerably, starting with another string of imperatives:

האזינה אלהים תפלתי   Give ear to my prayer, O God
ואל תתעלם מתחנתי   And do not brush aside my appeal
הקשיבה לי וענני   Pay attention to me! Answer me!
אריד בשיחי ואהימה   I ramble on in my complaint, distraught
כי ימיטו עלי און   As they stir up trouble against me[142]
ובאף ישטמוני   Angrily nursing grudges against me[143]
לבי יחיל בקרבי   My heart twists within me
ואימות מות נפלו עלי   As the terrors of death fall upon me[144]
יראה ורעד יבוא בי   Fear and trembling seize me
ותכסני פלצות   And horror clings to me
ואמר מי יתן לי אבר כיונה   I ask, "Who will give me wings like a dove

---

139. Reflecting on the trinitarian motto of the French revolution (*liberté, égalité, fraternité*), Margalit (*Betrayal*, 2) argues that compared to the first two notions the third tends to be most misunderstood because few realize that *fraternité* has a dark side, betrayal.

140. Ps 41:9 (lit., "the man of my peace"). OG ὁ ἄνθρωπος τῆς εἰρήνης μου ἐφ᾽ ὃν ἤλπισα ("the man of my peace in whom I hope"); Vg *homo pacis meae in quo speravi* ("Man of my peace in whom I hope"); Syr ܓܒܪܐ ܕܫܠܡܐ ܫܐܠ ("the man who asks for my peace"); Tg גבר דתעב שלומי ("the man who loathes my peace").

141. Ps 41:9 (lit., "he lifts the heel against me"); cf. the PN יעקב, "Jacob," "heel grabber," Gen 25:26). Jeremiah laments that Yhwh has "enticed" (פתה, Jer 20:7) him, but whether he feels *betrayed* is disputed (cf. Moore, *Babbler*, 81–93).

142. Ps 55:3. One Qumran psalmist parallels the "breakers of death" (משברי מות) with his "couch breaking into lament" (ערשי בקינה) and "the sound of sighing" (קול אנחה, 1QH 17.4).

143. Ps 55:3. This description of enemies rather precisely mirrors the behavior of Daniel's Persian rivals (Dan 6:4–15; cf. van der Toorn, "Lions," 626–40), not to mention the religious parties opposed to the Nazarene. In GNT Judas Iscariot is repeatedly called ὁ παραδιδούς ("the betrayer"—Matt 26:25; 27:3; Mark 3:19; Luke 22:48; John 6:71; 12:4; 13:2; 18:2, 5; cf. also Acts 1:16).

144. Puzzled by the absence of a "god of death" in Mesopotamia, Smith (*History*, cited in Healey, "Mot," 601) suggests that the Mesopotamian myth of a hero-figure seeking to engage and rescue a spouse trapped in the netherworld later evolves into a conflict between Death (Mot) and his counterpart (Ba῾al).

אעופה ואשכנה	That I may fly away and nest?"[145]
הנה ארחיק נדד	For I could fly far, far away
אלין במדבר	To nest in the wilderness
אחישה מפלט לי	I could promptly build for myself a shelter
מרוח סעה מסער	From the raging winds and storms
בלע אדני פלג לשונם	Confuse and confound their speech,[146] O Lord
כי ראיתי חמס וריב בעיר	For I see violence and strife in the city
יומם ולילה יסובבה על חומתיה	Day and night they crouch upon its walls
ואון ועמל בקרבה	Trouble and disaster in their midst
הוות בקרבה	Chaos lodged at its center[147]
ולא ימיש מרחבה תך	Coercion and deceit packing the marketplace[148]
כי לא אויב יחרפני	For you see, it is not an enemy who betrays me—
ואשה	That I could handle.[149]
לא משנאי עלי הגדיל	It is not an adversary who vaunts himself against me—
ואסתר ממנו	That I could deflect.[150]
ואתה אנוש כערכי	No, it is you, my partner,
אלופי ומידעי	My colleague, my friend[151]
אשר יחדו נמתיק סוד	The one with whom I keep close counsel,[152]

145. Ps 55:6. N.B. that the following psalm (Ps 56) is to be sung to the tune "Dove on Distant Oaks" (56:1 יונת אלם רחקים).

146. Ps 55:9. Theodore of Mopsuestia (d. 428 CE) reads this verse as alluding to the Tower of Babel saga in Torah (Gen 11:1–9) because of the way it focuses on "the differences of tongues" (τῇ διαιρέσει τῶν γλωσσῶν, *Psalms*, 710).

147. Cf. Moore, *Chaos*, 13–26.

148. Ps 55:9–11. Much of this section sounds like Zephaniah's description of Jerusalem as a "soiled, defiled dove" (מראה ונגאלה העיר היונה). HAL reads יונה as a m. ptc. of ינה ("to oppress"), but the versions of Zeph 3:1 all read "dove" (OG ἡ περιστερά; Vg *columba*; Syr ܝܘܢܐ). In other words, both Zephaniah and this psalmist emphasize the contrast between peace and violence.

149. Ps 55:12. Hossfeld and Zenger note the changes in person and number (*Psalms* 2.52), but as Dahood recognizes (*Psalms* 1.34; 2.34), such changes occur not only in the Psalter, but in ANE funerary inscriptions (e.g., from 3rd to 2nd person in *KAI* 225.4–5, and from 3rd to 1st person in *KAI* 226.3–4).

150. Ps 55:12. Theodore of Mopsuestia (*Psalms*, 714) comments: "'If it had been an enemy who reproached me,' he is saying, 'I could have put up with it, and if it had been a loudmouth (that is, a boaster), I would have withdrawn without responding, reasoning that as an enemy he does things consonant with his attitudes.'"

151. Ps 55:13. In Ruth 3:2 Naomi calls Boaz מדעתנו (lit., "our known one," usually translated "kinsman"). Theodore of Mopsuestia (*Psalms* 714) reads ἰσόψυχε ("soulmate"). Kselman and Barré ("Psalm," 449) see a connection between the "frenemy" in vv. 13–15 and the enemies in v. 3.

152. Ps 55:14. Reid ("Frenemy," 134) calls this section "the fulcrum of the psalm" because "it speaks to the heart of anyone who has survived trauma and betrayal at the hands of a trusted friend or relation. This is the part of the psalm that especially captures the voices of victims of child abuse and domestic violence, whose 'companions'

בבית אלהים נהלך ברגש   With whom I mill through the crowds in God's house
יש מות עלימו   May death come upon them!¹⁵³
ירדו שאול חיים   May they plummet alive into Sheol!
כי רעות במגורם בקרבם   For evil stains their dwellings to the core[154]
אני אל אלהים אקרא   But I call unto God
ויהוה יושיעני   And Yhwh saves me
ערב ובקר וצהרים אשיחה ואהמה   Evening, morning, and noon I moan and sigh
וישמע קולי   And he hears my voice
פדה בשלום נפשי   He ransoms my soul with compensation[155]
מקרב לי   From those who would threaten me
כי ברבים היו עמדי   For many stand against me
ישמע אל ויענם   The God forever enthroned
וישב קדם   Hears and humbles them[156]
אשר אין חליפות למו   There is nothing to exchange for them[157]
לא יראו אלהים   They do not fear God
שלח ידיו בשלמיו   He assaults his partners[158]
חלל בריתו   He profanes his covenant[159]
חלקו מחמאת פיו   His speech is smoother than butter[160]

---

have betrayed them with abuse and violence." Following Cottrill's (*Violence*, 13–15) division of human violence into three types (*direct/immediate, textual/symbolic, structural/cultural*), deClaissé-Walford ("Violence," 214–16) reads Ps 55 as an example of the first type (cf. Bail, *Gegen*, 173).

153. Ps 55:15 (lit., "be upon them"). N.B. the abrupt change in number and person both here and elsewhere in the Psalter (e.g., Pss 7:2–3; 17:11–12; 35:7–8; 55:20–21; 109:5–6).

154. Ps 55:15 (lit., "for evil is in their dwellings in the midst of them").

155. Ps 55:18. Cf. Syr ܠܝ ܡܢ ܐܝܠܝܢ ܕܩܪܒܝܢ ("from the practitioners plotting against me"). On שלם as "compensation" cf. Moore, *WealthWarn*, 159n24.

156. Ps 55:19. With NRSV and NIV the ET here reverses the syntactical order of these phrases.

157. Ps 55:19. MT חליפות ("exchange"); OG ἀντάλλαγμα ("exchange"); Vg *commutatio* ("exchange"); Syr ܚܘܠܦܐ ("exchange, substitute"). N.B. the parallel with חלל ברית ("profane the covenant") in v. 21, the preeminent Hebrew institution of peaceful "exchange."

158. Ps 55:20 (lit., "he sends forth his hand against those at peace with him"). It's not entirely clear whether this statement refers to the behavior of the "frenemy" in v. 13, but there seems little reason to doubt it.

159. Ps 55:21. Syr ܐܘܫܛ ܐܝܕܗ ܥܠ ܫܠܡܗ ܘܐܚܠ ܩܝܡܗ ("he sends forth his hand against his friend and profanes his covenant"; note the alliterative wordplay between ܫܠܡܗ and ܐܚܠ). The phrase חלל ברית ("profane the covenant") recurs in Ps 89:35 and Mal 2:10.

160. Ps 55:21. Kirkpatrick (*Psalms*, 314) defines "smoothness" as referring to "false and hypocritical flattery." Addressing various definitions for "praise" Simmons (*Talking*, 199) observes that some ANE "people seek God in ways that make sense to them or seem to work in their time. Flattering authority figures with authoritarian power that

וקרב לבו   But his heart is at war
רכו דבריו משמן   His words, more soothing than oil,
והמה פתחות   Are drawn swords[161]
השלך על יהוה יהבך   Cast your anxiety upon Yhwh[162]
והוא יכלכלך   And he will sustain you
לא יתן לעולם מוט לצדיק   He will not let the righteous be forever shaken[163]
ואתה אלהים תורדם לבאר שחת   But may you, O God, cast into the deepest Pit[164]
אנשי דמים ומרמה   The bloodthirsty[165] and the treacherous
לא יחצו ימיהם   Whose lives inevitably run short[166]
ואני אבטח בך   But for my part, I put my trust in you.[167]

COMMUNAL LAMENT

Communal laments tend to materialize at moments of national crisis.[168] Sumerian laments over fallen cities take standardized forms, the most

---

is used arbitrarily makes sense." Today, however, "the problem with this outmoded use of praise is the assumption that God wants or even needs ego gratification through flattery."

161. The "frenemy," in other words, is profoundly duplicitous in his dealings with others, a quality sharply condemned by Pascal, who observes that "man is nothing but disguise, falsehood and hypocrisy, both in himself and with regard to others. He does not want to be told the truth. He avoids telling it to others, and all these tendencies, so remote from justice and reason, are naturally rooted in his heart" (cited in Wood, *Pascal*, 103).

162. Ps 55:22. OG τὴν μέριμνάν σου, Vg *curam tuam*, and Syr ܨܦܬܟ all read "your anxiety."

163. Ps 55:22. OG σάλος, as in the phrase σεισθῆναι σάλῳ ("to shake violently," Eur. *Iph. taur.* 46).

164. Ps 55:23. One Qumran jurist draws a sharp contrast between the "paths of life" (דרכי חיים) and the "highways to the Pit" (נתיבות שחת, 4Q270 2.2.20; cf. Matt 7:13).

165. Ps 55:23 (lit., "men of bloods").

166. Ps 55:23. MT "who attain less than half their days."

167. Ps 55:23. For Pascal, "human life is nothing but a perpetual illusion. there is nothing but mutual deception and flattery. No one talks about us in our presence as he would in our absence . . . and few friendships would survive if everyone knew what his friend said behind his back" (cited in Wood, *Pascal*, 102).

168. Lee (*Singers*, 33) distinguishes *lament* (both individual and communal) from *dirge*: "Both genres deal with suffering and loss, the lament prayer (modeled in many psalms) is essentially a plea (that is, a prayer) addressed to the deity for intervention for help (thus it is characterized by 2nd person speech). The dirge, on the other hand, forewarns against or commemorates a death and/or destruction (and usually employs 3rd person speech)."

common being the BALAĜ (from the Sumerian word for "harp")¹⁶⁹ and the ERŠEMMA (from the Sumerian word for "tambourine").¹⁷⁰ Each *can* include a praise component,¹⁷¹ but unlike their Hebrew counterparts it is not obligatory.¹⁷² Paul Ferris subdivides the Psalter's communal laments into two categories, one for the demise of city-states, and the other for smaller communities.¹⁷³

Psalm 12

Psalm 12 is a good example of the latter:¹⁷⁴

הושיעה יהוה כי גמר חסיד	Save, O Yhwh, for the *ḥasidîm* are defeated¹⁷⁵
כי פסו אמונים מבני אדם	The faithful of humanity are vanished¹⁷⁶
שוא ידברו איש את רעהו	People say useless things to their neighbors¹⁷⁷
שפת חלקות בלב ולב ידברו	Muttering duplicitously through greasy lips¹⁷⁸
יכרת יהוה כל שפתי חלקות	May Yhwh cut off all greasy lips¹⁷⁹

169. Cohen (*BALAĜ*, 11) points out that *BALAĜ* texts, while national in scope, differ from communal laments over fallen cities in that the latter tend to focus on a specific historical event.

170. Krecher (*Kultlyrik*, 21) translates ER-ŠEM⁵-MA as "wail of the *šem* drum"). Cohen (*ERŠEMMA*, 5) points out that ERŠEMMA texts serve (a) as funeral dirges; (b) as incantations to ward off evil demons; (c) as dirges designed to pacify deities whose temples are for whatever reason being torn down; and (d) to engage in calendrical celebrations designed to maintain prophylactic protection against the anger of such deities.

171. Cooper (*Agade*, 20) views the *Curse of Agade* as a combination of BALAĜ and ERŠEMMA. Cf. Shipp, *Dirges*, 47–50.

172. Belnap ("Lament," 1–34) sees structural parallels between Hebrew communal laments and Hittite treaty formulae.

173. Ferris, *Lament*, 6–17, 145–46.

174. Dahood (*Psalms* 1.73) misreads Ps 12 as a "lament against personal enemies."

175. Ps 12:2. MT גמר can mean "to complete," as in Ug *gmr* (*UT* 592), but it can also mean "to end, destroy," esp. when paired with a verb like אסף ("to cease," Ps 77:8). On the *ḥasidîm*, see below.

176. Ps 12:1. MT פסס ("to vanish, disappear"); OG ὀλιγόω ("to lessen, diminish"); Vg *deminutae* ("to diminish"); Syr ܒܟܠܝ ("to cease, fail, come to nought").

177. Ps 12:2. MT (lit., "worthless," though the parallel with "duplicity" in the next line would suggest a meaning closer to "vileness"); OG μάταια ("empty things"); Vg *vana* ("vain things"); Syr ܣܪܝܩܐܬܐ ("idle, vain things").

178. Ps 12:2. One mentor at Qumran advises, "Do not rely on a man with twisted lips" (לוז שפתים) for "at your trial he will certainly use those lips to distort . . . the truth" (אמת משפטך הליו ילוז, 4Q424 1.8–9). Cf. *TEP* 131, "Are not those who twist the truth destined for destruction?"

179. Ps 12:3. MT כרת ("to cut"); OG ἐξολεθρεύω ("to destroy utterly"); Vg *disperdat* ("to scatter"); Syr ܒܣܪ ("to destroy"); Tg סוף ("to finish, destroy, ruin, diminish"). One

לשון מדברת גדולות	And tongues prone to arguing about "great things"[180]
אשר אמרו ללשננו נגביר	Who say, "*We* dictate policy with *our* decrees.[181]
שפתינו אתנו מי אדון לנו	*Our* lips are *ours*.[182] Who will stop us?"[183]
משד עניים	Because of violence against the poor
מענקת אביונים	And the groaning of the needy[184]
עתה אקום יומר יהוה	Yhwh says, "I will now arise,
אשית בישע יפיח לו	And provide the salvation for which they long."[185]
אמרות יהוה אמרות טהרות	Yhwh's words are pure[186]
כסף צרוף בעליל לארץ	Like silver purified in a furnace,
מזקק שבעתים	Purified seven times
אתה יהוה תשמרם	You, O Yhwh, protect us[187]
תצרנו מן הדור לעולם	You guide us from one generation to the next
סביב רשעים יתהלכון	Everywhere the wicked prowl
כרם זלות לבני אדם	As worthlessness is promoted among men.[188]

Qumran maven (4Q424 1.7–10) compares a man with "twisted lips" (לוז שפתים) to one who is "contentious" (תלונה) and has an "evil eye" (רע עין).

180. Ps 12:3. One Qumran commentator describes the individual in Hab 2:5 who "widens his throat like Sheol" (הרחיב כשאול נפשו) as the "Wicked Priest" (1QpHab 8.3–13), a character sometimes identified with Jonathan the High Priest (1 Macc 12:3l; cf. Lim, "Wicked," 973–76; Moore, *WealthWatch*, 182–88).

181. Ps 12:4 (lit., "with our tongues we conquer").

182. In other words, "We will say whatever we want." A more glaring rejection of "dialogical speech" (Buber) is hard to imagine.

183. Ps 12:4 (lit., "Who is *our* lord?"). Cf. Prov 26:23, "Like the glaze covering an earthen vessel are smooth lips covering an evil heart."

184. Ps 12:5. Zenger (*Vengeance*, 26) interprets this to be "a protest against the violence of violent people."

185. Ps 12:5 (lit., "to pant"). Cf. Eg. *m ʿwn ḥwrw ḥr jḥt=f*, "Do not defraud a poor man of his possessions" / *ꜣw pw n mꜣr jḥt=f*, "A pauper's belongings are his breath" / *dbb fnḏ=f pw nḥm st* "To seize them is to suffocate him" (TEP 262–65). In light of Ug *yph* ("witness," DULAT 974) Miller ("*Yāpîaḥ*," 497) translates, "I will put in safety the witness in his/her behalf."

186. Ps 12:7. OG τὰ λόγια ("the sayings"). The sudden shift to a listing of Yhwh's attributes mirrors the shift in 19:7.

187. MT reads a 3 m pl suffix ("you protect *them*"), but OG, Vg, and Syr all read a 1 c pl suffix ("you protect *us*"). Tg omits the 3 m pl suffix but retains the 2 m pl verb (תנתרנון לצדיקיא, "you guard the righteous"). On the "refuge" motif, cf. below.

188. Ps 12:8. Syr ܚܕܪܢ ܒܝܫܐ ܘܡܣܠܝܐ ܘܡܢ ܒܢܝ ܐܢܫܐ ܐܬܬܪܝܡܬ ("evil and abomination encircle us as corruption is promoted among men"); Tg חזור חזור רשיעיא מהלכין כעלוקא דמצצא דמיהון דבינשא ("the wicked walk around like leeches sucking out the blood of men").

Psalm 79

Manipulating the same components in an extended, more flexible way,[189] Ps 79, like Ps 74, laments one of Israel's most painful national tragedies—the destruction of the temple at the hands of foreign armies. Unlike Ps 74, though, Ps 79 avoids the mythopoeic language often used to depict the chaos-creation polarity in biblical texts like Genesis:[190]

אלהים באו גוים בנחלתך	O God, the nations[191] assault your heritage[192]
טמאו את היכל קדשך	They defile your holy temple[193]
שמו את ירשלים לעיים	They reduce Jerusalem to rubble
נתנו את נבלת עבדיך מאכל לעוף השמים	Feeding[194] your servants' bodies to the birds of the air
בשר חסידיך לחיתו ארץ	The flesh of your *ḥasidîm* to the beasts of the land.[195]
שפכו דמם כמים סביבות ירושלים	They pour out their blood[196] like water around Jerusalem
קובר ואין	And no one covers it.[197]
היינו חרפה לשכנינו	We are the target of our neighbors' reproach
לעג וקלס לסביבותינו	Mocked and ridiculed by those surrounding us.
עד מה יהוה תאנף לנצח	How long, O Yhwh? Will your anger burn forever?[198]
תבער כמו אש קנאתך	Will your fiery jealousy go on burning?
שפך חמתך אל גוים	Pour out your wrath upon the nations

---

189. Ferris (*Lament*, 7) recognizes the pattern in communal laments of structural components like divine invocation, lament proper, and appeal but is justifiably wary of calcifying it.

190. Cf. Sylva, "Discourse," 244–67; Basson, "Ruins," 128–37; Moore, *Chaos*, 13–26.

191. Ps 79:1. Vg translates *gentes* here and in Rom 15:11, which NRSV transliterates as "Gentiles" while KJV and Dahood (*Psalms* 2.249) read "heathen."

192. Ps 79:1. In light of the construct usage of אלהים + נחלת in 2 Sam 14:16, Lewis ("Estate," 597–612) argues that "ancestral estate" includes much more than just land possession (cf. Brichto, "Afterlife," 1–54).

193. Ps 79:1. N.B. that the Psalmist imagines the temple as "defiled" (טמא), not destroyed. Josiah uses this same verb (טמא, 2 Kgs 23:8) to label the "high places" littered throughout Judah.

194. Ps 79:2 (lit., "they give").

195. Ps 79:2. On *ḥasidîm* cf. footnote on 86:2 and below.

196. CAT 1.18.4.23–24 employs the metaphorical phrase *špk km šiy dm*, "pour out blood like an assassin."

197. Dahood (*Psalms* 2.251) notes that the Eshmunazar tombstone pronounces a curse on anyone robbing *his* grave that *they* "not be buried in a grave" (אל יקבר בקבר, KAI 14.8), and Tobit bitterly condemns the Assyrian policy of leaving the corpses of dead Jews in the streets (Tob 1:17–19; cf. Deut 21:23; Moore, *WealthWarn*, 145).

198. Ps 79:5. Cf. Ps 13:1, עד מה יהוה תשכחני נצח ("How long Yhwh? Will you forget me forever?"); Ps 85:5, הלעולם תאנף בנו ("Will you be angry with us forever?").

אשר לא ידעוך	Who do not recognize you,[199]
ועל ממלכות אשר בשמך לא קראו	Upon the kingdoms who do not call upon your Name[200]
כי אכל יעקב	For they devour Jacob[201]
ואת נוהו השמו	And destroy his habitation.
אל תזכר לנו עוונת רשונים	Remember not against us our former sins
מהר יקדמונו רחמיך	But expedite your compassion towards us
כי דלונו מאד	For we are very poor.[202]
עזרנו אלהי ישענו	O God of our salvation, help us!
על דבר כבוד שמך	According to the glory of your Name[203]
והצילנו וכפר על חטאתינו למען שמך	Deliver us! Paint over our sins for the sake of your Name[204]
למה יאמרו הגוים איה אלהיהם	Why should the nations say, "Where is their God?"[205]
יודע בגוים לעינינו נקמת דם עבדיך השפוך	Let the retribution for your servants' spilt blood Be exacted from the nations as we look on.[206]
תבוא לפניך אנקת אסיר	As the prisoners' groans ascend before you

199. Ps 79:6 (lit., "do not know you"). Note the wordplay: even as the nations "pour out" (שפך) the blood of the innocent, Yhwh is asked to "pour out" (שפך) his wrath on *them*.

200. Ps 79:6. What upsets Zionist extremists is that prophetic voices like Isaiah and Ezra unapologetically highlight Yhwh's determination to execute justice in Assyria (Isa 7:17) and Babylon (Ezra 5:12). They find this upsetting because they believe (a) that Yhwh cares about nobody except Hebrews and (b) that the nations can do nothing at Yhwh's behest without their permission (cf. Moore, *Babbler*, 226–27).

201. Ps 79:7. Isaiah laments that despite the fact that the Arameans on the east and the Philistines on the west "devour Israel," Israel refuses to change its ways (Isa 9:11), and one Qumran commentator applies this to the "Teacher of Lies" (מורה שקר, 4Q163 1.7).

202. Ps 79:8 MT דלל, "to be poor, humble"; OG ἐπτωχεύσαμεν σφόδρα ("made very poor"); Vg *pauperes facti sumus nimis* ("become extremely poor"); Syr ܐܬܡܟܟܢ ܠ ("brought quite low"); Tg לחדא אתמסכננא ("reduced to utter poverty").

203. Ps 79:9. Ezekiel is the biblical source most dramatically focused on Yhwh's "glory" (כבוד; cf. 3:12, 23; 8:4; 9:3; 10:4 *et passim*), but the Psalter is a close second (cf. Ps 8:1, 5; 19:1; 24:7–10; 29:2, 3, 9 *et passim*).

204. Ps 79:9. MT כפר (lit., "cover"; יום כפרים is the "Day of Covering," Lev 23:28); OG ἱλάσθητι, "to expiate"; Vg *propitius esto peccatis nostris*, "propitiate our sins"; Syr ܦܣܝ ܠܝ ܡܢ ܚܛܗܝ, "absolve me and deliver me from my sins"; Tg פרוק יתנא וכפר על חובנא, "deliver us and blot out our debt." On השם (*Ha-Shem*, "the Name") cf. below.

205. Ps 79:10. This question reappears in 115:2 and Joel 2:17.

206. Ps 79:10, lit., "be made known to our eyes"; OG ἐνώπιον τῶν ὀφθαλμῶν ἡμῶν ("before our eyes"); Syr ܐܬܝܕܥ ܒܥܡܡܐ ܠܥܝܢܝܢ (Let it be made known to the eyes of the Gentiles"); Tg פורענות למחמינא יתגלי בעמיא ("let an appearance of retribution be revealed to the Gentiles"; cf. Moore, *Retribution*, 97). The desire for retributional justice becomes even more pronounced in the reprisal psalms (see below).

כגדל זרועך הותר בני תמותה	By your great power spare those condemned to die[207]
והשב לשכנינו שבעתים אל חיכם	Pin onto our neighbors' chests
חרפתם אשר חרפוך אדני	Seven times the reproach they pin on you, Lord![208]
ואנחנו עמך וצאן מרעיתך	Then we your people, the sheep of your pasture
נודה לך לעולם	Will forever give you thanks
לדר ודר נספר תהלתיך	And declare your praise to future generations[209]

REPRISAL PSALMS

Vengeance is a dark, foul desire, and in spite of the fact that worshipers are repeatedly warned to avoid it,[210] it hovers over the margins of many lament psalms. In the so-called reprisal psalms it emigrates to the center,[211] but whether this emigration is healthy is a question often debated, especially among postmodern "progressives."[212] Some, like Franz Buggle, go out of their way to vilify the reprisal psalms as texts "dominated by primitive and uncontrolled feelings of hatred, a desire for vengeance, and self-righteousness."[213] Others, like Dietrich Bonhoeffer, contend (a) that the Psalms are simultaneously "the word of human beings and the Word of God;" and (b) that the psalmist's prayer is in fact the prayer of Jesus Christ, the "Word become flesh" (John 1:14).[214] Emphasizing the distance between premoderns and postmoderns, C. S. Lewis reminds the latter that the psalmists "live in a

---

207. Ps 79:11. The phrases "prisoner's groans" and "those doomed to die" recur in parallel in 102:21.

208. Ps 79:12 (cf. Ps 41:9). One Qumran psalmist complains, "I am the target of sl[ander for my rivals,] a cause for quarrel and argument to my neighbors, for jealousy and anger to those who join my cause, for challenge and grumbling to all my followers. Ev[en those who e]at my bread raise their heel against me, 'sneering at me with an evil lip'" (שפת עול ויליזו עלי, 1QH 13.22–24).

209. Ps 79:13. Echoing Girard (*Psaumes*, 376–81) Auffret ("Grandeur," 57) sees "a concentric arrangement of material around v. 7, and that vv. 1–6 and 8–13 respectively also form a parallel." Citing several parallels, Hossfeld and Zenger (*Psalms* 2.305) suggest that "overall this psalm is in an intertextual conversation with the book of Jeremiah" (cf. Moore, *Babbler*, 58–121).

210. Rom 12:19 (citing Deut 32:35).

211. Cf. Pss 57–59, 69, 109, 137, 139, and 149 (Wälchli, *Zorn*, 146–49). Seerveld ("Church," 150) contends that "it is scriptural . . . for God's people to utter ritual curses at critical times against Evil Incorporated."

212. Olson (*Progressive*, 1–2) insightfully defines the terms "progressive" and "liberal."

213. Buggle, *Wissen*, 22.

214. *DBWE* 14.387.

world of savage punishments, of massacre and violence, of blood sacrifice in all countries and human sacrifice in many," and further, that "we are, after all, blood-brothers to these ferocious, self-pitying, barbaric men."[215] Others, like Erich Zenger, argue that the reprisal psalms, bloody as they are, serve a twofold purpose: (a) to show that divine wrath is an outgrowth of divine love and should therefore be characterized not as irrational passion but as justifiable anger emanating from the heart of a protective Father; and (b) to show that mercy and wrath are ultimately rooted in what is certainly one of the most important of all divine attributes: *justice*.[216] Thus, Zenger argues, the reprisal psalms are intentionally designed to "rob the aggressive images of the enemies of their destructiveness and transform them into constructive forces."[217]

Drawn to Zenger's explanation, Gary Anderson applies it to Pss 57 and 58 to explain the dynamics of David's ingrained but prudently suppressed desire to take vengeance on his enemies, in this case his father-in-law King Saul.[218] What draws Anderson to these psalms is his concern that the Roman Liturgy of the Hours no longer requires the reading of the reprisal psalms "for priests and monastics who are obliged to pray this office daily" and that for all intents and purposes they have been "removed" from "the practice of the religious life."[219] Casey Barton also rejects this cancel-culture mentality, contending that faithful preaching "of the whole canon" must include a willingness "to preach these hard and sad texts to our listeners."[220] To this end Geoffrey Boyle highlights a decidedly pastoral rationale for singing the reprisal psalms, arguing that these "divine words" are specifically designed to help innocent sufferers discover "the missing armor, the comfort that has

---

215. Lewis, *Psalms*, 27.

216. In Egypt, Gestermann ("Zorn," 43) argues that "wrath" is but "one side of the divine double-nature," and Assmann (*Herrschafft*, 54) embellishes, arguing that divine anger includes the "anger of the judge who intervenes to save and the wrath of the Lord who confronts renegade vassals." Cornell (*Psalms*, 200) asks whether Yhwh's aggression is unique; i.e., "Does Yhwh alone damn his own king and country?" McCarter ("Temper," 87–88), on the other hand, argues that because Canaanite myths so systematically equate divine anger with divine "sickness," this suggests the possibility that Yhwh's anger may somehow be "a hypostatic or quasi-independent entity" which, in spite of his "beneficent regard for people, can be provoked into destructive activity by certain forbidden human activities."

217. Zenger, *Vengeance*, vii.

218. Anderson ("Imprecation," 272–77) observes that the tune title אל תשחת ("Do Not Destroy") appears in both 1 Sam 26:9 and in the superscriptions of Pss 57 and 58.

219. Anderson, "Imprecation," 267.

220. Barton, "Willows," 83.

been deprived to those who need it most."[221] Ellen Charry summarily agrees that "the reprisal psalms, if used to cling to anger and hurt may support unhealthy emotions, but when employed judiciously they can provide for catharsis and a way beyond pathological grief and anger, leaving God to resolve complicated situations."[222] Weighing these options carefully, Nadine Hamilton concludes that Bonhoeffer's approach is the "only" way "to understand how . . . the Christian can . . . pray the reprisal psalms."[223]

Psalm 58

At any rate, Ps 58 begins with pointed questions about (in)justice:

האמנם אלם צדק תדברון   Rulers, do you truly advocate for justice?[224]
מישרים תשפטו בני האדם   Do you judge people fairly[225]
אף בלב עולות תפעלון   When you devise evil in your hearts
בארץ חמס ידיכם תפלסון   And promote violence in the land?[226]
זרו רשעים מרחם   The wicked go astray from the womb[227]
תעו מבטן דברי כזב   Errant from birth, they speak lies[228]

221. Boyle, "Wellness," 193; cf. Hankle, "Psalms," 275–80.

222. Charry, "Psalm 35," 127.

223. Hamilton, "Psalms," 380. Maré ("Pray," 443) argues that the lament in Ps 22 "paves the way for all believers to use it in times of suffering" because "all believers have the right to pray as Jesus prayed."

224. Ps 58:1 (lit., "Do you truly, O gods, speak justice?"). A. Anderson's (*Psalms*, 430) translation of אלם as "be silent" is problematic (*HAL* 55 reads אלים as "gods, rulers"; cf. אלהים in 82:1), as is Dahood's convoluted reading of אמנם as "counselors" (*Psalms* 2.57), esp. in light of the parallel with מישרים ("uprightness") in the next line. Kraus (*Psalms 1–59*, 535) thinks that efforts to identify the meaning of אלים should attend more carefully to the mythopoetic idea that the gods are responsible for the execution of justice, especially the solar deities Šamaš (Mesopotamia), Ra (Egypt) and Šapšu (Canaan). Codex Hammurabi, e.g., is dedicated to Šamaš, and Arneth (*"Gerechtigkeit,"* 17) observes that alongside the rejection of Assyrian solar religion in 8th-century Yahwism (2 Kgs 23:11), "there is also a positive reception of Assyrian Šamaš–ideas with anti-Assyrian intentions." On צדק ("justice"), cf. below.

225. Ps 58:1. The word משפט ("justice, judgment") is the nominal form of the verb שפט ("to judge").

226. Ps 58:2 (lit. "when your hands weigh out violence"). This question stands at the center of *TEP, DILA, BT, Lud*, the Hebrew prophets, the book of Job, and other ANE texts (cf. discussion in Moore, *Retribution*, 71–116).

227. Ps 58:3. One of the most violent Canaanite deities, the virgin goddess Anat "deeply yearns" (Ug *agzrt*) to bear a child, but when "her womb experiences no conception" (Ug *kbdh lyd` hrh, CAT* 1.13.31) this "proves" that her violence can be "controlled."

228. Ps 58:3. One Qumran commentator interprets the individual condemned in Ps 37:7 as a reference to the contemporary individual called the "Man of Lies" (איש הכזב,

חמת למו כדמות חמת נחש	Their poison is like that of snakes[229]
כמו פתן חרש יאטם אזנו	Like deaf adders without ears
אשר לא ישמע לקל מלחשים	Unresponsive to the charmer's voice
חובר חברים מחכם	Or the sorcerer's spell.[230]
אלהים הרס שנימו	Shatter their teeth, O God
בפימו מלתעות כפירים נתץ יהוה	Tear out the lions' fangs, O Yhwh
ימאסו כמו מים יתהלכו למו	Melt them down like water
ידרך חציו כמו יתמללו	And trample them underfoot like dead dry grass[231]
כמו שבלול תמס יהלך	Like a snail dissolved in its own slime
נפל אשת בל חזו שמש	Like a miscarried baby never seeing the sun[232]
בטרם יבינו סירתיכם אטד	Before your cooking pots feel the brambles
כמו חי כמו חרון	When they start burning
ישערנו	Let them be swept away
ישמח צדיק כי חזה נקם	The righteous rejoice when they see retribution[233]
פעמיו ירחץ בדם הרשע	Washing their feet in the blood of the wicked,[234]
ויאמר אדם	So that a person might confess,
אך פרי לצדיק	"Surely there is a reward for the just[235]
אך יש אלהים שפטים הארץ	Surely there is a God who judges the earth."[236]

Psalm 35 begins with a petition to Yhwh that he might fight against the psalmist's enemies:

ריבה יהוה את יריבי	Contend, Yhwh, with those who contend against me[237]

4Q171.1.26; CD 20.15), a character often identified with the "Spouter of Lies" (מטיף הכזב, 1QpHab 10.9) and the "Wicked Priest" (הכוהן הרשע, 1QpHab 8.8; cf. discussion in Lim, "Liar," 493–94; "Priest," 973–76).

229. Ps 58:4. In Canaanite myth, Ba'al and Mot "bite each other like 'snakes'" (*b*ṯ*nm*, CAT 1.6.6.17–19).

230. Ps 58:6. Torah makes it clear that sorcerers and mediums will be allowed to "test whether you indeed love Yhwh your God with all your heart and soul" (Deut 13:3).

231. Ps 58:8 חציו ("arrows"), but *HAL* 329 suggests חציר ("grass").

232. Ps 58:9. Job uses many of these same images in his opening lament (Job 3:16).

233. Ps 58:10 is, in Maré's words ("Vengeance," 322), "quite disturbing" because "it is disturbing to read a psalm in which the psalmist prays for vengeance on his enemies, using a series of highly dramatic images to pray for their complete destruction."

234. Ps 58:10, reading "of" (instead of "in") with Dahood (*Psalms* 2.63).

235. Ps 58:11 (lit., "fruit to the *ṣadîq*"). In 56:7 "deliverance" (פלט) occurs with the release of divine "wrath" (אף). In 76:7 no one can stand before divine "wrath" (אף), and in 76:10 the purpose of "human wrath" (חמת אדם) is to generate "thanksgiving" (ידה). Retribution and compensation are two sides of the same coin (cf. Moore, *Retribution*, 97).

236. Lewis (*Pain*, 91–92) speaks of "the universal human feeling that bad men ought to suffer," and that "it is no use turning up our noses at this feeling, as if it were wholly base," because "on its mildest level it appeals to everyone's sense of justice."

237. Ps 35:1. The noun ריב ("lawsuit") structurally bookends this psalm by

חם את לחמי	Fight off those who plot war against me[238]
החזק מגן וצנה	Take up shield and javelin[239]
וקומה עזרתי	Rise up! Help me!
והחזק חנית וסגר לקראת רדפי	Take up hammer and shield against my pursuers[240]
אמר לנפשי ישעתך אני	Say to my soul, "*I am your salvation!*"[241]
יבשו ויכלמו מבקשי נפשי	May those who despise me be shamed and dishonored[242]
יסגו אחור ויחפרו חשבי רעתי	May the plotters of my ruin be ashamed and repelled
יהיו כמץ לפני רוח	May they become like chaff in the wind
ומלאך יהוה דוחה	Whisked away by Yhwh's angel
יהי דרכם חשך וחלקלקות	May their path be dark and slippery[243]
ומלאך יהוה רדפם	As Yhwh's angel pursues them[244]
כי חנם טמנו לי שחת	For they seek to entrap me for no reason[245]
רשתם חנה חפרו לנפשי	And for no reason they cast nets for my soul[246]

---

appearing here and in v. 23. Interestingly, one Qumran writer thinks that the phrase ריב אל ("Lawsuit of God") should be written on one of the banners carried into the final battle against the "sons of darkness" (1QM 4.12).

238. The psalmist's demands are hardly unprecedented, given the fact that Yhwh himself is called a "man of war" (איש מלחמה, Exod 15:3).

239. In the final battle against the world's infidels the "sons of light" hurl "seven javelins of war" (שבעה זרקות מלחמה) against the "sons of darkness" (1QM 6.2).

240. Ps 35:2. Listing offensive as well as defensive weapons, Fretz ("Weapons," 893) distinguishes four types of ANE weaponry: (a) projectile; (a) shock; (c) mobile; and (d) protective.

241. Ps 35:3. On ישוע ("salvation") cf. below.

242. Olyan ("Honor," 201–18) analyzes the contours of several honor-shame substrata covering ancient Israel.

243. Ps 35:6. At Qumran "straying from the path" (סרי דרך) involves several things, including "seeking easy interpretations" (דרשו חלקות), "choosing illusions" (יבחרו בהמהלות), "looking for loopholes," (יפצו לפרצות), "choosing the handsome neck" (יבחר בטוב הצואר), "acquitting the guilty" (יצדיקו רשע), and "sentencing the just" (ירשיעו צדיק), CD 1.13–19).

244. Ps 35:6. Yhwh's "angel" both protects (Exod 23:20) and destroys (Num 22:31), but in Qur'an an "angel" (ملك) is *never* sent to accompany divine revelation because such a strategy is perceived to make it more difficult for non-believers to convert, seeing as the angel's presence would instantly kill them (Q 6.8).

245. Ps 35:7. Kirta commands his army to "attack" (Ug wgr) the outlying towns and "entrap" (šrn) the villages surrounding Udum, the capital city of his rival Pabuli, the father of his future wife, Lady Ḥuraya (CAT 1.14.3.6, 39).

246. Ps 35:7. That חנם occurs twice seems no accident because synonyms for this semitic term are difficult to find. N.B. the similar repetition of חנם in the Prologue to Job (Job 1:9; 2:3l; cf. Moore, *Retribution*, 25–30).

תבואהו שואה לא ידע	May Shoah catch them off guard[247]
ורשתו אשר טמן תלכדו	May the nets they are hiding entrap *them*
בשואה יפל בה	May they fall into them as into their own Shoah[248]
ונפשי תגיל ביהוה	Then my soul will rejoice in Yhwh
תשיש בישועתו	And take delight in his deliverance,
כל עצמותי תאמרנה	Crying out with all my being,[249]
יהוה מי כמוך	"Who is like you, O Yhwh
מציל עני מחזק ממנו	Savior of the oppressed and needy[250]
ועני ואביון מגזלו	And the miserably exploited poor?"[251]
יקומון עדי חמס	Villainous witnesses arise
אשר לא ידעתי ישאלוני	Grilling me on things about which I know nothing
ישלמוני רעה תחת טובה	Repaying me evil for good
שכול לנפשי	Placing my soul at a loss
ואני בחלותם לבושי שק	For *I* don sackcloth when they are ill
עניתי בצום נפשי	I humble my soul with fasting
ותפלתי על חיקי תשוב	And when my prayers return unanswered
כרע כאח לי התהלכתי	I mourn as if for a friend or brother
כאם קדר שחותי בל	Disheveled, *I* weep for his mother
ובצלעי שמחו ונאספו	But at *my* stumbling they gather gleefully
נאספו עלי נכים ולא ידעתי	Secretly[252] recruiting thugs[253] against me[254]
קרעו ולא דמו	Always seeking to tear me down
בחנפי לעגי מעוג	Callously mocking me
חרק עלי שנימו	Gnashing their teeth at me
אדני כמה תראה	How long, Lord, will you continue to look on?

247. Ps 35:8a. N.B. that the phrase שואה לא ידע (lit., "Shoah he does not know") appears also in Isa 47:11. In contemporary Holocaust literature many Jewish writers prefer to describe what happens in 1930s-1940s Europe via the Heb term שואה ("Shoah") instead of the Lat term *holocaustum* (lit., "whole burnt offering"; cf. Baron, *Shoah*, 7–8; Gutmann, *Reckoning*, 107–25).

248. Ps 35:8. What might be described as the "Law of Redirection" ("may-that-which-is-planned-to-destroy-us-be-redirected-against-them") is in many ways the beating heart of retribution theology generally and the reprisal psalms specifically.

249. Ps 35:10 (lit., "all my bones").

250. Ps 35:10. MT מציל is the nominal/participial form of the verb נצל ("to save, deliver"). Cf. below on the "salvation" motif.

251. Ps 35:10 (lit., "robbed").

252. Ps 35:13, lit., "without my knowing."

253. Ps 35:15. MT נכים ("broken ones"; Tg רשיעיא, "evil ones") is ambiguous. OG reads μάστιγες ("whips"; Vg *flagella*), but Syr reads an adverb, ܐܓܪܐ ("at length"), omitting the verse's last two words. NIV reads "assailants" and NRSV "ruffians," but Thomas ("Psalm 35:15f," 51) emends to כנכרים ("like foreigners").

254. Ps 35:15. Jezebel's methods come to mind when reading this text, particularly her decision to hire two "sons of Belial" (בני בליעל) to testify against Naboth (1 Kgs 21:10; cf. Moore, *Faith*, 37–44).

הָשִׁיבָה נַפְשִׁי מִשֹּׁאֵיהֶם	Rescue my soul from their violence[255]
מִכְּפִירִים יְחִידָתִי	My life from the lions[256]
אוֹדְךָ בְּקָהָל רָב	I will thank you in the great assembly[257]
בְּעַם עָצוּם אֲהַלְלֶךָּ	I will praise you in the great throng
אַל־יִשְׂמְחוּ־לִי אֹיְבַי	Let not my enemies gloat over me
שֶׁקֶר שֹׂנְאַי חִנָּם יִקְרְצוּ־עָיִן	Or those who hate me roll their eyes for no reason
כִּי לֹא שָׁלוֹם יְדַבֵּרוּ	For they talk not about holistic peace
וְעַל רִגְעֵי־אֶרֶץ	But against the land's welfare
דִּבְרֵי מִרְמוֹת יַחֲשֹׁבוּן	Devising fraudulent messages[258]
וַיַּרְחִיבוּ עָלַי פִּיהֶם אָמְרוּ	They open their mouths wide, saying,
הֶאָח הֶאָח רָאֲתָה עֵינֵינוּ	"Aha! Aha! See what we mean?"[259]
רָאִיתָה יְהוָה	Do *you* see, Yhwh?
אַל־תֶּחֱרַשׁ אֲדֹנָי	Do not stay silent, Lord!
אַל־תִּרְחַק מִמֶּנִּי	Do not distance yourself from me!
הָעִירָה וְהָקִיצָה לְמִשְׁפָּטִי אֱלֹהַי	O my God! Rise up! Prepare my defense,
אֲדֹנָי לְרִיבִי	Defend me, Lord!
שָׁפְטֵנִי כְצִדְקְךָ יְהוָה	Judge me according to *your* justice,[260] O Yhwh
אֱלֹהַי אַל־יִשְׂמְחוּ־לִי	O my God, do not let them gloat over me
אַל־יֹאמְרוּ בְלִבָּם	Let them not say in their hearts,[261]
הֶאָח נַפְשֵׁנוּ	"Here we go again!"[262]
אַל־יֹאמְרוּ בִּלַּעֲנוּהוּ	Let them not say, "Let's *Balaam* him!"[263]
יֵבֹשׁוּ וְיַחְפְּרוּ יַחְדָּו	Let those who rejoice over my calamity
שְׂמֵחֵי רָעָתִי	Be shamed and rebuked[264]
יִלְבְּשׁוּ־בֹשֶׁת וּכְלִמָּה	May those who exalt themselves against me
הַמַּגְדִּילִים עָלָי	Be clothed with shame and regret[265]
יָרֹנּוּ וְיִשְׂמְחוּ חֲפֵצֵי צִדְקִי	May those who desire my vindication rejoice
וְיֹאמְרוּ תָמִיד	And continuously say,

---

255. Ps 35:17. Reading Syr ܐܢܫܐ.

256. Ps 35:17. Cf. the same נפש // יחיד parallel in 22:21.

257. Ps 35:18. OG reads ἐξομολογήσομαί σοι κύριε ("I will confess you, Lord"). Cf. footnote on 22:26.

258. *Example*: "US Teacher Charged."

259. Ps 35:21 (lit., "our eyes see"). Syr reads ܐܗܐ ܐܗܐ ("aha, aha"). The ET here is attempting to be as idiomatic as possible.

260. Ps 35:24. On צדק ("justice, righteousness"), cf. below.

261. Ps 35:25 (lit., "in their heart").

262. Ps 35:25 (lit., "Aha, our soul"). OG reads εὖγε εὖγε ("well, well," followed by Vg), but Syr more idiomatically reads ܐܟܣܘܗܝ ("here we go again").

263. Ps 35:25. MT בלע means "to swallow up," but since בלע is the root of the PN Balaam (בלעם = בלע + עם, "swallower of the people"), the ET here is less a translation than a paraphrase (cf. Moore, *Balaam*, 97–109).

264. Ps 35:26. This ET reverses the order of these two clauses.

265. Ps 35:26. The order is reversed here as well.

יגדל יהוה   "Great is Yhwh
החפץ שלום עבדו   Who delights in the welfare of his servant!"
ולשוני תהגה צדקך   Then my tongue will tell of your justice
כל היום תהלתך   And praise you every day[266]

Psalm 137

Psalm 137 is widely considered to be the quintessential psalm of reprisal:[267]

על נהרות בבל שם ישבנו   There, by the Babylonian canals, we sat down[268]
גם בכינו בזכרנו את ציון   And wept in remembrance of Zion[269]
על ערבים בתוכה תלינו כנרותינו   On the poplar trees we hung up our instruments[270]
כי שם שאלונו שובינו דברי שיר   When our captors demanded the lyrics of a song,[271]
ותוללינו שמחה   Our tormentors grunted,
שירו לנו משיר ציון   "Sing us one of those Zion songs!"

---

266. Charry ("Psalm 35," 127) observes that "like all the imprecatory psalms, Ps 35 invokes God as the agent of retribution for the humiliated speaker," thereby "enabling the speaker to express his hurt safely in the presence of those who empathize with him (God and his supporters, v. 27)."

267. Vv. 1–4 focus on "we"; vv. 5–6 focus on "I"; and vv. 7–9 are imperatives instructing Yhwh on what to do with Edom and Babylon (cf. Hossfeld and Zenger, *Psalms* 3.513).

268. Beaucamp (*Psautier* 2.266) observes that "Ps 137 occupies a unique place in the Psalter. It is the only one which can be dated with absolute certainty," and "there is certainly no question that it is the product of singers within the deported groups of 597 or 586." Cf. Barton, "Willows," 83–101; and Ahn, "Laments," 267–89.

269. Ps 137:1. Alroey (*Zionism*, 1–6) carefully distinguishes between Zion (the name of the Jebusite stronghold colonized by David, 2 Sam 5:7) and Zionism, a sociopolitical movement begun in response to 19th-century CE territorial proposals like the so-called Uganda Scheme to create a Jewish homeland in a portion of British East Africa. Though presented to the Sixth World Zionist Congress in Basel, this and all other schemes are rejected by Theodor Herzl, the founder of the Zionist movement, in favor of a Jewish homeland in the land originally settled by the twelve tribes of Israel (Josh 11:23).

270. Ps 137:2. MT כנור (Syr جنة; Tg כנר) refers to a stringed instrument like a harp or lyre, instruments eventually evolving in the East into the tanbur, oud and balalaika, and in the West into the lute, banjo and guitar. OG ὄργανον (Vg *organum*; cf. the English term "organ") broadly refers to a musical instrument of some kind.

271. Ps 137:3. In a hymn addressed to several Canaanite deities one Ugaritic writer specifies that it be accompanied by *knr wtlb btp wmṣltm mrqdm dšn* ("lyre and flute, tambourine and cymbals, even ivory castanets," *CAT* 1.108:4–5).

איך נשיר את שיר יהוה	But how can we sing a Zion song, O Yhwh,[272]
על אדמת נכר	On foreign soil?
אם אשכחך ירשלם	If I forget you, O Jerusalem,
תשכח ימיני	May my right hand be severed[273]
תדבק לשוני לחכי	May my tongue stick to the roof of my mouth
אם לא אזכרכי	If I do not remember you
אם לא אעלה את ירושלם	If I do not exalt Jerusalem
על ראש שמחתי	Above my highest joy[274]
זכר יהוה לבני אדום	Remember, O Yhwh, the Edomites[275]
את יום ירשלם האמרים	Who on the day of Jerusalem's fall[276] cried out,
ערו ערו עד היסוד בה	"Tear it down! Tear it down to its foundations!"
בת בבל השדודה	O daughter of Babylon![277] O Destroyer!
אשרי שישלם לך	Happy is the one who rewards you
את גמולך שגמלת לנו	With the "reward" with which you have "rewarded" us[278]
אשרי שיאחז ונפץ	Happy are those who seize your children
את עלליך אל הסלע	And dash them up against a rock![279]

272. The first word in this phrase is the adverb איך ("How!"), the first word in the Book of Lamentations.

273. Syr ܐܠܗܐ ܡܢܝ, "let my right hand perish"; OG ἐπιλησθείη ἡ δεξιά μου, "let my right hand forget"; Tg אנשיה לימיניה, "let my right hand be removed."

274. Ps 137:6. Focusing on the psalmist's repeated mention of Jerusalem in vv. 5–7, Goldingay (*Psalms* 3.599) suggests that this psalm is not so much about retribution for Edom and Babylon (vv. 7–9), but about "being mindful of Jerusalem."

275. Ps 137:7. Unlike the on-again, off-again relationship between Israel and Moab, the Israel-Edom relationship tends to be uniformly negative (cf. Amos 1:11; Bartlett, "Edom," 289–93; Moore, *Babbler*, 197–211).

276. MT and the vss. read "the day of Jerusalem," but Tg reads דאחריבו ירושלם, "when they (the Edomites) destroyed Jerusalem."

277. Ps 137:8. Babylon is sometimes called "Lady Babylon" (ᴰGAŠAN-KÁ.DIN-GIR.KI) in NA poetry (SAA 3.9.25).

278. Lit., "the compensation with which you compensated us" (N.B. the repetition of the root גמל for emphasis).

279. Ps 137:9. To those who find this psalm too violent for the canon, Hossfeld and Zenger (*Psalms* 3.523) point out that it "does not ask for power to carry out punishment against the enemies by one's own initiative, but leaves it to God," so "to that extent the psalm is an implicit rejection of violence."

2

Why Praise?

BETWEEN PRAISE AND THANKSGIVING

RESISTING ANY AND ALL boundaries between "praise" and "lament,"[1] Erhard Gerstenberger insists that the two genres have something in common in that both "engage in modes of human conduct fully responsible for life's good order," adding that "in contrast to Western... dogmatic narrowness, Near Eastern theology implicitly acknowledges the unfathomable depth of being which cannot be harmonized into a human, rational system."[2] To the question, "Why is praise such an important aspect of worship?" Edward Simmons suggests that the answer "lies not in God's nature, but in human need. Just as the desire for God is built into the human brain, so the need for praise as part of relationship is a built-in human need." Though often overlooked, it's obvious that "no God of holiness and separateness from all of creation... needs to be praised by his creatures."[3] Building on the praise-lament polarity resisted by Gerstenberger, Westermann attempts to

---

1. Westermann (*Praise*, 15–32), e.g., posits more form-critical divisions in the Psalms than do most other readers.

2. Gerstenberger, *Praise*, 13. (cf. his *Theologies*, 283–306). Pondering the impact of such polarized thinking on Western theologians, Stepaniants (*Eastern*, 81) cautions that "the stereotyped appraisal of the Western mode of thought as primarily "rationalistic" is obviously prompted by trends in the development of European philosophical thought in modern times. But such a designation is undoubtedly inapplicable to, say, medieval philosophy in Europe... Having found no Cartesian trend in the East, some scholars are prone to drawing hasty conclusions according to which rationality is in principle alien to the 'Oriental' mentality."

3. Simmons, *Bible*, 200.

draw another boundary between "thanksgiving" and "praise,"[4] basically dismissing Mowinckel's insight that "human thankfulness, when deepened and spiritualized . . . *becomes* praise."[5]

Psalm 103

Pondering these taxonomical options, Robert Foster reads Ps 103 as an archetypal *praise psalm* because it so obviously contains "numerous references to attributes and actions of Yhwh that serve as *reasons* for praise."[6]

ברכי נפשי את יהוה	Bless Yhwh, O my soul[7]
וכל קרבי את שם קדשו	Let everything within me bless his holy Name[8]
ברכי נפשי את יהוה	Bless Yhwh, O my soul
ואל תשכחי כל גמוליו	And overlook none of his rewards:[9]
הסלח לכל עונכי	He forgives all your sins
הרפא לכל תחלאיכי	He heals all your illnesses

---

4. Westermann, *Praise*, 25–30.

5. Mowinckel, *Psalmenstudien* 2.143 (emphasis added). Porter ("Music," 76) marvels at how "many of the psalms interweave joyful praise with cries of utter despair, anguish, and even anger at God's willful silence." Estes ("Transformation," 163) contends that "believers today can move from pain into praise through the process of meditation."

6. Foster, "Praise," 80 (emphasis added). Goldingay ("Cycle," 86) distinguishes between Babylonian and Israelite psalmody in that "Babylonian psalmody moves in one . . . direction (from praise to prayer)" while "Israelite psalmody is cyclic," i.e., "that the end of one psalm can be the beginning of another." Gerstenberger (*Praise*, 14), however, challenges this analysis, arguing that both Babylonian and Hebrew psalmody demonstrate the workings of cultures (a) "committed to creating and maintaining that harmonic order intended by the great deities and inherent in all being," because (b) "humans on all social levels take co-responsibility to ward off destructive forces ('petition') and strengthen the beneficial ones ('praise')."

7. Psalm 103 both begins and ends with the same ברך-blessing (cf. Scharbert, "ברך," 279–308). Willis ("Psalm 103," 526) subdivides the psalm into five strophes "marked most often, though not always, by stylistic features found at the beginning of cola." Goldingay (*Psalms* 3.164–65) views it as a "cross between a testimony psalm and a praise psalm, structurally moving from 'you' (the self; vv. 1–5) to 'they' (Israel of the past; vv. 6–9) to 'we' (Israel of the past and present; vv. 10–14) to humanity (vv. 15–18) to the heavenly and earthly cosmos (vv. 19–22)."

8. Ps 103:1. On השם (*Ha-Shem*, "the Name") cf. below.

9. Ps 103:2. MT גמוליו ("benefits, compensations"); OG ἀνταποδόσεις ("rewards, compensations"); Vg *retributiones* ("retributions"); Syr ܦܘܪܥܢܐ ("rewards, compensations"); Tg חסולוי ("his finished works"). Cf. the recurrence of גמל in v. 10 and N.B. that (a) the positive connotations appear in the PN גמליאל ("Gamaliel," "God is my reward"), while (b) the negative connotations emerge in the placarded phrase אל גמול ("Retribution of God," 1QM 4.12; cf. Seybold, "גמל," 33).

הגואל משחת חייכי	He redeems your life from the Pit[10]
המעטרכי חסד ורחמים	He crowns you with *ḥesed* and mercy[11]
המשביע בטוב עדיך	He satisfies your bodies with good things[12]
תתחדש כנשר נעוריכי	He renews your youth like the eagle's[13]
עשה צדקות יהוה	Yhwh works for vindication[14]
ומשפטים לכל עשוקים	And justice for all the oppressed[15]
יודיע דרכיו למשה	He makes known his ways to Moses,
לבני ישראל עלילותיו	His deeds to the children of Israel[16]
רחום וחנון יהוה	Yhwh is merciful and gracious
ארך אפים ורב חסד	Slow to anger and abounding in *ḥesed*
לא לנצח יריב	He does not always prosecute[17]
ולא לעולם יטור	Nor is he always angry[18]
לא כחטאינו עשה לנו	He does not treat us as our sins deserve
לא כעונותינו גמל עלינו	Nor does he compensate us for our iniquities *quid pro quo*
כי כגבה השמים על הארץ	For as high as the heavens are above the earth
גבר חסדו על יראיו	So is the power of his *ḥesed*-loyalty to those who fear him
כרחק מזרח ממערב	As far as the east is from the west[19]
הרחיק ממנו את פשעינו	He eradicates our transgressions
כרחם האב על בנים	Like a father compassionate toward his children
רחם יהוה על יראיו	So is Yhwh compassionate toward those who fear him

10. Ps 103:3–4. As "benefits" (גמולים, v. 2) go, forgiveness, healing and redemption are hardly peripheral (cf. Moore, *Wealth Watch*, 148–67).

11. Ps 103:4. N.B. that the D form of עטר ("to crown") recurs in 8:6. Playing off v. 15, Weiser (*Psalms*, 657) calls this psalm "one of the purest blossoms on the tree of biblical faith." On *ḥesed*, cf. below.

12. Ps 103:5. Reading with Syr ܡܣܒܥ ܒܛܒܬܐ ܨܒܝܢܟ.

13. Ps 103:5. Goldingay (*Psalms* 3.169) dismisses any mythopoetic referral to the life-renewal motif symbolized by eagles (cf. Job 29:18; Gunkel, *Psalmen*, 445), but N.B. that in one Canaanite myth Baʻal searches for prince Aqhat's bones in the gullets of suspected eagles, and when no bones are found he "rebuilds" (Ug *bn*; cf. Heb בנה) their bodies and wings and sends them on their way revived (*CAT* 1.19.3.12–13).

14. Ps 103:6. OG reads ποιῶν ἐλεημοσύνας ὁ κύριος ("the LORD extends mercies, alms") followed by Vg *misericordias* ("mercies"), but Syr ܘܬܒܥܬܐ ("vindication") and Tg צדקתא ("vindication, justice") follow MT.

15. Ps 103:6. On the "justice" motif spotlighted by the word-pair צדקה // משפט, cf. below.

16. Ps 103:7. "Ways" and "deeds" seem tame compared to God's promise at the burning bush; viz., that in Egypt Moses will witness נפלאתי ("my wonders," Exod 3:20; cf. Vg *mirabilibus meis*, "my miracles"; Syr ܐܬܘܬܐ, "the signs"; Tg פרשוותי, "my wonders").

17. Ps 103:9. On the judicial nuance of ריב as "prosecute" see footnote on 35:1.

18. Ps 103:9. Cf. McCarter, "Temper," 78–91.

19. Ps 103:12. Cf. "I tell you, many will come from east and west to eat with Abraham and Isaac and Jacob in the kingdom of heaven" (Matt 8:11).

WHY PRAISE? 55

כי הוא ידע יצרנו	For he knows our limitations[20]
זכור כי עפר אנחנו	He remembers that we are but dust
אנוש כחציר ימיו	A man's days are like grass
כציץ השדה כן יציץ	Like a wildflower in bloom
כי רוח עברה בו ואיננו	When the wind blows it disappears
ולא יכירנו עוד מקומו	And its place is no longer recognized[21]
וחסד יהוה מעולם ועד עולם	But Yhwh's *ḥesed* goes on forever
על יראיו	For those who fear him
וצדקתו לבני בנים	And his justice is for the grandchildren
לשמרי בריתו	Who keep his covenant
ולזכרי פקדיו לעשותם	And remember to obey his commandments[22]
יהוה בשמים הכין כסאו	Yhwh establishes his throne in the heavens
ומלכותו בכל משלה	And his kingship dominates everything[23]
ברכו יהוה מלאכיו	Bless Yhwh, O you his messengers[24]
גברי כח עשי דברו	You mighty ones who do his will
לשמע בקול דברו	Who obey his spoken word
ברכו יהוה כל צבאיו	Bless Yhwh, all you his armies
משרתיו עשי רצונו	You ministers who do his will
ברכו יהוה כל מעשיו	Bless Yhwh, all his works
בכל מקמות ממשלתו	In all the places where he rules
ברכי נפשי את יהוה	Bless Yhwh, O my soul.

20. Ps 103:14. OG πλάσμα ἡμῶν (lit., "our plasma"); Syr ܚܒܠܢ ("our moulding"); Tg יצרנא ("our inclination"). N.B. the "two inclinations" in 1QS 3.13–14, the יצר הטוב ("good inclination") vs. the יצר הרע ("bad inclination"). Cf. van der Horst, "Inclination," 318).

21. Ps 103:14–16 (cf. John 3:8). Charnock's (*Discourses*, 489) comments remain relevant: "He not only remembers our sins, he remembers our frame of formation, what brittle but clear glasses we were by creation, how easy to be cracked! He remembers our impotent and weak condition by corruption; what a sink we have of vain imaginations that remain in us after regeneration . . . Had he lost the knowledge of how he first framed us, did he not still remember the mutability of our nature, as we were formed and stamped in his mint, how much more wretched would our condition be than it is!"

22. Ps 103:17–18.

23. Ps 103:19. On the "kingship" motif cf. below.

24. Ps 103:20–22. The psalm's final verses pronounce a blessing upon Yhwh's angels, armies, ministers and works.

Psalm 30

Mitchell Dahood finds in Ps 30 a "tightly structured psalm of thanksgiving for recovery from illness,"[25] a conclusion shared by Franz Delitzsch and Klaus Seybold:[26]

ארוממך יהוה כי דליתני	I lift you up, Yhwh, for you allowed me to fail[27]
ולא שמחת איבי לי	But did not permit my enemies to gloat over me
יהוה אלהי שועתי אליך	O Yhwh, my God, I cried out to you for help
ותרפאני	And you healed me
יהוה העלית מן שאול נפשי	You lifted up my soul from Sheol, Yhwh
חייתני מירדי בור	You revived me from among those gone down to the Pit
זמרו ליהוה חסידיו	Let the *ḥasidim* chant before Yhwh[28]
והדו לזכר קדשו	And give thanks to commemorate his holiness[29]
כי רגע באפו	For his anger is momentary[30]
חיים ברצנו	But his favor lifelong
בערב ילין בכי	Weeping may linger in the evening
ולבקר רנה	But joy comes in the morning
ואני אמרתי בשלוי	When things are going well I think,[31]
בל אמוט לעולם	"I will never stumble[32]

---

25. Dahood, *Psalms* 1.182.

26. Delitzsch, *Psalms*, 453; Seybold, *Studien*, 274. Fohrer (*Introduction*, 287) reads Ps 30 as an individual psalm of thanksgiving, Westermann (*Psalter*, 65) as an individual declarative psalm of praise, and Craigie (*Psalms*, 251) as an individual psalm of thanksgiving/praise (cf. Becker, *Psalmenexegese*, 52–57).

27. Ps 30:1. MT דליתני may derive from either דלה ("to draw up") or דלל ("to make small"). The vss. tend to go with the first option, but Goldingay (*Psalms* 1.423) suggests that the second more strikingly connotes the recognition that things sometimes go down before they go up. Whatever the case, the psalmist seems ambivalent because in v. 3 he is grateful not to be in the pit, but in v. 9 he seems to be asking whether the pit is still an option. Thus Craigie's subtitle seems to be most *apropos*: "Praise for Deliverance from the Danger of Death" (*Psalms*, 250).

28. Ps 30:4. On זמר as "chant" cf. OG ψάλλω, Vg *psallite*, and Syr ܙܡܪ. On *ḥesed*, see footnote on 86:2 and discussion below.

29. Ps 30:4. Ridderbos (*Psalmen*, 224) identifies ידה ("to thank") as both the "keyword" and the "closing word," seeing as it occurs three times in the psalm (Ps 30:4, 10, 12). Sukenik (d. 1953) chooses the term הודיות (*Hodayot*, 'thanksgiving') to describe the sectarian hymnal retrieved from Qumran Cave 1 because so many of its songs begin with some form of ידה (cf. VanderKam and Flint, *Scrolls*, 6–7; Moore, *Babbler*, 94–121).

30. Ps 30:5. Baʿal's anger, on the other hand, is something in which he "languishes" (Ug *anš*, CAT 1.2.1.38), as does Mot (*anšt*, 1.6.5.21; cf. McCarter, "Temper," 78–91), Marduk (*Erra* 1.32–38), and esp. Erra ("when Erra is enraged, no one can advise him," *Erra* 5.12; cf. Krebernik, "Zorn," 55–66; Moore, *WealthWatch*, 89–98).

31. Ps 30:6 (lit., "Now I say in my prosperity").

32. Ps 30:6. Cf. the use of מוט ("to falter") in 10:6; 13:5; 16:8; 62:3, 7.

יהוה ברצונך	For through your favor, Yhwh
העמדתה להררי עז	You stand me up like a strong mountain."[33]
הסתרת פניך	But when you hide your face[34]
הייתי נבהל	I become dismayed
אליך יהוה אקרא	I call on you, O Yhwh
ואל אדני אתחנן	And to the Lord I make supplication:
מה בצע בדמי	What profit is there in my death?[35]
ברדתי אל שחת	If I sink into the Pit[36]
היודך עפר	Will the dust give you thanks?
היגיד אמתך	Will it tell of your faithfulness?[37]
שמע יהוה וחנני	Listen, Yhwh, and be gracious to me
יהוה היה עזר לי	Help me, Yhwh!
הפכת מספדי למחול	Let my mourning be transformed into dancing
פתחת שקי ותעזרני שמחה לי	Take away my sackcloth and clothe me with joy
למען יזמרך כבוד	So that I may chant "Glory" to you[38]
ולא ידם	And not remain silent
יהוה אלהי	O Yhwh my God

33. Ps 30:6–7. Whereas the biblical psalmist attributes his good fortune to Yhwh, one Qumran poet exhorts listeners to rely on themselves: "May your own hand deliver you" (תושעך ידך, 4Q380 1.2.4).

34. Ps 30:7. The Isaianic tradition makes it clear that the Holy One will on occasion "hide himself" (מסתתר, Isa 45:15; cf. 104:29; Miskotte, *Silent*, 267; Burnett, *Absence*, 2; Podella, *Trauer*, 33–70; Gerstenberger, *Petition*, 15–26). Critical of Luther's theology of *deus absconditus* ("absentee God"), Barth (*Dogmatik*, 179) insists that overemphasis on it is Christologically problematic (cf. discussion in Brian, *Luther*, 1–7).

35. Ps 30:9. Judah asks a similar question of his brothers with regard to Joseph: "What 'profit' (בצע, same word) is there in murdering our brother and concealing his blood?" (Gen 37:26).

36. Ps 30:9. Charry's structural analysis (*Psalms*, 99–100) helps explain why the two mentions of "Pit" in this psalm hold different connotations: (a) vv. 4–5 urge the audience to praise God for rescue from the pit; and (b) vv. 6–12 go into "lament mode" where the pit seems again to be an option. Loader ("Psalm 30," 293) calls this "structural inversion."

37. Daschbach (*Father*, 54) contends that these verses "deny the afterlife," but what it in fact denies is a vacuous *understanding* of the afterlife. Several Canaanite texts testify to the belief that life continues after death. When Baʻal pleads to El on behalf of a barren King Danel, e.g., he asks that El provide, among other things, someone to (a) "bring up his funerary incense from the earth/netherworld (Ug *arṣ*), (b) protect his 'tomb' (lit., "place," *mqm*, as in *KAI* 214.14) from the dust (ʻ*pr*), (c) dismiss the reproaches of his enemies, and (d) shut the jaws of his detractors" (*CAT* 1.17.1.27–29). Hays (*Death*, 349) contends that while "ancestor cults," at least among royal families, "are largely obscured in the present form of the biblical texts, they probably coexist alongside Yhwh's cult in Jerusalem and elsewhere mostly without incident until the eighth century, when a combination of social and religious forces brings them into official disfavor."

38. Ps 30:11. Cf. Syr ܐܘܕܐ ܠܟ ܐܝܩܪܟ ("praise your glory"). Cf. the continuous chanting of קדוש ("Holy") by the *seraphim* in Isa 6:3.

לעולם אודך   I will forever give you thanks.

Psalm 107

Psalm 107 is a thanksgiving psalm structured around four recurrences of the word ידה ("to give thanks") scattered over four "stanzas"[39] designed to show how Yhwh rescues four groups of people: (1) enslaved souls in need of redemption (vv. 2–9); (2) prisoners suffering for rebellious deeds (vv. 10–16); (3) sick folks suffering from disease (vv. 17–22); and (4) seafarers suffering the fear of drowning on the job (vv. 20–32).[40]

Stanza 1—Redemption

הודו ליהוה כי טוב	Give thanks to Yhwh, for he is good
כי לעולם חסדו	For his *ḥesed* lasts forever
יאמרו גאולי יהוה	Let those redeemed by Yhwh speak up[41]
אשר גאלם מיד צר	Those who have been redeemed from trouble
ומארצות קבצם	Gathered from lands[42]
ממזרח וממערב	East and West
מצפון ומים	North and South

---

39. Raabe (*Psalms*, 21–28) defines a "stanza" as (a) a metrical unit comprised of one or more strophes, and (b) often isolated by refrains, like the one in Pss 42:5, 11; 43:5: "Why are you cast down, O my soul, and why are you disquieted within me? Hope in God; for I shall again praise him, my help and my God." The Sumerian Lamentation Over the Destruction of Ur (*COS* 1.166.535–38; Michalowski, *Lamentation*) consists of eleven KI-RU-GU$_2$ "stanzas" (Ferris, "Lamentations," 411).

40. Dahood (*Psalms* 3.80) views this psalm as a prologue, four stanzas, and a closing hymn, "which, in the style of Wisdom literature, develops the theme of reversal of fortunes." Broyles (*Psalms*, 408) subtitles it "The Lord of Reversals: Thanksgiving of Desert Wanderers, Prisoners, the Sick, and Sailors." Wilson (*Psalter*, 187–90) agrees that Ps 107, the first psalm in Book 5, uses language most likely drawn from the wisdom tradition, pointing out that the first psalms of Book 1 (Ps 1) and Book 4 (Ps 90) are wisdom psalms. Tucker (*Power*, 16), however, thinks that the purpose of Book 5 (beginning with Ps 107) is to "construct a subtle anti-imperial ideology in response to the threats imposed from all empires both past and present, but in particular the Persian empire." Beyerlin (*Werden*, 1) lists several redactoral theories designed to explain the structure of Ps 107, and Allen (*Psalms*, 63) suggests that "an older poem (vv. 1, 4–32) appears to have been taken over and re-used for a new situation."

41. On the theological motif of "redemption," cf. Moore, *WealthWatch*, 148–58.

42. Ps 107:3. To "gather from the lands" parallels the phrase in the previous psalm (106:47, "to gather from the nations"). Both phrases feature the verb קבץ ("to gather").

תָּעוּ בַּמִּדְבָּר בִּישִׁימוֹן Wandering the wastelands of the wilderness[43]
דֶּרֶךְ עִיר מוֹשָׁב לֹא מָצָאוּ Finding no path to a settled city
רְעֵבִים גַּם צְמֵאִים Hungry and thirsty
נַפְשָׁם בָּהֶם תִּתְעַטָּף Their souls fading fast[44]

Chorus:[45]

וַיִּצְעֲקוּ אֶל יְהוָה בַּצַּר לָהֶם But then they cry out to Yhwh in their distress
מִמְּצוּקוֹתֵיהֶם יַצִּילֵם And he delivers them from it
וַיַּדְרִיכֵם בְּדֶרֶךְ יְשָׁרָה Guiding them on a straight path
לָלֶכֶת אֶל עִיר מוֹשָׁב Toward city settlements[46]
יוֹדוּ לַיהוָה חַסְדּוֹ Let them thank Yhwh for his *hesed*-loyalty
וְנִפְלְאוֹתָיו לִבְנֵי אָדָם And his wondrous deeds for humanity
כִּי הִשְׂבִּיעַ נֶפֶשׁ שֹׁקֵקָה For he satisfies the soul of the thirsty
וְנֶפֶשׁ רְעֵבָה מִלֵּא טוֹב And fills the hungry with good things[47]

Stanza 2—Emancipation

יֹשְׁבֵי חֹשֶׁךְ וְצַלְמָוֶת Some sit in darkness on death row[48]

43. Ps 107:4. N.B. (a) that the מדבר/ישימון parallel recurs in 78:40 and 106:14, two psalmic summaries of the wilderness period (basically, Exodus-Deuteronomy; cf. Moore, *Chaos*, 51–129); and (b) that the verb used here is תעה ("to stray, err"), not עבר ("to wander"; an עברי is a "Hebrew," a "wanderer").

44. Psalm 107:1–5 succinctly describes a homeless population (a) scattered to the four corners; (b) astray and lost; (c) hungry and thirsty; and (d) weak. Whether this refers to Zedekiah's imprisonment at the beginning of the Babylonian exile is possible (so Tg), but homelessness is hardly limited to one time or place (cf. discussion in Goldingay, *Psalms* 3.247–48). Allen (*Psalms*, 60) thinks that "all four accounts are concerned with everyday occurrences, with reality in its manifold fullness."

45. The chorus is the component of a song which repeats multiple times. Not all songs have choruses, but the general rule of thumb is that in those which do, the chorus is the place to showcase the song's main theme(s). What makes the four choruses in Ps 107 interesting is the way in which the psalmist artfully engages the main theme of "deliverance/salvation."

46. Ps 107:7. In other words they become "city-dwellers" (*ša ašib ali*, Erra 1.55), a positive appellation in the Gilgamesh Epic (Gilgamesh is a "city-dweller," Enkidu is a "field-dweller"), but a negative one in the Epic of Erra (vis-à-vis "field-dwellers," *ša akil šēri*, Erra 1.56; cf. Moore, *WealthWatch*, 89–99).

47. Ps 107:7. Both Landy ("Cities," 79) and Matthews ("Threshing," 25–40) highlight the interdependence between threshing floors and city settlements.

48. MT צלמות is a compound noun meaning "shadow of death" (Ps 23:4), but "death

אסירי עני וברזל	Prisoners in misery and in irons
כי המרו אמרי אל	For having rebelled against God's words
ועצת עליון נאצו	And spurning the counsel of the Most High[49]
ויכנע בעמל לבם	Their hearts broken by toil,
כשלו ואין עזר	Struggling with no one to help[50]

CHORUS:

ויזעקו אל יהוה בצר להם	Then they cry out to Yhwh in their pain[51]
וממצבותיהם יושיעם	And he delivers them from their distress
יוציאם מחושך וצלמות	He escorts them out of death row darkness
ומוסרותיהם ינתק	And breaks their chains
יודו ליהוה חסדו	Let them thank Yhwh for his *ḥesed*-loyalty
ונפלאותיו לבני אדם	And his wondrous deeds for humanity
כי שבר דלתות נחשת	For he breaks down bronze doors
ובריחי ברזל גדע	And cuts through iron bars[52]

Stanza 3—Healing

אולים מדרך פשעם	Some fools chase sinful paths

---

row" is more idiomatically relevant today.

49. Prior to the exile, Jeremiah asks, "Who has stood in the council of Yhwh so as to see and hear his word?" (Jer 23:18), and DH explains that the exile occurs "because the people of Israel sinned against Yhwh their God, who had brought them up out of the land of Egypt from under the hand of Pharaoh king of Egypt, worshiping other gods and walking in the customs of the Gentiles" (2 Kgs 17:7–8; cf. Moore, *Faith*, 343–50).

50. Ps 107:12. OG ἀσθενέω ("they were weak"); Vg *infirmati sunt* ("they were infirm"); Syr ܐܬܟܪܗܘ ("they were sick"); Tg אתקילו ("they were degraded"). That the vss. tend to associate illness with imprisonment is not unusual because, as Dahood (*Psalms* 3.85) points out, the "causal relationship between sin and sickness" is universally presumed in the ancient world. In the Kirta Epic, e.g., Prince Yaṣṣib presumes that his father's *zblh* ("sickness") is because *ltdn dn almnt lttpt tpt qṣr npš* ("you do not judge the widow's case or try the case of the less fortunate," CAT 1.16.6.45–47). Only later does the Nazarene prophet debunk the sin < sickness equation (John 9:1–3).

51. Ps 107:13. The greatest example of this in Tanak, of course, is the cry of the Hebrew prisoners in Egypt: "I have seen the pain of my people in Egypt; I have heard their cries on account of their taskmasters, and I truly understand their suffering" (Exod 3:7; cf. Moore, *Chaos*, 51–66).

52. Ps 107:16. Isaiah uses this same couplet in his commissioning of Cyrus "to subdue nations before him and strip kings of their robes" (Isa 45:1–2).

ומעונותיהם יתענו	And suffer affliction for their iniquitous deeds[53]
כל אוכל תתע בנפשם	Their souls reject all food
ויגיעו עד שארי מות	As they begin to approach the gates of death[54]

Chorus:

ויזעקו אל יהוה בצר להם	Then they cry out to Yhwh in their pain
ממצכותיהם יושיעם	And he delivers them from their distress
ישלח דברו וירפאם	He sends forth his word and heals them
וימלט משחיתותם	He rescues them from the Pit
יודו ליהוה חסדוב	Let them thank Yhwh for his *ḥesed*-loyalty
ונפלאותיו לבני אדם	And his wondrous deeds for humanity
ויזבחו זבחי תודה	Let them offer sacrifices of thanksgiving
ויספרו מעשיו ברנה	And recount his works with joy

Stanza 4—Calming the Storm

יורדי הים באניות	Some march down to ships on the sea[55]
עשי מלאכה במים רבים	To do business on dangerous waters[56]
המה ראו מעשי יהוה	They see the works of Yhwh
ונפלאותיו במצולה	His marvelous accomplishments in the deep
ויאמר ויעמד רוח סערה	He speaks and the winds begin to blow
ותרומם גליו	Stirring up the waves of the sea
יעלו שמים	Rising up to the heavens
ירדו תהומות	And plunging down to the depths
נפשם ברעה תתמוגג	Their souls paralyzed by distress,
יהוגו וינועו כשכור	They stumble and stagger like drunkards

---

53. Ps 107:17. See footnote on v. 12.

54. Ps 107:18 (lit., "touch the gates of death"). Elsewhere in the Psalter the phrase "the gates of death" (9:13) stands in contrast with "the gates of Daughter Zion" (9:14), an obvious life-vs.-death polarity. N.B. (a) that עיר מתים ("the city of the dead," Job 24:12) has walls and gates just like the cities above ground; and (b) that the heavens also possess a "gate" (שאר השמים, Gen 28:17).

55. Ps 107:23. "Sea" (ים) is one of the "big three" deities in the Canaanite pantheon ("Sea," "Land," and "Death"; cf. *CAT* 1.2.3.7, 8, 12, 16, 21; Stolz, "Sea," 737–42).

56. Ps 107:23. Cf. footnote on 29:3, but in all likelihood מים רבים ("great waters") refers not so much to chaos as to the dangerous storms seafarers regularly have to face on the Mediterranean, memorably depicted in the book of Jonah (cf. Knapp, *Seafaring*; Beresford, *Sailing*; R. Anderson, *Sailing*).

וכל חכמתם תתבלע   As all their capabilities are swallowed up[57]

Chorus:

ויזעקו אל יהוה בצר להם   Then they cry out to Yhwh in their pain
ממצבותיהם ויוציאם   And he releases them from their distress[58]
יקם סערה לדממה   He quiets the storm
ויחשו גליהם   And calms the waves
וישמחו כי ישתקו   They rejoice as things quiet down[59]
וינחם אל מחוז חפשם   And he leads them into their desired port[60]
יודו ליהוה חסדוב   Let them give thanks to Yhwh for his *ḥesed*-loyalty
ונפלאותיו לבני אדם   And his wondrous deeds for humanity
וירממוהו בקה לעם   Let him be celebrated in the people's assembly
ובמושב זקנים הללוהו   And praised in the council of the elders[61]

Closing Hymn[62]

ישם נהרות במדבר   He turns rivers into desert
ומצאי מים לצמאון   And wellsprings into wasteland
ארץ פרי למלחה   Fertile land into salt flats

---

57. Ps 107:25–27. Cf. Jonah 1:4–5—"Yhwh hurled a great wind upon the sea, and such a mighty storm came upon the sea so that the ship threatened to break apart. Then the mariners were afraid, and each cried out for his god."

58. N.B. that whereas the previous refrains repeat the verb ישע ("to save, deliver"), the verb here is יצא ("to go out").

59. Ps 107:30. Cf. Jonah 1:15—"So they grabbed Jonah and threw him into the sea, and the sea ceased from its raging." Mark 4:39—"He woke up and rebuked the wind, and said to the sea, 'Peace! Be still!' Then the wind stopped, and there was a dead calm."

60. Ps 107:30. In v. 7 Yhwh leads wanderers out of the wilderness into settled cities; here he leads them out of a raging sea into a safe haven.

61. At first glance these four groups seem to have little in common, yet each (a) faces a serious threat (b) cries out for help, and (c) is divinely delivered. This sequence abbreviates the pattern framing the savior-stories in the book of Judges: (a) Israel does evil; (b) God allows an enemy to punish Israel; (c) Israel cries out to Yhwh; (d) Yhwh sends a savior to deliver them; and (e) the land has peace. (Cf. Brown, "Judges," 127).

62. Kim ("Psalms," 143–57) sees a structural parallel between the closing hymn of Ps 92 and the closing hymn of Ps 107, not to mention several other parallels between Books 4 and 5. Within this closing hymn two sections focus on what Hackett (*Balaam*, 75) calls "upheavals in nature," the first on *un-creation* (vv. 33–34, 39–40), the second on *re-creation* (vv. 35–38, 41–42).

מרעת ישבי בה	Because of their wicked inhabitants[63]
ישם מדבר לאגם מים	He turns wilderness into wetlands
וארץ ציה למצא מים	And dry land into pools of water
ויושב שם רעבים	He settles there the hungry
ויכוננו עיר מושב	And establishes city settlements
ויזרעו שדות	They sow fields
ויטעו כרמים	And plant vineyards
ויעשו פרי תבואה	Which produce fruitful yields
ויברכם וירבו מאד	With his blessing they produce a huge yield
ובהמתם לא ימעיט	And their livestock does not die off[64]
וימעטו וישחו	When they are demeaned and belittled
מעצר רעה ויגון	Whether through oppression, grief, or sorrow
שפך בוז על נדיבים	He pours contempt on patrician folk
ויתעם בתהו לא דרך	And sends them straying into trackless wastes[65]
וישגב אביון מעני	But the needy he lifts out of affliction
וישם כצאן משפחות	And establishes families like productive flocks
יראו ישרים וישמחו	The upright see it and rejoice
וכל עולה קפצה פיה	And everything evil is forced to shut up![66]

Concluding proverb

מי חכם וישמר אלה	Whoever is wise,[67] listen carefully to these things
ויתבוננו חסדי יהוה	And thoughtfully reflect on Yhwh's *ḥesed*[68]

---

63. Ps 107:33–34. These verses bear witness to the deity's power to *un*-create. Cf. Isa 27:10—"For the fortified city will become solitary, a deserted and forsaken settlement, like the wilderness."

64. Ps 107:35–38. These verses bear witness to the deity's power to *re*-create. Cf. Ezekiel's vision of a blooming desert (Ezek 47:1–12).

65. Ps 107:40. The intertextual reworking of this verse in Job 12:21, 24 prompts Clines (*Job* 1.297) to remark that "the connections with Ps 107 are so close and numerous that it seems right to term it a 'source'" of the material in Job 12 "in the way that Ps 8 is the 'source' of Job 7:17–18."

66. Ps 107:39–43. These verses contrast the fate of oppressive noblemen vs. those oppressed by them. In Anatolia an irate prince reprimands several "noblemen" because "you continually oppress your workers (to the point that) they start oppressing others" (*KBo* 22.1.3′) ... "When my father convenes the assembly will he not investigate your corruptions?" (*KBo* 22.1.16′–17′; cf. Moore, *WealthWise*, 47–49).

67. Cf. the beginning of another conclusion: "Everyone then who hears these words of mine and acts on them will be like a wise man" (Matt 7:24).

68. Ps 107:43. Cf. footnote on 86:2 and below on *ḥesed*.

HYMNS

Ascertaining the structural differences between "praise psalms" and "hymns" can be challenging sometimes,[69] yet most readers agree that the primary goal of a hymn is simply and only *to ascribe glory to God*, not implore him or thank him for anything. For James Mays, "the function of praise in the Psalter belongs first of all to the hymn,"[70] but for Walter Brueggemann, "hymn" denotes a "public (as distinct from personal or intimate) song that is sung with abandonment in praise to God for the character of God's person or the nature of God's creating and liberating actions."[71]

Psalm 29

Whatever the interpretive possibilities, Ps 29 is widely considered a classic hymn:[72]

הבו ליהוה בני אלים	Let the children of God[73] ascribe[74] to Yhwh
הבו ליהוה כבוד ועז	Ascribe to Yhwh glory and strength
הבו ליהוה כבוד שמו	Ascribe to Yhwh the glory of his Name[75]
השתחוו ליהוה בהדרת קדש	Worship Yhwh in holy splendor[76]

---

69. Westermann (*Psalms*, 31) distinguishes between two kinds of "thanksgiving psalms" (תודה) in the Psalter, one *descriptive* ("thanksgiving song"), the other *declarative* (i.e., the "hymn"). Assigning 1QH to "the genre of hymns," Puech ("Hodayot," 365) describes the "poetic compositions" in the Qumran sectarian songbook as "imitations of the biblical Psalms in giving thanks to God the Creator and the one who exercises Divine Providence for his deeds of kindness."

70. Mays, *Psalms*, 26.

71. Brueggemann, *Message*, 158. Watson (*Hymn*, 1) understands that the English hymn can be problematic because "it has traditionally been regarded as a second-rate poetic form, limited in its aims and expressions, and disfigured by sentimentality, inflexible meters, self-congratulation, and religiosity."

72. Emanuel (*Psalter*, 23) points out several close parallels between Pss 29 and 96.

73. Ps 29:1 (lit., "sons of gods"). OG υἱοὶ θεοῦ ("sons of God"); Vg *filii Dei* ("sons of God"); Syr ܒܢܝ ܓܒܐ ("sons of sorrow"); Tg הבון קדם יי תושבחתא כתי מלאכיא בני אלים ("Ascribe to Yhwh, O bands of angels, sons of God"). N.B. that in Canaanite myth Ba'al is attended by the *pḫr bn ilm* ("council of the sons of the gods," *CAT* 1.4.3.14). Craigie (*Psalms*, 246–47) points out several parallels between the mythopoetic language in Ps 29 and the Song of Victory in Exod 15.

74. Ps 29:1 MT הבה ("to give, go, come"); OG ἐνέγκατε (2nd aor ipv of φέρω, "to bear, bring"), not δίδωμι ("to give"); Vg *adverte* ("to turn or direct something toward, pay attention, recognize"); Syr ܐܝܬܘ is a Š ipv of ܐܬܐ ("to come").

75. Ps 29:2. On the significance of השם (*Ha-Shem*, "the Name"), cf. below.

76. Ps 29:2. OG ἐν αὐλῇ ἁγίᾳ αὐτοῦ ("in his holy court"); Vg *in atrio sancto eius* ("in his holy chamber"); Syr ܒܗܝܟܠܐ ܩܕܝܫܐ ("in his holy chamber"). Tg בשבהורת קודשא ("in

קוֹל יְהוָה עַל הַמָּיִם	The voice of Yhwh is upon the waters[77]
אֵל הַכָּבוֹד הִרְעִים	The God of glory thunders
יְהוָה עַל מַיִם רַבִּים	Yhwh stands on the mighty waters[78]
קוֹל יְהוָה בַּכֹּחַ	Yhwh's voice is strong
קוֹל יְהוָה בֶּהָדָר	Yhwh's voice is majestic
קוֹל יְהוָה שֹׁבֵר אֲרָזִים	Yhwh's voice shatters cedars
וַיְשַׁבֵּר יְהוָה אֶת אַרְזֵי הַלְּבָנוֹן	Yhwh splinters the cedars of Lebanon
וַיַּרְקִידֵם כְּמוֹ עֵגֶל לְבָנוֹן	He makes Lebanon skip like a calf
וְשִׂרְיֹן כְּמוֹ בֶן רְאֵמִים	And Sirion like a young ox[79]
קוֹל יְהוָה חֹצֵב לַהֲבוֹת אֵשׁ	Yhwh's voice quenches fiery flames
קוֹל יְהוָה יָחִיל מִדְבָּר	Yhwh's voice shakes the wilderness
יָחִיל יְהוָה מִדְבַּר קָדֵשׁ	Yhwh shakes the holy desert[80]
קוֹל יְהוָה יְחוֹלֵל אַיָּלוֹת	Yhwh's voice shakes the mighty oaks[81]
וַיֶּחֱשֹׂף יְעָרוֹת	And strips the forests bare
וּבְהֵיכָלוֹ כֻּלּוֹ אֹמֵר כָּבוֹד	In his temple all cry, "Glory!"
יְהוָה לַמַּבּוּל יָשָׁב	Yhwh sits enthroned upon the Flood[82]
יְהוָה מֶלֶךְ לְעוֹלָם	Yhwh is the eternal king
יְהוָה עֹז לְעַמּוֹ יִתֵּן	May Yhwh strengthen his people

---

his holy splendor"). The versions take הדר to refer to *Yhwh's* "splendor" (i.e., not his heavenly retinue of worshipers—*pace* MacLaren, *David*, 32).

77. Ps 29:3. Psalm 29 may well be subtitled the "Voice of Yhwh" because the phrase קול יהוה occurs no less than seven times in eleven verses. Whether קול refers to a divine "voice" or "sound" (like thunder) is left unspecified, regardless of the debate among the church fathers Basil, Theodoret, Diodorus and Theodore (cf. discussion in Gibson, "Voice," 28–29).

78. Ps 29:3 (cf. 93:4). MT מים רבים ("mighty waters") is mythopoeic shorthand for "the disorderly, insurgent elements" of chaos (May, "Waters," 10). Van der Toorn (*Religion*, 325) notes that in the תפלה ("psalm") of Habakkuk (Hab 3:1) "other elements are involved in the conflict (Sun and Moon, Mountains and Deep)," but Yhwh's "real adversary is the Sea with its mighty waters." Cf. the later-fully-domesticated θάλασσα ὑαλίνη ("sea of glass") in Rev 4:6. Chisholm ("Myth," 75–84) suggests that unlike the lament psalms, the praise psalms tend to demythologize the primordial battle with the Sea in order to affirm the unconditional character of Yhwh's sovereignty.

79. The Sidonians call Mt. Hermon Sirion, while the Amorites call it Senir (Deut 3:9).

80. Ps 29:8 (or, "the desert at Kadesh"); OG Καδης; Vg *Cades*; Syr ܩܕܫ; Tg רקם (Rekem). Tg's choice may or may not refer to a GN (like OG and Vg; cf. *DTTM* 1497). On קדש ("holiness"), cf. below.

81. Ps 29:9. OG (ἐλάφους) and Vg (*curvos*) read MT אילות as "deer" (KJV "calves"), but איל as "mighty tree" (Isa 1:29; 61:3) seems the best fit here.

82. Ps 29:10. OG τὸν κατακλυσμὸν ("the cataclysm"); Vg *diluvium* ("the deluge/flood"); Syr ܛܘܦܢܐ ("the flood/deluge"); Tg יי בדר טופנא יתיב על כורסי דדינא למתפרע מנהון ("Yhwh scatters the Flood and sits upon the throne of judgment to destroy them"). MT מבול ("Flood") is an obvious parallel to מים רבים ("mighty waters") in v. 3.

יהוה יברך עמו בשלום   May Yhwh bless his people with peace.[83]

Psalm 8

Another classic hymn is Ps 8:[84]

יהוה אדנינו   O Yhwh, our Lord[85]
מה אדיר שמך בכל הארץ   How majestic is your Name in all the earth![86]
אשר תנה הודך על השמים   I will serve your majesty above the heavens[87]
מפי עללים וינקים   Through the mouths of babes and infants
יסדת עז למען צורריך   You build barricades against your foes
להשבית אויב ומתנקם   To silence the enemy and the avenger[88]
כי אראה שמיך   When I look at your heavens
מעשי אצבעתיך   The works of your fingers
ירחו וכוכבים   The moon and the stars
אשר כוננתה   Which you establish
מה אנוש כי תזכרנו   What is man that you are mindful of him?

---

83. Ps 29:11. The Pardees ("Glory," 122) note that the description of Yhwh here finds "unmistakable echoes in the character of Baʿal in *CAT* 1.4.7.14–52, but Amzallag (*Canaanite*) reads Ps 29 as a hymn hailing Yhwh as a southern deity responsible for the invention of metallurgy.

84. Tournay ("Psaume 8," 18) calls Ps 8 a "hymne"; Craigie (*Psalms*, 106) calls it a "hymn of praise"; Westermann (*Psalter*, 78) calls it a "psalm of creation"; Goldingay (*Psalms* 1.154) calls it "the Psalter's first actual praise song, though both its form and its subject are atypical"; Schmidt ("Erwägungen," 1–15) sees in this psalm a mixture of hymnic, wisdom, and lament elements.

85. Craigie (*Psalms*, 104) translates "O Lord, our governor."

86. Tournay ("Psaume 8," 20) contends that "the cult of the Name is ineffably developed up to the rabbinic and GNT periods," arguing that "the Name is like a type of hypostasis, analogous to the Spirit or Wisdom" (cf. Galling, "Ausrufung, 65–70). On השם ("the Name"), cf. below.

87. Ps 8:1. Dahood (*Psalms* 1.49) and Craigie (*Psalms* 1.105) read MT אשר תנה as one word—אשרתנה ("I will serve, worship," 1 c. sg. ipf of שרת; cf. *HAL* 1532–33). Mays (*Psalms*, 66) sees this text focusing on "Yhwh as cosmic ruler establishing sovereignty by subjecting the hostile powers of chaos" (cf. Moore, *Chaos*, 13–26).

88. Ps 8:3. For Craigie (*Psalms*, 107) "the essence of the enemies of God is that they do not recognize the Name of God or the revelation that comes through that Name, for if they had come to such full recognition, they would desist from their enmity. Babes, on the other hand, symbolize human weakness and humility, but they have a strength greater than that of God's enemies when they take the Name ... on their lips; that is, in speaking the Name, they acknowledge and in some sense understand the majesty and revelation of God implicit within that Name. Thus God may utilize the weak of this world, even the child, both to establish his strength, reflected in his nature and in his creation, and at the same time 'put to rest' the opposition of enemies."

ובן אדם כי תפקדנו   Or the son of man that you engage him?[89]
ותחסרהו מעט מאלהים   You make him a little less than God
וכבוד והדר תעטרהו   Crowning him with glory and honor
תמשילהו במעשי ידיך   You cause him to rule over the works of your hands
כל שתה תחת רגליו   And place everything under his feet[90]
צנה ואלפים כלם   All sheep and oxen
וגם בהמות שדי   Also the beasts of the fields
צפור שמים ודגי הים   The birds of the air and fish of the sea
עבר ארחות ימים   Even that which passes through the seas.[91]
יהוה אדנינו   O Yhwh, our Lord
מה אדיר שמך בכל הארץ   How majestic is your Name in all the earth!

WISDOM PSALMS

The wisdom psalms are not as prevalent as other types of psalms, but when they do appear they play a strategic role in the editorial shaping of the Psalter as a "book."[92] The entire collection begins with a wisdom psalm (Ps 1), for example, and wisdom helps shape its longest composition (Ps 119).[93]

---

89. Ps 8:4–5. N.B. how Job parodies these lines in his first response to Eliphaz (Job 7:17–18; cf. Kynes, *Psalm*, 63–79). Craigie's (*Psalms*, 108) comment is insightful: "In contrast to God, the heavens are tiny, pushed and prodded into shape by the divine digits. But in contrast to the heavens, which seem so vast in the human perception, mankind is tiny. The response to this heavenly panorama is a response which so many humans feel, whether or not they encounter Ps 8." The GNT *Letter to the Hebrews* cites this verse to argue that even though humankind is a little "lower than the angels," they are still worth saving (Heb 2:6–7).

90. Paul cites this passage to show (a) that the Son of Man is powerful, and (b) that his subjection to the Almighty is voluntary (1 Cor 15:27–28). Another GNT writer cites it to make the christological point that the Son of Man "is *temporarily* made lower than the angels," not so much to manage "the works of your hands" as to finish his mission of redemption, which unavoidably includes his "tasting of death for everyone" (Heb 2:9).

91. Ps 8:5–8. In contrast to this "high anthropology" Bildad asks: "If the moon is not radiant enough, nor the stars bright enough in God's eyes, how much less a maggoty mortal, or the wormy spawn of a hominid?" (Job 25:5–6; cf. Moore, *Retribution*, 56).

92. Truth be told, sapiential motifs help shape many biblical texts, not just the Psalms. Cf. Longman (*Wisdom*, 65–77); Crenshaw (*Wisdom*, 165–83); Sheppard (*Wisdom*, 136–44); and Moore (*WealthWise*, 92–98). Dell ("Riddle," 445–58) challenges Mowinckel's ("Psalms," 205–44) view that the late wisdom psalms are completely non-cultic, heartily agreeing with Murphy ("Psalms," 166–67) and Perdue (*Wisdom*, 267–68) that the boundaries between wisdom and worship are too porous to support such a claim.

93. *Contra* Soll (*Psalm 119*), Murphy ("Wisdom," 162–67), Engle (Delight) and Reynolds (*Torah*, 29), Scott (*Wisdom*, 199–200), Allen (*Psalms 101–150*, 139), and A. Anderson (*Psalms*, 806) classify Ps 119 as a "wisdom psalm." Mays ("Torah-Psalms," 7)

Psalm 49

Psalm 49 is a wisdom psalm shaped by the question "What is the value of a human being?"[94] because the keyword יקר ("value") anchors each of its two sections:

ואדם ביקר בל ילין	Human beings do not understand their "value"
נמשל כבהמות נדמו	They are like fragile beasts.[95]

Like many other wisdom texts, Ps 49 ponders the meaning and mystery of the human condition:[96]

שמעו זות כל העמים	Listen up, everyone!
האזינו כל ישבי חלד	Give ear, all inhabitants of the world[97]
גם בני אדם גם בני איש	Both high and low[98]
יחד עשיר ואביון	Rich and poor together
פי ידבר חכמה	My mouth will utter wisdom
והגות לבי תבונות	And the meditation of my heart[99] understanding
אטה למשל אזני	I will incline my ear to a proverb,
אפתח בכנר חידתי	Whisper my riddle to a lyre[100]
למה אירא בימי רע	Why should I fear evil days?
עון עקבי יסובני	When the iniquity of my oppressors engulfs me[101]
הבטחים על חילם	When those who put their trust in wealth

---

and van der Ploeg ("Sagesse," 85) see it as a *sui generis* composition.

94. Prinsloo (*Psalms*, 392–93) sees this psalm as a text dealing "with the question of the value of wealth" (cf. Moore, *WealthWise*, 95–97).

95. Ps 49:14, 21 (with slight differences). Cf. OG καὶ ἄνθρωπος ἐν τιμῇ ὢν οὐ συνῆκεν ("humans do not understand their value"); Syr ܒܪ ܐܢܫܐ ܠܐ ܐܣܬܟܠ ܒܐܝܩܪܗ ("a son of man does not understand his value"); Vg *homo cum in honore esset non intellexit* ("humans with in [sic] honor/value do not understand"); Tg גברא חיבה ביקרא לא יבית עם צדיקיא ("a sinful man does not dwell with the righteous").

96. Cf. Moore, *WealthWise*, 59–128.

97. Ps 49:1. Like most wisdom texts the intended audience is not just Israel or Judah, but "all peoples."

98. Ps 49:2 (NRSV). MT is less than clear, and the vss offer little help. Tg interprets this phrase to mean אוף בני אדם קדמאה אוף בנוי דיעקב ("both the sons of the first man and the sons of Jacob").

99. Ps 49:3. MT הגות is a nominal form of the verb הגה ("to meditate, groan"), a catchword linking Ps 1 (v. 3) to Ps 2 (v. 1).

100. Ps 49:4, reading אפתח with Dahood (*Psalms* 1.297) as an infixed-*t* conjugation of פוח ("to breathe, blow"). MT כנר ("harp, lute"); OG ψαλτηρίῳ ("psaltyrion, stringed instrument"); Vg *psalterio* (transliteration of OG); Syr ܟܢܪܐ ("herp"); Tg כנר ("harp, lute"); cf. footnote on 137:2.

101. Ps 49:6. Cf. Syr ܒܥܠܕܒܒܝ, "my enemies" (derived from ܒܥܠ, *baʿal*); Tg reads אלהי דחובת סורחני ("gods of the sin of my corruption").

וברב עשרם יתהללו	Praise themselves for their great fortunes[102]
אח לא פדה יפדה	The truth is that no one can engineer redemption[103]
איש לא יתן לאלהים כפרו	Nor can anyone ransom themselves before God[104]
ויקר פדיון נפשם	For the soul's redemption is expensive[105]
וחדל לעולם	And always will be[106]
ויהי עוד לנצח	No one continues on forever[107]
לא יראה השחת	Without seeing the grave
כי יראה חכמים ימותו	For anyone can see that the wise die
יחד כסיל ובער יאבדו	That both fool and dolt perish together
ועזבו אחרים חילם	And leave their wealth to others[108]
קרבם בתימו לעולם	Their graves become their permanent residences
משכנתם לדר ודר	Their dwellings for coming generations
קראו בשמותם עלי אדמות	Though they name lands after themselves[109]
ואדם ביקר בל ילין	Human beings do not understand their value[110]
נמשל כבהמות נדמו	For they are like fragile beasts
זה דרכם כסל למו	Such is the path of the fool
ואחריהם בפיהם ירצו	And anyone else who uses their mouth to gratify[111]
כצאן לשאול שתו	Like sheep bound for Sheol
מות ירעם	So Death will shepherd them[112]

102. Ps 49:7. Most ETs read "boast in their great fortunes," but N.B. that יתהללו is reflexive (cf. Prov 11:28). Smith (*Redemption*, 1) calls Ps 49 "a priest's invective against the wealthy elite who live carelessly, trusting in their own self-importance."

103. Ps 49:7 (lit., "redeem redemption"; i.e., infinitive absolute + finite verb of the same root, GKC 113*l*). Cf. the "pious sufferer's" lament over being denied Marduk's "redemption" (Akk *paṭāru*, Lud 1.56).

104. Ps 49:8. OG ἐξίλασμα, "propitiatory offering, ransom"; Syr ܠܐ ܢܬܠ ܦܘܪܩܢܐ ("one cannot give a ransom to God as the ransom"; so Tg).

105. Ps 49:8 (the last letter in נפשם is likely an enclitic *mem*; WOC 9.8). Tg ויהי יקיר פורקניה ויפסוק בישוותיה ("for its redemption is valuable when he cuts away its wickedness"). Again, N.B. that the MT root יקר ("to value") recurs in vv. 12 and 20.

106. Ps 49:9 (lit., "never changes"). Tg ופורענותה לעלם ("and he will forever pay it").

107. Ps 49:9 (lit., "for the duration").

108. Ps 49:11. N.B. King Munbaz's critique of "earthly treasure" (*t. Peʾah* 4.18), i.e., how (a) it is "vulnerable to human hands," (b) cannot produce genuine "benefits," (c) has more to do with *mammon* than souls, and (d) benefits only "others" (Moore, *WealthWarn*, 164). On "wealth," cf. below.

109. Ps 49:11. N.B. the parallel motifs of land, judgment, death, loss of wealth, and loss of status in Isa 14:11–21 (cf. Shipp, *Dirges*, 162–63).

110. Ps 49:12. Whereas this verse reads בל ילין ("cannot abide"), the psalm's final verse (49:20) reads לא יבין ("does not understand").

111. Ps 49:13. In GNT another sage warns that "the tongue is a small thing bragging about great things" (Jas 3:5).

112. Ps 49:14. Mot (DN) is the name of the god of Death in Canaanite myth (Heb מות), so in a way this verse is a negative echo of the more familiar Ps 23:1: "Yhwh is my

וירדו בם ישרים לבקר	As they descend straight to the grave
וצירם לבלות	Where their form decays
שאול מזבל לו	Sheol is their home[113]
אך אלהים יפדה נפשי	But God redeems *my* soul[114]
מיד שאול	From the power of Sheol
כי יקחני	When he takes me[115]
אל תירא כי יעשר איש	So do not worry when someone else becomes rich[116]
כי ירבה כבוד ביתו	When the wealth of their house compounds[117]
כי לא במותו יקח הכל	For when they die they take nothing
לא ירד אחריו כבודו	None of their wealth descends after them
כי נפשו בחייו יברך	Even though their souls in this life seem blessed
ויודך כי תיטיב לך	(For you are praised when you do well for yourself)
תבוא עד דור אבותיו	They will go into the company of their ancestors
עד נצח לא יראו אור	Where they will never again see light[118]
ואדם ביקר ולא יבין	Human beings do not understand their value
נמשל כבהמות נדמו	For they are like fragile beasts.

---

shepherd" (i.e., not Death).

113. Ps 49:15. מות ירעם ("Death is their shepherd") echoes Mot's activity in Canaanite myth, particularly when he swallows up Baʿal in a clash between the gods (*CAT* 1.5.1.7; cf. Dahood, *Psalms* 1.300). For Craigie (*Psalms* 1.360) Ps 49:15 has to do with "dumb sheep, on their way to slaughter (cf. 44:12), not realizing where they are going. But while they 'graze' in the pleasant pastures of their life, thinking all is well with them, 'death' is already 'grazing' on them (v 15b)!"

114. Ps 49:16. MT יפדה ("he will redeem"); OG λυτρώσεται ("he will redeem"); Syr ܢܦܪܩܝܘܗܝ ("he will ransom/redeem it"); Vg *redimet manu inferi* "he will buy back from the hand of hell"); Tg יפרוק ("he will tear away, rescue"). Qur'an allows that in lieu of fasting, those who can afford it can "ransom a poor person by feeding him"(فديه طعام مسكين, Q 2.184). Rosenzweig's *Star of Redemption* is widely perceived to be one of the most significant modern interpretations of the *redemption* motif.

115. Ps 49:16. Because לקח occurs below in v. 18, "take" seems the best ET here. Cf. OG ὅταν λαμβάνῃ με ("whenever he takes me"); Vg *acceperit me* ("accepts me"); Tg יפרוק נפשי מן דין גהנם ארום ילפנני אוריתיה לעלמין ("He will sever my soul from the judgment of Gehenna, I will arise, and he will impart to me his teachings forever"). Craigie (*Psalms* 1.360) imagines these words in the mouths of the foolish rich who imagine escape from Death as something easily "purchased."

116. Ps 49:17. In GNT the acquisition of wealth can be problematic in itself (Jas 2:6–7; cf. Moore, *WealthWise*, 176–87).

117. Ps 49:17. A similar sentiment occurs in 73:12, הנה אלה רשעים ושלוי עולם ה שגו חיל ("Look at these wicked people, always at ease, increasing in wealth"). Cf. Sir 4:27—5:8; Moore, *WealthWise*, 144–46.

118. Ps 49:19. For Kellermann ("Auferstehungsglauben," 275), "Death is . . . the great leveler."

Psalm 37

Psalm 37 is an acrostic poem[119] focused upon the question of "economic power, a prominent theme in biblical wisdom literature."[120] Other motifs animate this psalm as well, but "land possession,"[121] a socioeconomic motif recurring no less than six times, is its thematic backbone:

בטח ביהוה ועשׂה טוב	Trust in Yhwh and do good
שׁכן ארץ ורעה אמונה	Colonize[122] land and manage its wealth[123]
כי מרעים יכרתון	The wicked will be cut off
וקוי יהוה המה יירשׁו ארץ	While those who hope in Yhwh will possess land[124]
ועוד מעט ואין רשׁע	A little while longer and the wicked will be gone
והתבוננת על מקומו ואיננו	You will stare at their place, but find it empty[125]
וענוים יירשׁו ארץ	The poor will possess land[126]
והתענגו על רב שׁלום	And enjoy its rewards.[127]
חרב פתחו רשׁעים ודרכו קשׁתם	The wicked draw the sword and bend the bow
להפיל עני ואביון	To strike down the poor and needy,[128]

---

119. Cf. Botha, "Wealth," 105–28.

120. Kuntz (*Wisdom*, 139). Goldingay (*Psalms*, 514–35) entitles it "The Weak Will Take Possession of the Land" and Cheung (*Wisdom*, 53) entitles it "The ABCs of Living in the Land."

121. Citing ANE texts in which land is never sold by one person to another unless first sanctioned by the king/overlord, Lohfink ("ירשׁ," 385; followed by Joosten, *Land*, 186–87), argues that Yhwh's giving of land, particularly in Torah, is modelled on the same royal grant system.

122. Ps 37:3. Görg ("שׁכן," 695) nuances a semantic distinction between ישׁב and שׁכן, positing the first to signify "permanent dwelling," but the second to signify "an apparently secure but in reality endangered existence" (i.e., "colonization"; cf. Lohfink, "ירשׁ," 385).

123. Ps 37:3. MT is difficult ("pasture its substance?"). Cf. OG ποιμανθήσῃ ἐπὶ τῷ πλούτῳ αὐτῆς ("shepherd its wealth"), followed by Vg *divitiis eius* ("its riches"). On "wealth," cf. below.

124. Ps 37:9. MT קוה ("to hope/wait") appears again in 37:7, 34. Cf. Syr ܡܣܒܪ̈ܐ, "endure"; OG ὑπομένοντες ("endure"); Vg *sustinentes* ("forbear"); Tg ודסברין במימרא דיי ("those who hope in the Memra/'Word' of Yah").

125. Ps 37:10. Cf. Prov 23:5 and 4Q171.2.7. אתבוננה, "I will stare" (1 p. sg.).

126. Ps 37:11. OG οἱ πραεῖς, "the meek" (cf. Syr ܡܟܝ̈ܟܐ, "the poor man" (sg.); 4Q171.2.9 ענוים (same as MT) is defined by one commentator as עדת האביונים, "the congregation of the poor" (4Q171.2.10; cf. Matt 5:5).

127. Ps 37:11 (cf. the identical phrase, רב שׁלום, in 72:7); Syr ܒܣܘܓܐܐ ܕܫܠܡܐ evidently takes MT על רב adverbially, reading "enjoying themselves in peace." 4Q171.2.11–12 employs this motif not from a metaphorical, but a socioeconomic perspective, insisting that no slaveowner/landowner/creditor will ever again be allowed to force the poor to do their bidding.

128. Ps 37:14. OG πτωχὸν καὶ πένητα, "beggar and day-laborer"; Syr ܡܣܟܢܐ ܘܒܝܫܐ,

לטבוח ישרי דרך	And slaughter those who navigate the straight path[129]
טוב מעט לצדיק	But better is a little with the righteous
מהמון רשעים רבים	Than a lot with the wicked[130]
לוה רשע ולא ישלם	The wicked borrow without repayment
וצדיק חונן ונותן	While the righteous give generously[131]
כי מברכיו יירשו ארץ	Those blessed by him will possess land[132]
ומקלליו יכרתו	But the accursed will be cut off
לעולם נשמרו	The righteous will always be protected[133]
וזרע רשעים נכרת	But the descendants of the wicked will be cut off
צדיקים יירשו ארץ	The righteous will possess land[134]
וישכנו לעד עולם	And colonize it forever.
קוה אל יהוה ושמר דרכו	Hope in Yhwh and stay on his path
וירממך לרשת ארץ	And he will enable you to possess land.[135]

Psalm 19

Psalm 19 is a hybrid composition comprised of a Yahwicized solar hymn (vv. 1–6) sutured onto a wisdom manifesto (vv. 7–14):[136]

השמים מספרים כבוד אל	The heavens declare the glory of God[137]

"poor and unfortunate"; Tg למקטול עניי וחשיכי למכוס, "to kill the poor and those 'held hostage' (lit., 'darkened') by the customs-house."

129. Ps 37:14.

130. Ps 37:16 (cf. Prov 15:16). Like Sirach, the sage in 4Q171.2.23 manipulates the tradition by identifying the צדיק as "anyone who does Torah."

131. Ps 37:21. 4Q171.3.10–11 applies this text to the "congregation of the poor . . . inheriting the high mountain of Israel."

132. Ps 37:22. Ross (*Psalms*, 803) emphasizes that "one of the key considerations of the study of Psalm 37 is the intriguing emphasis on the blessing of the land."

133. Ps 37:28. Creach (*Refuge*, 17) contends that "the ideas expressed by חסה/מחסה and a related field of words for 'refuge' represent an editorial interest that may be observed throughout the Psalter."

134. Ps 37:29. Tg למחסן ארעא, "take possession of the land" (cf. Tg 37:34).

135. Ps 37:34 (lit., "he will exalt you to inherit," Vg *exaltabit*).

136. Dahood (*Psalms* 1.121) takes vv. 1–6 to be a Yahwistic redaction of an originally Canaanite solar hymn, and Wyatt ("Liturgical," 103–32) imagines a contextual history of this hymn with the Jerusalem cult, but Arneth ("Sonne," 5, 201) suggests a closer relationship with Assyrian solar tradition (e.g., SAA 3.11; cf. Moore, "Sonne," 541–42).

137. Ps 19:1. C. S. Lewis (*Psalms*, 73) calls Ps 19 "the greatest poem in the Psalter and one of the greatest lyrics in the world." *Personal note:* Ps 19 is the first psalm I ever memorized, having been asked by my school principal to recite it from memory into the PA system during the announcements one morning.

ומעש ידיו מגיד הרקיע	The sky bears witness to his handiwork[138]
יום ליום יביעה אמר	Day after day it pours forth words
ולילה ללילה יחוה דעת	Night after night it proclaims knowledge[139]
אין אמר אין דברים	There is no speech nor language
בלי נשמע קולם	Where their voice is not heard[140]
בכל הארץ יצא קום	Their sound penetrates into all the earth[141]
ובקצא תבל מליהם	And their language to the ends of the world
לשמש שם אהל בהם	He pitches a tent for the sun in them[142]
והוא כחתן יוצא מחפתו	Like a bridegroom emerging from the bridal tent
ישיש כגבר לרוץ ארח	Or an athlete running track with joy
מקצא השמים מוצאו	It advances from one end of the heavens
ותקפותו על קצותם	And loops its way over to the other end[143]
תורת יהוה תמימה משיבת נפש	Yhwh's law revives the soul
עדות יהוה נאמנה מחימת פתי	Yhwh's statutes teach the teachable
פקודי יהוה ישרים משמחי לב	Yhwh's precepts gladden the upright of heart
מצות יהוה ברה מאירת עינים	Yhwh's commands make the eyes sparkle
יראת יהוה טהורה עומדת לעד	The fear of Yhwh is forever pure
משפטי יהוה אמת צדקו יחדו	Yhwh's decrees are altogether pure and just[144]
הנחמדים מזהב ומפז רב	More desirable than gold, even much fine gold

138. Paul repeats this sentiment in Rom 1:19–20.

139. Ps 19:2. Data is broadcast during the day, but knowledge accumulates at night.

140. Ps 19:3. N.B. the equation *words < declaration < voice*. Attempting to explain these lines, Tg reads דתורעמתא ולית מלי דשגושא דלא משתמע קלהון לית מימור ("there is no puzzling term, nor are there perplexing words where their voice is not heard").

141. Ps 19:4. MT קום is problematic. OG ὁ φθόγγος αὐτῶν ("their voice"); Vg *sonus eorum* ("their sound"); Syr ܣܒܪܗܘܢ ("their announcement"). N.B. that קול in the previous verse suggests that an original קולם ("their voice/sound") becomes קום ("their line") through scribal dittography (*pace* Dahood's attempt to read קום as "their call," *Psalms* 1.121–22). Evidently aware of the problem, Tg omits the word altogether, reading בכולא ארעא נפק מתת ענינהון ("the extent of their answer goes out into all the earth").

142. Ps 19:4. MT בהם ("in them") can refer to מליהם ("their words") or השמים ("the heavens," vv. 1, 6). The psalmist appears to be revealing in this song several hitherto inconspicuous connections between word, voice, knowledge, the heavens and the sun, all in a bold attempt to Yahwicize the solar theologies surrounding Israel; i.e., Eg *Ra*, Akk *Š amaš*, Ug *Šapšu* (cf. Ps 72:5, 17; Stähli, *Solare*, 28–39; Arneth, "Sonne," 17).

143. Where Eg sources depict Ra traversing the sky in a sailboat and Gk sources depict Apollo traversing the sky in a flaming chariot, Ps 19 depicts the sun as an athlete running from one horizon to the other. However similar, each depiction reflects its own set of cultural cues.

144. Ps 19:7–9 lists several aspects of Yhwh's character, each connected in some way with the "words" in vv. 2–4: *torah, statutes, precepts, commands, fear,* and *decrees*. N.B. (a) the similar pattern of connections between *word* and *flesh* in John 1:1–14; so that (b) this latter use of the pattern need not necessarily reflect Hellenistic fusion (*pace* Argyle, "Philo," 385–86). On צדק ("justice"), cf. below.

ומתוקים מדבש ונפת צופים	Sweeter than honey or the drippings of the honeycomb
גם עבדך נזהר בהם	By them your servant is warned
בשמרם עקב רב	For in keeping them there is great reward
שגיאות מי יבין	Who understands wrongdoing?
מנסתרות נקני	Blot out my occult activities[145]
גם מזדים חשך עבדך	Spare your servant from insolent men
אל ימשלו בי	Do not let them have control over me
אז איתם ונקיתי מפשע רב	So that I may be innocent of great transgression
יהיו לרצון אמרי פי	Let the words of my mouth[146]
והגיון לבי	And the meditation of my heart
לפניך	Be acceptable to you
יהוה צורי וגאלי	O Yhwh, my rock and my redeemer.

Psalm 39

Psalm 39 is a hybrid psalm melding together components from both wisdom and lament.[147]

מרתי אשמרה דרכי מחטוא בלשוני	I thought, "I will guard my ways from verbal sin[148]
אשמרה לפי מחסום בעד רשע לנגדי	I will muzzle my mouth when dealing with evil"[149]
נאלמתי דומיה החשיתי מטוב	So I stay silent,[150] avoiding saying anything beneficial
וכאבי נעכר	But my pain increases
חם לבי בקרבי	My heart burns within me

---

145. Ps 19:12. Cf. OG κρύφιος ("concealed"); Vg *ab occultis* ("from the occult"); Syr ܡܢ ܟܣܝܬܐ ("from concealment"); Tg מטמירתה ("from secrecy").

146. Ps 19:14. The mention of אמר ("word") here at the end of the wisdom manifesto firmly connects it to the Yahwicized solar hymn by its repetitive use of אמר/דבר ("word," vv. 3, 4).

147. Jacobson ("Psalm 39," 364) thinks that it "borrows a rhetorical structure from the song of thanksgiving," but García-Bachman ("Silence[s]," 365) sees "no consensus regarding its genre."

148. Ps 39:1 (lit., "from sin with my tongue"). Like Ps 19, Ps 39 manipulates the speech-vs.-silence polarity, a main theme of the wisdom tradition (e.g., Job 6:24; 13:5, 19; 33:31, 33; Ps 39:2, 9; 50:21; Prov 11:12; 17:28).

149. Ps 39:1 (lit., "as long as evil is before me"). Seerveld ("Church," 146) suggests that "vigorous, no-nonsense Welsh tunes mesh well with God's psalms" because "they are not bubbly or upbeat, but vigorous, supple, with grit. And you need grit to voice Psalm 39."

150. Ps 39:2. N.B. the threefold recurrence of terms for "silence": דומיה, אלם, and חשה.

WHY PRAISE? 75

בהגיגי תבער אש	While I groan, the fire burns[151]
דברתי בלשוני	So I start speaking with my tongue:
הודיעני יהוה קצי	"Show me my end, Yhwh:
ומדת ימי מה היא	How many days do I have left?[152]
אדעה מה חדל אני	Let me know: What do I lack?[153]
הנה טפחות נתתה ימי	You delimit my days to a handbreadth
וחלדי כאין נגדך	My lifespan is of little consequence to you[154]
אך כל הבל כל אדם נצב	Surely[155] all is futile[156] for every living person[157]
אך בצלם יתהלך איש	Yes, people do cultivate images[158]
אך יהמון הבל יצבר	Yes, they frantically heap up treasure[159]
ולא ידע מי אספם	Not knowing who will receive it[160]
ועתה מה קויתי אדני	Now, what do I wait for, Lord?[161]
תוחלתי לך היא	My hope is in you
מכל פשעי הצילני	Save me from all my sins
חרפה נבל אל תשימני	Let me not become the butt of fools' jokes
נאלמתי לא אפתח פי	I was mute, not opening my mouth
כי אתה עשית	While you were hard at work[162]
הסר מעלי נגעך	Remove from me your plague
מתגרת ידך אני כליתי	Lest the blow from your fist knock me out[163]
בתוכחות על עון יסרת איש	With punishments for sin you discipline people

151. Ps 39:3 (lit., "in my groaning").

152. Ps 39:4 (lit., "the number of my days—what is it?").

153. Ps 39:4. OG τί ὑστερῶ ἐγώ ("What do I lack?"); Vg *quid desit mihi?*

154. Ps 39:5. OG ὑπόστασις ("substance, existence, property"); Vg *substantia* ("substance"); Syr ܡܫܘܚܬܐ ("measure, extent, anointing"); Tg סדרתא יומי קלילין ("you have arranged/established my days to be few." Cf. Ps 8:4, "What is man that you are mindful of him?"

155. Ps 39:5. The adverb אך ("surely, indeed, yes") repeats three times in this passage (then again in v. 11) to indicate that each of these sentiments "goes without saying."

156. Ps 39:5. The term הבל ("vapor, futility, meaninglessness") is one of Qohelet's keywords (Qoh 1:2, 14; 2:1, 15, 17, 19, 21, 26; cf. Moore, *WealthWise*, 98–110).

157. Ps 39:5 (lit., "standing man"). OG πᾶς ἄνθρωπος ζῶν ("every living human"); Syr ܐܢܫܐ ܟܠ ܗܒܠܐ ܩܐܡ ("surely standing men are a vapor").

158. Ps 39:6 (lit., "a man walks back and forth with an image").

159. On "wealth" cf. below.

160. Ps 39:5–6. Qur'an posits that "those who constantly argue about Alla" will suffer "wrath and punishment" because their arguments are "futile" (داحضة); and those who desire only the "harvest of this world" (حرث الدنيا) may receive a share here, "but no share in the hereafter" (Q 42.16, 20).

161. Ps 39:7. In other words, "if not treasure to insure financial security, then what?"

162. Ps 39:9 (lit., "for you are doing").

163. Ps 39:10. Cf. Job 6:4, "The arrows of Šadday are in me. My spirit drinks their poison."

ותמס כעש חמודו   Squashing their toys like so many bugs[164]
אך הבל כל אדם   Indeed, every man is but a vaporous mist
שמעה תפלתי יהוה   O Yhwh, hear my prayer
ושועתי האזינה   Give ear to my cry for help
אל דמעתי אל תחרש   Be not deaf to my cries
כי גר אנכי עמך   For I am a stranger before you
ככל אבותי   Like all my forebears
השע ממני ואבליגה   Look away from me so that I may smile[165]
בטרם אלך ואינני   Before nothing is left of me inside[166]

164. Ps 39:11 (lit., "you crush their delight like a moth").

165. Ps 39:13 (lit., "be blind to me"; N.B. the deafness-blindness sequence in these verses).

166. Ps 39:13 (lit., "before I walk and I am not").

3

Primary Theological Motifs in the Psalter

As the previous pages try to show, the Psalter covers a great deal of theological ground. Not every motif can be fully expounded in a "short theological introduction,"[1] of course, yet the following motifs beg primary attention:

LOYALTY

Of the 245 times חסד (*hesed*) appears in the Bible, approximately half occur in the Psalter (127 times), far more than any other book.[2] In the sampling of psalms above it appears fifteen times (Pss 13:5; 51:11; 86:5, 13, 15; 103:4, 8, 11, 17; 107:1, 8, 15, 21, 31, 43) and its derivative *ḥasid* (חסיד) four times.[3] Further, it often appears in synonymous word-pairs with חנן ("grace"),[4] רחם ("mercy"),[5] אמת ("truth, faithfulness"),[6] אהב ("love"),[7] שלם

---

1. Jacobson ("Psalms," 499–512) lists three approaches to constructing a theology of the Psalter: (a) historical-reconstruction approaches; (b) canonical-narrative approaches; and (c) key-concept approaches. The pages below exemplify this third category.
2. Cf. Zobel, "חסד," 45.
3. Ps 12:2; 30:4; 79:2; and 86:2.
4. Ps 86:15, 103:8; 145:8. Cf. the comparison of חסד and חנן in Moore, "Ruth," 303–5.
5. Ps 86:15; 103:4, 8; 109:12; 145:8.
6. Ps 25:10; 61:8; 85:11; 86:15; 89:3, 15.
7. Ps 33:5.

("to compensate, complete"),[8] סלח ("to forgive"),[9] משפט ("justice"),[10] and צדק ("righteousness").[11]

Nelson Glueck contends that "the constituent parts of the comprehensive term *ḥesed* ... are principally reciprocity, then mutual service, uprightness, friendliness, brotherliness, duty, faithfulness, and love,"[12] and further, that חסד, unlike, say, רחם ("mercy")[13] or אהב ("love"),[14] tends to be "obligatory" in character.[15] Affirming this analysis, Norman Snaith translates חסד as "covenant-love," and אהב as "election-love."[16] Resisting Glueck's emphasis on "reciprocity" and "obligation," however, Felix Asencio contends that *ḥesed* simply denotes "mercy-*feeling*," a trait anticipatory to the doing of "mercy-*work*."[17] Hans Joachim Stoebe also believes that *ḥesed* focuses "predominantly" (*übergeordnete*) on "good-hearted sentiment or kindness" (*gütige Gesinnung oder Freundlichkeit*) but that רחם more often than not denotes the *activation* of this "sentiment."[18] Uku Masing thinks that חסד manifests itself primarily in relationships between superior entities and politically or socially inferior entities,[19] and building on the unpublished work of Sidney Hills,[20] Kathy Sakenfeld concludes that *ḥesed* is less an attitude

---

8. Ps 62:13.

9. Ps 86:5.

10. Ps 89:15; 101:1.

11. Ps 89:15; 141:5. On the prevalence and significance of word-pairs cf. Watters (*Formula*, 146–47). On צדק cf. below.

12. Robinson (*Inspiration*, 57) similarly highlights the "elements of loyalty, or moral obligation, (and) social bond." On the mentioning of these and related notions in the Amarna correspondence, cf. Moore, *Babbler*, 140–55.

13. The Sefire inscription compares the "kings who love (*rḥm*) me" with the kings who serve only to profit as trading partners (*KAI* 224.8).

14. Cf. Ug *ahb(t)* in *CAT* 1.4.4.39; 1.5.5.18 (both passages referring to the physical act of "love," *DULAT* 31).

15. Glueck, *Ḥesed*, 21, 34. Cf. Eichrodt, *Theology*, 1.36–45. Mendenhall ("Covenant," 1179) points out that "covenant-based relationships in the West have become almost obsolete, the fragile institution of marriage being the most noteworthy vestige of such relationships. Thus, one legitimate issue in the study of biblical covenant must be the extent to which modern and Western students of the Bible can conceive and imagine relationships built upon little more than promises reliably made and honorably kept."

16. Snaith, *Ideas*, 99. Cf. Wallis, "אהב," 101–18.

17. Asencio, *Misericordia*, 32–38.

18. Stoebe, "Bedeutung," 247–48.

19. Masing, "*Ḥesed*," 27–63.

20. Cited in Sakenfeld, *Ḥesed*, 10–11.

than an action performed by a "situationally superior party for one who is completely lacking in present resources or future prospects."[21]

Whatever its nuances, חסד (*ḥesed*) fundamentally denotes "covenant *loyalty.*" Not just "love." *Loyalty.* Unlike other words for "love" *ḥesed* presumes a commitment to a particular *kind* of loyalty; viz., *covenant* loyalty. Psalm 86 points out that the greatness of Yhwh's *ḥesed* is actively demonstrated by the decisions he makes to protect his children from bullies and rescue their souls from Sheol.[22] Psalm 62 contrasts faith in Yhwh's *ḥesed* with faith in riches, especially when it is so easy for wealth-formation to degenerate into something corrupt.[23] Psalm 89 insists that because Yhwh's *ḥesed* is eternal his covenant with David is irrevocable,[24] the result being that his covenant people can never be denied access to the light of his presence.[25] Psalm 103 points out that Yhwh's *ḥesed* automatically prohibits him from over-exercising his anger and rigidly punishing his children, even though they sometimes deserve it.[26]

TRUST

The root בטח ("to trust") appears thirty-two times in the Psalter,[27] sometimes in parallel with אמונה ("security"). Psalm 4 depicts "offering just sacrifices" as a matter of "trust."[28] Psalm 9 parallels it with "recognizing the Name."[29] Psalm 25 contrasts it with "being put to shame."[30] In Psalm 31 the poet laments his "sorrow, sighing, and wasting away," not to mention his being surrounded by worthless idolaters intent on plotting his demise. But even in the midst of this, "I trust in you, Yhwh."[31] Psalm 32 contrasts "trust in Yhwh" with "the torments of the wicked."[32] Psalm 37 teaches that

21. Sakenfeld, *Ḥesed*, 12.
22. Ps 86:13–15. In 103:4 the psalmist is redeemed from the pit.
23. Ps 62:10–12. Cf. below and Moore, *WealthWatch*, 45–47, 55–57, 137–40.
24. Ps 89:2–4. To quote Paul's Letter to the Romans, "The call and the gifts of God are irrevocable" (Rom 11:29).
25. Ps 89:15. Cf. Moore, "Presence," 166–70.
26. Ps 103:8–10.
27. Three of these come in the noun מבטח (Ps 40:5; 65:6; and 71:5, with תקוה, "hope").
28. Ps 4:5.
29. Ps 9:10.
30. Ps 25:2.
31. Ps 31:6–14; cf. 40:3–4.
32. Ps 32:10.

those who trust in Yhwh and do good will dwell "securely" (אמונה) in the land, and those who "commit their way" (גלל, lit., "cause it to roll") to Yhwh will see him "respond."[33] Psalm 44 insists that "trust" cannot be successfully invested in weapons (like the bow and arrow) as it can in Yhwh.[34]

Psalm 51 correlates trust in Yhwh with proclamation of the Name.[35] In Psalm 55 the psalmist insists that even though his "best friend" betrays him, "I will trust in Yhwh."[36] In Ps 56 the poet declares that even though he has to face fearful situations, such will not dissuade him from keeping his trust in Yhwh, because after all, "What can flesh do to me? . . . What can a mere mortal do to me?"[37] Psalm 78, a historical psalm, explains Israel's wilderness wandering period as a time when the chosen people had to decide whether to "test" God or "trust" God.[38] Psalm 125 simply states that those who put their trust in Yhwh are immovable, like Mt. Zion.[39]

IDENTITY

Naming is important business. As Janet Finch observes, "naming" (a) "personifies individuals" by "encapsulating their essence"; and (b) "embodies a sense of connectedness between individuals and their families, including the parents who give the name as well as others in domestic arrangements or kin networks with whom . . . the name is shared."[40] Readers of the Bible are aware of this because biblical tradition often attends to the business of naming and re-naming,[41] sometimes to the point of exposing tensions within families.[42]

---

33. Ps 37:3–5.

34. Ps 44:6. Not in "wealth and riches" (49:6; 52:7), nor "trust" in chariots (Isa 31:1).

35. Ps 52:8–9.

36. Ps 55:11–23 (see above).

37. Ps 56:3–4, 11 (cf. Matt 10:28). Such trust should be constant, not haphazard (Ps 62:8; 115:8–11).

38. Ps 78:18–22.

39. Ps 125:1. For more on the "trust" motif, cf. Moore, *Faith*.

40. Finch, "Names," 711. In other words "naming" involves both individual and corporate aspects.

41. In the book of Ruth, e.g., Naomi (נעם, "sweet") re-names herself Mara (מרא, "bitter"), even as she works to preserve the name of her dead husband, Elimelek (Ruth 1:20; 4:5–10; cf. Ps 109:13).

42. The naming of John the Baptist, for example, occurs in spite of the fact that the community expects a different name, arguing "there is no one among your relatives who is called by this name" (Luke 2:16).

The word שֵׁם ("name") occurs 778 times in Tanak and 109 times in the Psalter (more than any other book). In Torah the term is crucial to describing the implementation of Moses' "theological corrective";[43] i.e., the material in Deuteronomy which dissociates the deity from any earthly "place," thereby dismissing, according to Moshe Weinfeld, "the ancient belief that the deity actually dwells in the sanctuary."[44] In the Second Temple period some communities expand on this "corrective" by mandating that all public reading of scripture substitute the generic title אדוני ("Lord") in place of the DN יהוה (Yhwh).[45] Another way Israel attempts to "consecrate" the name occurs when scribes decide to write the Tetragrammaton in paleo-Hebraic script, as attested in fragmentary texts found at Qumran and Naḥal Ḥever.[46] Each of these efforts, one oral and one scribal, represent well-meaning, albeit primitivist attempts to "consecrate" the name using secretive techniques practiced by Mesopotamian priests as early as the OB period.[47]

Yhwh's identity—his *name*—is sacred and holy, but the Psalter emphasizes its power to protect, not its "need" to be protected.[48] Psalm 20 mentions *Ha-Shem* ("the name") three times in nine verses, conferring upon it

43. Von Rad, *Deuteronomium-Studien*, 25–30. Reiterer ("שֵׁם," 134) emphasizes that the use of *Ha-Shem* can and does "function as a substitute for the person in question," and further, that such usage "takes on particular importance in the theological domain."

44. Deut 12:1–11; Weinfeld, "Deuteronomy," 175; Richter, *Name*, 127. N.B. that Ps 74:7 explicitly parallels מקדשך ("your sanctuary") with משכן שמך ("the dwelling-place of your Name"), and in Ps 75:1 Yhwh dwells in the heavens, but the Name is "near." Jesus revisits the "where to worship" question in his conversation with the Samaritan woman at Jacob's well (John 4:20–22).

45. Talmud attributes the beginning of this substitutionary practice to the year of the death of the high priest Simon the Just, c. 290 BCE (*b. Yom.* 39b; cf. Josephus, *A. J.*12.43; Sir 50:1–29). First revealed to Moses, the name יהוה (Yhwh) is sometimes referred to as the Tetragrammaton (Lat *tetra*, "four," + *grammatos*, "letter"). Cross (*CMHE* 60–75) discusses several interpretations of אהיה אשר אהיה ("I am who I am") in Exod 3:14, but Surls ("Name," 287–90) contends that the DN יהוה is not *formally* revealed until 34:6.

46. The Psalms Scroll from Qumran Cave 11 shows the Tetragrammaton written out in paleo-Hebraic script (e.g., in Ps 119:64), and the same practice occurs even in Greek (!) texts from Naḥal Ḥever. Talmud explains: "Torah was given to Israel in *Ivrit* script (עברי; i.e., paleo-Hebrew) . . . But in the days of Ezra it was given to them in *Assyrian* script" (אשורית, *b. Sanh.* 21b), referring to the square Aramaic script adopted by Hebrew exiles in Assyria, and still used today.

47. Diviners of various stripes claim to be able to discern the secrets of the gods from a "vertical" perspective, while *ummânū*-scholars try to control this "secret knowledge" from a "horizontal" perspective by (a) complicating the character of cuneiform script and language to make literacy itself a "secret"; and (b) inserting warnings onto tablets warning the "unknowing" (*la mudû*) not to try to become part of the "knowing" (*mudû*; cf. examples cited in *CAD* M/2 163–68 and Lenzi, *Secrecy*, 378).

48. Kalman ("Iyov," 77) argues that the primary goal of Job's counselors is "to defend God at Job's expense" (cf. Job 34:10–12; Moore, *Retribution*, 64–65).

the power to "protect," "fulfill petitions," and "commemorate" the activity of worshipers.[49] Psalm 22 begins its "vow of praise" section with a promise to "recount your Name."[50] Psalm 44 affirms that it is "through your Name that we tread on our assailants and push down our enemies." In fact, "if we ever forget the Name," the psalmist says, God will sooner or later make sure it is "rediscovered."[51] Recognizing the inherent power of "the Name," soon-to-be King David asks God to use it to "deliver" and "vindicate" him before King Saul and his army.[52] Psalm 68 insists that "the 'cloud-rider's' Name is Yhwh" (i.e., not Ba'al).[53] Psalm 74 contrasts the *wicked* (who "revile the Name") with the *needy* (who "praise it").[54] Psalm 79 presumes (a) that forgiveness of sins justifies every attempt to consecrate the name; and (b) that divine anger will be poured out on "those kingdoms who refuse to do so."[55] Psalm 86 refers to *Ha-Shem* three times, the first in a jussive command to the nations to glorify it, the second in a confession from the psalmist demanding that it be feared, and the third in a thanksgiving pledge.[56] Psalm 99 mentions three heroes of the past who "call on the Name": Moses, Aaron, and Samuel.[57] Psalm 102 draws a sharp contrast between the psalmist's name (susceptible to curse) and the Name (unsusceptible to curse) to make it clear that the nations should fear the Name dwelling on Mt. Zion over any other.[58] Psalm 115 uses "name" language to distinguish the "cart" from the "horse": "Not to us, O Yhwh, not to us, but to your Name give glory, for the sake of your *ḥesed* and faithfulness."[59]

---

49. Ps 20:2, 5, 7.

50. Ps 22:22.

51. Ps 44:5, 20.

52. Ps 54:1.

53. In Ps 68:4, MT רכב בערבות is an obvious Yahwicization of Ug *rkb 'rpt*, the "cloud-rider" epithet attributed to Ba'al in Canaanite myth (cf. *CAT* 1.2.4.8 *et passim*; Herrmann, "Rider," 703–5).

54. Ps 74:21.

55. Ps 79:10, 6.

56. Ps 86:9, 11, 12; cf. 96:8; 97:12.

57. Ps 99:6.

58. Ps 102:8, 12, 15, 21.

59. Ps 115:1 (cf. Clifford, "Translation," 293–301).

SALVATION

Several words populate the semantic field of "salvation" in the Psalter, including ישע ("to save"), נצל ("to deliver"),[60] חלץ ("to rescue"),[61] מלט ("to save, make escape"),[62] and פלט ("to deliver, make escape").[63] In addition, several synonyms hover over its semantic margins; e.g., עזר ("to help"),[64] ענה ("to answer"),[65] פדה ("to redeem"),[66] and שמר ("to guard, protect").[67] Not unexpectedly, most "salvation" petitions occur in the laments, especially the sections focused on "supplication."[68] In the first of the so-called "penitential psalms,"[69] for example, the poet laments his pain and suffering ("my bones shudder in terror") before crying out, "Deliver my soul! Save me for the sake of your *ḥesed*."[70] The lament in Ps 22 employs the word-pair ישע ("save!") and ענה ("answer!") in the last line of the supplication section.[71] Psalm 28 acknowledges in Yhwh (a) a strong shield who "helps" (עזר) his people, and (b) a "saving refuge" for his Messiah.[72] Psalm 31 manipulates a triad of "salvation" synonyms: פלט ("deliver"),[73] נצל ("rescue")[74] and ישע ("to save") before pronouncing the now-famous words, "into your hand I commit my

---

60. Ps 7:1; 59:2; 142:7; 143:9.

61. Ps 6:5.

62. Ps 33:17; 116:4.

63. Ps 71:12.

64. Ps 46:1 (cf. the PN "Ezra").

65. Ps 86:7. Cf. Moore, "Anomalies," 234–43.

66. Ps 25:22.

67. Ps 86:2. The participial/nominal form of ישע (מושיע, "Savior") occurs twice (Pss 17:7 and 106:21).

68. Gamberoni ("חסה," 66) notes the same for חסה ("refuge").

69. Dahood (*Psalms* 1.38) lists these as Pss 6, 32, 38, 51, 102, 130, and 143.

70. Ps 6:4, using the word-pair חלץ/ישע. Psalm 7:1 repeats this word-pair, but reverses the order. Ps 109:26 also petitions Yhwh's salvation "according to your *ḥesed*-love."

71. Ps 22:21.

72. Ps 28:8 (מעוז ישועות, lit., "a refuge of salvations"). OG ὑπερασπιστὴς τῶν σωτηρίων τοῦ χριστοῦ αὐτοῦ ("a champion of the saving deeds of his Christ"); Vg *protector salvationum christi sui* ("guarantor of the salvation of his Christ"); Syr ܚܣܝܢܐ ܘܦܪܘܩܐ ܕܡܫܝܚܗ ("the help and Savior of his Messiah"). With regard to the thorny hermeneutical questions attending the question of messianic "prophecy," Niebuhr (*Destiny*, 2.15) pointedly observes that "no Christ could validate himself as the disclosure of a hidden divine sovereignty over history or as a vindication of the meaningfulness of history, if a Christ were not expected."

73. Ps 31:1.

74. Ps 31:3, 15.

spirit."[75] Psalm 57 correlates Yhwh's heavenly "salvation" (ישע) with the "putting to shame" of those creatures who take delight in "trampling" him.[76]

Psalm 69 produces another "salvation triad" of words spaced at the beginning, middle, and end of the psalm: (a) It begins with the imperative "Save me!" (ישע) from "the waters reaching up to my neck"; then (b) pleads for "rescue" (נצל) from the sticky mire beneath; then (c) shares the hope that God will someday "save" (ישע) Zion from her enemies.[77] Psalm 76 depicts the execution of "justice" (משפט) and "salvation" (ישע) of the oppressed" as two sides of the same coin.[78] Psalm 106, an historical psalm highlighting Israel's sinful behavior, succeeds Ps 105, a psalm celebrating the nation's positive accomplishments. Near the end of these two psalms the psalmist spotlights Yhwh's decision to "deliver" (נצל) and "save" (ישע) his rebellious children[79] because their disloyalty can never annul, rescind, or even marginalize his *ḥesed*-loyalty.[80]

REFUGE

Jerome Creach spotlights "refuge" as a central motif in the Psalter, both semantically and structurally.[81] Kenneth Kuntz doubts there is enough evidence to support this claim,[82] but William Brown agrees with Creach that the "refuge" motif is "an important root metaphor."[83] The major synonyms in

---

75. Ps 31:3, 5, 16 (cf. Luke 23:46). "Salvation triads" are not uncommon in the Psalter. In Ps 71 the "salvation" synonyms are פלט, נצל, and ישע (all in v. 2). In Ps 80:2–3 the "salvation" motif permeates a triad of verbs: ישע, "save"; שוב, "restore" and ישע, "save"). In 31:21 the psalmist specifies that the saved *stay* saved because Yhwh hides them from harm in a "shelter" (סתר, lit., "hiding place") / "booth" (סכה; cf. חג הסכות, "feast of booths," Lev 23:34).

76. Ps 57:3. Psalm 59:2 emphasizes that such "trampling" is the work of "wicked and bloodthirsty men."

77. Ps 69:1, 14, 35.

78. Ps 76:9 (i.e., one is impossible without the other; cf. Matt 25:31–46).

79. Ps 106:43.

80. Ps 106:47. Brueggemann's (*Astonishment*, 13–14) approach to the *historical psalms* is that while some interpreters give precedence to autonomous reason, and others anchor their understanding of history in experience (the pain and suffering of the oppressed), the better way to look at history is through eyes filled with "abiding astonishment" (a phrase coined by Martin Buber).

81. Creach, *Refuge*, 19.

82. Kuntz, *Refuge*, 740–42. Creach's approach brings to mind Eichrodt's (*Theology*, 206–88) attempt to isolate "covenant" as the central motif of the OT, or اسلام (*islam*, "submission") as the central motif of Qur'an (cf., e.g., Q 33.35).

83. Brown (*Metaphor*, 18) goes on to say that Creach has shown that "refuge," is, "in

the "refuge" semantic field are חסה ("to seek refuge"), עוז ("to seek shelter"), שמר ("to keep, guard"),[84] and סתר ("to hide").[85] Like justice, refuge is a universal longing, especially for those living in violent environments populated by greedy oppressors and demonic spirits,[86] whether the *modus operandi* is sociopolitical, socioeconomic, socioreligious, or all of the above. Yet Israel does not always appreciate the refuge Yhwh tries to provide. To cite Isaiah, even though Yhwh has "founded a throne in Zion" to give refuge to "the needy among his people,"[87] his "rebellious children" sometimes turn away from him to places like Egypt,[88] thereby prompting the prophet to warn them that if they continue to "seek refuge under Pharaoh's shadow," such "refuge" will quickly turn to "shameful humiliation."[89]

In Ps 7 King David responds to the incriminations launched against him by Cush the Benjaminite,[90] crying out, "O Yhwh my God, in you I take refuge (חסה); save (ישע) me from all my pursuers, and deliver (נצל) me."[91] Psalm 11 elaborates the fight-or-flight polarity as (a) "fleeing to the mountains" vs. (b) "taking refuge" (חסה) in Yhwh.[92] Psalm 14 warns all foolish evildoers that if they think they can "eat up my people as they would bread," they are in for a rude awakening. Why? Because the "refuge" (מחסה) of God's people is protected by the Name dwelling on Mt. Zion.[93] Psalm 18 uses no less than seven synonyms to describe Yhwh as "Refuge": "my strength" (חזקי), "my rock" (סלעי), "my fortress" (מצודתי), "my deliverer" (מפלטי), "my stronghold" (משגבי), "the horn of my salvation" (קרן ישעי), and "refuge in him" (אחסה בו).[94] Psalm 25 utilizes a triad of synonyms to

---

essence, a filter through which the Psalter in its entirety can be viewed theologically."

84. Ps 16:1 (// חסה).

85. Ps 17:7–8 (// שמר and חסה).

86. Noting that OG Ps 91:6 reads καὶ δαιμονίου μεσημβρινοῦ ("and/or the noonday demon"), Schmutzer ("Refuge," 107) argues that Ps 91 "can teach us how to relate to God in a world fraught with danger, including demonic oppression."

87. Isa 14:32.

88. Isa 30:1. Jeremiah similarly condemns his fellow exiles in Egypt for (a) forsaking Yhwh and (b) taking refuge in the "Queen of Heaven" (Jer 44:17).

89. Isa 30:2–3. N.B. the twice-repeated word-pair עוז ("seek shelter") // חסה ("seek refuge") in these two verses.

90. Cf. 2 Sam 16:5 (Shimei).

91. Ps 7:1.

92. Ps 11:1.

93. Ps 14:6–7. MT מחסה is the nominal form of חסה. Cf. OG ἐλπὶς αὐτοῦ ("his hope"); Vg *spes eius* ("his hope"); Syr ܣܒܪܗ ("his confidence").

94. Ps 18:1–2. "Shield" (מגן) repeats in v. 30 (cf. also the military language in 91:1–4). Brown (*Metaphor*, 18–30) identifies the theological contours of the "refuge metaphor" in some detail.

paint a contrast between "refuge" and "shame" (בוש).⁹⁵ Psalm 31 declares that the decision to seek Yhwh's "refuge" (חסה) is the only way for "those who fear him" to find "accomplishment" and "abundance."⁹⁶ Psalm 36 promises that someday "all the sons of Adam will 'take refuge' (חסה) in the shadow of his wings."⁹⁷ Psalm 37 specifies that Yhwh's "salvation" (ישע) is a "safety-net" (מעוז) designed to protect the oppressed; i.e., that he has an intense desire to "rescue" (פלט) and "save" (ישע) them.⁹⁸ Psalm 43 asks why "the God in whom I take refuge" would "reject" (זנח) him, especially when the enemy threatening him is so heartless and cruel.⁹⁹ Psalm 46 insists that even if the nations and the kingdoms roar, even if all the shields and spears shatter and burn, and even if the mountains shake and the seas boil, the God of Jacob remains the "refuge" (מחסה)¹⁰⁰ and "stronghold" (משגב) of his people.¹⁰¹ Psalm 52 condemns those in the habit of pushing Yhwh aside to make wealth their "refuge" (מעוז) instead.¹⁰² Psalm 73 discloses that without Yhwh's "refuge" (מחסה) it is impossible "to recount all his works."¹⁰³ Psalm 91 condemns various types of evil via a format much like that found in ANE incantation handbooks like *Maqlû* and *Šurpu*.¹⁰⁴ Psalm 118 famously spotlights the contrast, "It is better to 'take refuge' (חסה) in Yhwh than to trust in men; it is better to 'take refuge' (חסה) in Yhwh than to trust in princes."¹⁰⁵

WEALTH

Most books of the Bible attempt in some way to engage the poverty-wealth polarity, but the Psalter, to use a dreadful play on words, is a "gold mine" on

---

95. Ps 25:20, שמר ("guard"), נצל ("deliver"), and חסה ("refuge"). The same contrast occurs in 31:1; and v. 4 contrasts "refuge" with "entrapment." Cf. also the triad of words for "refuge" in 71:1 (חסה), 3 (מעון), and 7 (מחסה).

96. Ps 31:19.

97. Ps 36:7.

98. Ps 37:39–40.

99. Ps 43:2 (cf. 61:3–4). Gamberoni ("חסה," 73) argues that "the object in view is always some kind of enemy in human form, apparently never impersonal perils like disease or natural catastrophe," yet note the use of הוות ("disaster") in 57:1.

100. As Gamberoni ("חסה," 71) points out, "the fabric of associations (with מחסה) expresses more than the individual word."

101. Ps 46:1, 7, 12.

102. Ps 52:7. Cf. Moore, *WealthWise*, 92–98.

103. Ps 73:28.

104. Cf., e.g., the lists of evil things condemned in *Maq* 5.11–20 and *Šur* 2.33–46.

105. Ps 118:8–9.

the subject.[106] Psalm 10 makes it clear that persecution of the poor is due to the greediness of the wicked, and further, that they manifest this greed in several ways: (a) by waiting in hiding-places to ambush the poor, lurking secretly like a lion in its den; and (b) by stooping, crouching, seizing, and dragging the helpless into nets, rationalizing their actions with "No one will find out . . . because God does not care about the poor."[107] In spite of all this, however, Ps 22 promises the poor that they will "eat and be satisfied,"[108] and Ps 41 pronounces a blessing on those who decide to help the poor *today*.[109] Psalm 49 (a) bids both rich and poor to understand that "their persecutors' iniquity" results from their decision to "trust in wealth and boast in riches"[110] and (b) ridicules those who think that their material wealth can somehow convince Yhwh to blot out all their sins and ransom their souls from Sheol.[111] *Application*: Do not worry when someone becomes richer than you because in Sheol there is no difference whatsoever between rich and poor.[112] Psalm 52 condemns the behavior of Doeg the Edomite, the infamous mercenary responsible for slaughtering eighty-five priests in the village of Nob after Saul's Hebrew soldiers refuse to do so.[113] Why does he kill these priests? The psalmist says that it's because he "trusts in abundant riches, and seeks refuge in wealth."[114] Psalm 113 describes Yhwh as a deity who "raises the poor from the dust and lifts the needy from the ash heap,"[115] and Ron Sider cites these and other texts to ask wealthy believers,

> We have the money. And we know what to do. Are we generous enough to do it?[116] . . . It's tragic that so many rich Christians are missing Jesus' path to joy and self-fulfillment . . . Millions are in despair as they seek in vain for happiness through ever-greater

---

106. For a more comprehensive look at the poverty-wealth polarity, see Moore, *WealthWatch*, *WealthWarn*, and *WealthWise*.

107. Ps 10:2–10; cf. 12:5; 14:6; 37:14.

108. Ps 22:26; cf. 132:15.

109. Ps 41:1; cf. 72:4; 74:19.

110. Ps 49:5–6.

111. Ps 49:7–9. V. 10 reports that some wealth-worshipers even believe that their money will accompany them to the grave, when in actuality it simply transfers to another mortal for a short period of time.

112. Ps 49:16–17.

113. 1 Sam 22:16–20.

114. Ps 52:7.

115. Ps 113:7. Cf. Job 42:10–12; and Moore, *Retribution*, 117–25.

116. Cf. Ps 37:21, "The righteous give generously."

material abundance," but "Jesus, on the other hand, offers true joy, not through getting, but through giving."[117]

KINGSHIP

The root word מלך ("king") appears in the Psalter twenty-six times. Of that number sixteen refer to the deity.[118] The phrase מלך יהוה ("Yhwh is king")[119] occupies a dense section of Book 4 (Pss 93:1; 96:10; 98:1; and 99:1),[120] and cognates appear in Amorite,[121] Ugaritic,[122] Ammonite,[123] Canaanite,[124] Aramaic,[125] Syriac,[126] and Arabic texts.[127] On occasion a Hebrew psalm will Yahwicize a phrase from a Gentile text. For example, where a line in the Canaanite Baʿal myth reads "Lift up your heads, O *gods*,"[128] the psalmist writes "Lift up your heads, O *gates* . . . that the king of glory may come in."[129] And lest there be any confusion as to who this "king of glory" might be, the psalmist declares that it is "Yhwh, strong and mighty; Yhwh, mighty in battle."[130]

Kingship is an important motif in the Bible generally, but nowhere is it more overt than in the Psalter.[131] Often the noun מלך ("king") is used to

---

117. Sider, *Christians*, xvi.

118. Childs, *Introduction*, 515–16; Wilson, "Royal," 85–94.

119. Also written as יהוה מלך.

120. N.B. that this phrase (יהוה ימלך, "Yhwh will reign") appears in the Israelite song of victory (Exod 15:18; cf. Moore, *Chaos*, 52).

121. Huffmon, *Amorite*, 230.

122. *CAT* 1.16.6.58.

123. *CAT* 137.4.3; 219.3. Cf. the name אלמלך (Elimelek, "my God is king") in Ruth 1:2; Ug *ilmlk* in *CAT* 1.6.6.53.

124. "Mightiest Baʿal is our king" (Ug *mlkn aliyn bʿl*, *CAT* 1.3.5.32); "the mountain of El, and entered the chapel of the king" (*ǵl il wybu qrš mlk*, *CAT* 1.2.3.5).

125. *DAT* 2.15.

126. *PSSD* 277.

127. One surah in Qurʾan begins with an acknowledgment of Allah as "the Holy One" (القدوس), "the All-Wise" (الحكيم), "the King" (الملك, Q 62.1).

128. Ug *šu ilm raštkm* (*CAT* 1.2.1.27).

129. שאו שערים ראשיכם . . . ויבוא מלך הכבוד (Ps 24:7).

130. יהוה עזוז וגבור יהוה גבור מלחמה (Ps 24:8). In an era when Israelites worship the chthonic deity Milcom (1 Kings 11:5), Tammuz (Ezek 8:14), the Queen of heaven (Jer 44:17) and many other gods, to emphasize that *Yhwh* is the "king of glory" is a minority opinion in some circles.

131. Based on the recurrence of the term אשרי ("blessed") in Pss 1:1 and 2:12 some argue that the Psalter as a whole is intentionally framed by the motifs of wisdom (Ps

describe the deity's identity,[132] but the verb מלך ("to rule") also describes that which is royally *done*.[133] In Ps 2, for example, Yhwh responds to the rebellious ruminations of Gentile kings by establishing *his* king on Mt. Zion,[134] then gives him whatever he needs to achieve "great victories."[135] Psalm 10 emphasizes that Yhwh, as eternal king, not only saves orphans from starvation but sometimes does so by "breaking the arm of the wicked."[136] Psalm 21 celebrates the king's trust in Yhwh because after throwing his enemies into a fiery furnace the Lord's wrath consumes them.[137] The aforementioned Psalm 24 announces Yhwh's arrival at the city gate, a military tradition (cf. Zech 9:9) which may or may not have been modified into a liturgical ceremony for ushering the ark into the holy of holies.[138] Psalm 47 celebrates the fact that Yhwh is a great king over all the nations of the earth, contending that this alone makes him worthy of praise.[139] Psalm 84 recognizes that despite his role as commander-in-chief, Yhwh still makes time to minister to the needs of sparrows and swallows.[140] Psalm 96 celebrates the fact that Yhwh's kingship is greater than that of any other king, divine or human, and warns that rejection of this claim is likely to be taken as a nascent indication of idolatry.[141] Psalm 29 links Yhwh's kingship to the power of his voice to

---

1) and kingship (Ps 2) or that "the first two psalms serve as an introduction to the entire book of Psalms" (Hakham, תהלים, 3). That this editorially indicates "an interest in choosing Yahweh as 'refuge' (cf. חסה in 2:12) because of the ineffectiveness of human rulers" is another possibility (Creach, *Refuge*, 104). Cf. discussions in Eaton, *Kingship*, 1–26; Grant, "King," 101–18; Wilson, "Seams," 85–94; and Miller, "Kingship," 127–42.

132. Pss 5:2; 24:7-10; 29:10; 44:4; 47:2, 6-7; 48:2; 68:24; 74:12; 84:3; 89:18; 93:1; 95:3; 98:6; 99:4; 145:1; 149:2. Interestingly, מלך appears 37 times in Ezekiel but never in a description of the deity. Cf. Howard, "Kingship," 197–207; Snearly, "King," 209–17.

133. Ps 10:16; 47:8; 96:10; 97:1; 99:1. Whether מלך is to be read as a noun or verb is largely determinable by (a) the versional translations (OG, Vg, and Syr) and (b) the masoretic pointings; i.e., מֶלֶךְ (noun) vs. מָלַךְ (verb).

134. Ps 2:2-6, after which he adds to this *political* title a *familial* one, "my son" (בני, v. 7). N.B. that the "Zion kingship" motif appears at both the beginning and end of the Psalter (149:1).

135. Ps 18:50 (ישועות, lit. "salvations"; cf. 44:4). Ps 20:9 reads הושיעה המלך ("let the king be saved"). Cf. 61:6; 63:11; 89:17-18; 98:1-9.

136. Ps 10:15-18.

137. Ps 21:7-10 (פרימו, lit. "his fruit").

138. Ps 24:7-10 (cf. 68:24-29 and 99:1-9). Following Gunkel (*Psalmen*) and Kraus (*Psalms*), Kroeger (*Bible*, 297) agrees that this psalm is probably modified to "celebrate the return of the Ark."

139. Ps 47:2-8; cf. 145:1.

140. Ps 84:1-3 (cf. Matt 6:26). The title יהוה צבאות ("Yhwh Ṣebaoth") in vv. 1 and 3 means "Yhwh of Hosts."

141. Ps 96:3-10; cf. 97:1-7.

shatter trees and shake deserts while enthroned upon the primeval waters of the flood.[142]

HOLINESS

The root קדש ("to make holy") appears in the Psalter fifteen times, six in the brief sampling above (Ps 22:3; 29:2, 8; 51:11; 79:1; 103:1).[143] Unlike חסד, cognates of קדש pop up regularly in the literature of Israel's neighbors, and while often referring to the consecration of sanctuaries, land, and temple paraphernalia,[144] they predominantly describe the identities of deities. For example, one Canaanite myth matter-of-factly refers to El's queenly consort (Athirat) as "the Holy One."[145] An Akkadian mouth-washing ritual lays out several must-do activities to ensure that "the mouth of the holy one" (i.e., the mouth of the humanoid image being prepared for public display) is properly "washed."[146] An Aramaic commentary on Genesis from Qumran Cave 1 designates the "daughters of men" as "holy ones,"[147] even as God is identified as "the Great Holy One, King of Heaven."[148] The Scroll of the Rule from Cave 1 calls the Dead Sea covenanters a "holy assembly" (עצת קודש).[149] In a series of blessings over the "sons of Zadok"[150] one instructor expresses

---

142. Ps 29:1–10 (cf. above). Cf. 74:12–15; 93:3–4; 95:5.

143. Cf. Otto, *Holy*; Gammie, *Holiness*; Eliade, *Sacred*.

144. A Phoenician inscription from Tyre reads *lrbty l'strt 'š bgw hqdš*: "To my lady Astarte who is (enthroned) in the holy place/sanctuary" (*KAI* 17.1), and in Qur'an Moses tells tired refugees, "O my people, enter the 'holy' (المقدسة) land which Alla has predestined for you" (Q 5.21, alluding to the root قدس, "holy").

145. Ug *ltpn wqdš*, "the Kindly One and the Holy One" (*CAT* 1.16.1.11).

146. Akk *pī qa-aš-di* LUḪ-*u* (text cited in *CAD* Q.147). Walker and Dick (*Image*, 57) point out that new and rehabilitated humanoid images are obliged to go through a special ritual called the *mīs pî* (lit., "mouth-washing") before they can be used in public worship. One Hebrew psalm satirically depicts the use of such images: "Their idols are silver and gold, the work of human hands. They have mouths, but do not speak; eyes, but do not see. They have ears, but do not hear; noses, but do not smell. They have hands, but do not feel; feet, but do not walk; they make no sound in their throats. Those who make them are like them; so are all who trust in them" (Ps 115:4–8).

147. 1QapGen 2.1 reads, "I thought in my heart that this conception (Gen 6:4) was the work of the Watchers (with regard to) the pregnancy of the 'Holy Ones'" (קדישין, f. pl. of קדש).

148. קדישא רבא במלך שמיא (1QapGen 2.4).

149. 1QS 2.24–25.

150. The PN Zadok (צדוק) in 1Q28b 3.22 comes from the root word for "justice, righteousness" (צדק).

the hope that the Zadokites (Sadducees)[151] might be appreciated "like an angel in the presence of the holy residence . . . like a crown in the holy of holies."[152]

Turning to the Psalter, Psalm 79 laments Jerusalem's demolition into rubble, the devouring of its children by ravenous beasts, and the draining of innocent blood into the street, regarding each of these violent acts as defilements of his "holy house."[153] Psalm 103 urges Israel to consecrate the Name responsible for forgiving sins, curing sickness, redeeming from the pit, and vindicating the oppressed.[154] Psalm 46 acknowledges that the mountains may fall and the seas may boil, but nothing can vanquish the "river whose streams make glad the city of God, the 'holy habitation' of the Most High."[155] Psalm 65 insists that even though sin can seem overwhelming, "happy are those whom you choose to come and live in your courts," the only place in the world where one can experience "satisfaction with the goodness of your house, your holy temple."[156] Psalm 29 describes Yhwh's voice as a force able to quench fiery flames and splinter cedars, and that the only appropriate response to such power is to fall down and worship the "splendor of his holiness."[157]

JUSTICE

Twenty-seven times the root צדק ("justice, righteousness") appears in the Psalter, and the term often found in parallel to it, משפט ("justice, judgment"), appears fifteen times. Both words can be translated into English as "justice," but where the second one can denote *acts* of justice, the first can denote the abstract *notion* of justice; i.e., "righteousness."[158] Justice is a universal

---

151. Cf. Flint, *Scrolls*, 133–36.
152. כמלאך פנים מעון קודש . . . נזר לקודש קודשים (1Q28b 4.25, 28).
153. Ps 79:1–3. Cf. Douglas, *Purity*; Moore, *Chaos*, 67–75.
154. Ps 103:1–6.
155. Ps 46:2–4.
156. Ps 65:3–4. Seerveld, ("Church," 152) writes that "I'm told that in darkened pubs today lonely persons are sometimes ready to tell their tale of woe to a perfect stranger as if in a confessional. They do this there because church worship services are often too brightly lit, too 'happy-happy' a place to bear your intimate sorrows to anybody."
157. Ps 29:2–9.
158. Cf. examples and variations of צדק listed in *HAL* 941–44, and in Johnson ("צדק," 243–64). According to Noonan (*Advances*, 69), "Synonyms, antonyms, and inclusion relations all facilitate the classification of meaning according to *semantic field* . . . Our understanding of something is often enhanced by comparing and contrasting it with something else, especially that which is similar. So, by juxtaposing word

longing in all cultures, so it's no surprise that it comes variously clothed in different texts. Cognates of צדק (ṣdq) appear in several semitic texts,[159] and although the ṣdq morpheme does not appear in Egyptian or Akkadian, the judicial texts of these cultures are hardly silent. Egyptian scribes, for example, use the word m3ʿt to signify a whole range of concerns associated with the problem of (in)justice. As Siegfried Morenz sees it, "m3ʿt is right order in nature and society, as established by the act of creation, and hence means, according to the context, what is right, what is correct, law, order, justice and truth."[160] Mesopotamian scribes navigate the "justice" semantic field with terms like *mīšaru*[161] and *kittu*,[162] and Qurʾan does the same with terms like صدق (ṣadq) and زكوه (zaqāh).[163]

In Psalm 7 the psalmist implores Yhwh to render "judgment" (משפט) against his enemies in order that the glory of his "righteousness" (צדק) might be clearly displayed, especially since he has worked so hard to simulate this "justice" (צדק) in his own life as a reflection of the *imago Dei*.[164] Psalm 9 observes that the wicked are ensnared by their own schemes whenever and wherever Yhwh decides to execute "justice" (משפט).[165] In Psalm 37 the "righteous" (צדיקים) are recognized by the fact that they (a) speak with wisdom and "justice" (משפט), and (b) give liberally to the poor.[166] Psalm 119 plaintively asks, "When will you execute justice (משפט) against my pursuers"... especially since "I am doing what is 'just' (משפט) and 'right' (צדק)?"[167] And Psalm 99 summarily states that Yhwh establishes "upright-

---

meanings in this way, semantic field theory enhances our understanding of each individual meaning."

159. Cf. examples cited in Ringgren, "צדק," 242–43.

160. Morenz, *Religion*, 113; cf. Smelik, "Maʿat," 534–35; Moore, *Retribution*, 72–80.

161. "Justice, righteousness" (Cf. *CAD* M/1.116-19).

162. "Truth, rightness, justice, loyalty, alliance." E.g., *i-pu-ša a-na-ku ki-ta it-ti abdi-a-ši-ir-ta ... bal-ṭati ša-ni-tu* ("send word back to me or I will make an alliance with Abdi-aširta ... and stay alive" (*EA* 83.25; cf. *CAD* K.468-72).

163. Arab. صدق (ṣadq) means "truth, truthfulness, sincerity, candor, veracity, correctness" (Wehr 508–9), and زكوه (zaqāh) means "justness, integrity, honesty, justification, vindication, alms-tax," as in the Qurʾanic instruction, "Establish prayer and pay the 'alms-tax'" (زكوه, Q 2.110). Taxation, in other words, is a matter of retributive justice.

164. Ps 7:6-8. N.B. that this "reflective justice" motif hardens somewhat in the Hodayot scroll from Qumran Cave 1; e.g., "You honor yourself through 'justice against the wicked' (משפט רשעים)" and "'strengthen yourself through me' (הגבירכה בי) before the sons of Adam" (1QH 10.24).

165. Ps 9:16.

166. Ps 37:26-30.

167. Ps 119:84, 121.

ness" (מישרים),¹⁶⁸ "justice" (משפט), and "righteousness" (צדקה) because he "is a mighty king who loves justice."¹⁶⁹

SUMMARY

To be sure, the foregoing comments and reflections only scratch the surface, but one would be hard-pressed to find other motifs more central to the Psalter's theological identity. The *historical* question is this: upon what do Second Temple worshipers focus in the Psalms if not the motifs of *loyalty, salvation, identity, trust, refuge, wealth, kingship, holiness,* and *justice*? The *contemporary* question is this: are these motifs prioritized in contemporary Christian worship?

---

168. Cf. Akk *mīšaru*; Ug *yšr* (*CAT* 1.14.1.13).
169. Ps 99:4 (עז מלך משפט אהב); cf. 37:28.

4

What Is Sung About Today in Congregational Worship?

MANY ARE SORELY DIVIDED, or at least deeply ambivalent, over how to conduct congregational worship today. On the one hand, some find "Contemporary Christian Music" (CCM)—the largest supplier of worship material since the 1960s—to be something created by the devil for the express purpose of poisoning the church.[1] Others see it, with Richard Mouw, as a precious gift bestowed by the Holy Spirit to help clear out the cobwebs and re-energize the church.[2] Most stand somewhere between these two extremes. According to pollster George Barna,

> the coverage afforded the so-called "worship wars" tends to exaggerate the scope of the problem while ignoring the real issues regarding worship;[3] viz., that the major challenge is not about how to use music to facilitate worship as much as it is to help people understand worship and have an intense passion to connect with God.[4]

---

1. Hyperbole intended (!), but cf. the more serious discussions in Howard and Streck, *Apostles*; Lucarini, *Music*; Lemley, *Sing*; Kelman, *Shout*; and Hart, *Exposed*.

2. Mouw ("Foreword," 5) admits that "I am a switch-hitter when it comes to worship music. I love the old hymns, but I also like the praise music," positively describing the latter as resulting from a "hunger for spiritual renewal."

3. Webber (*Blended*, 106–20) argues (a) that simplistic polarities like "traditional-vs.-contemporary" or "formal-vs.-vernacular" or "liturgical-vs.-contemporary" do relatively little to bring peace to congregations caught up in the "worship wars," but (b) that "blended services" can help bring healing where it's most needed.

4. Barna, *Music*, cited in Woods and Walrath, "Introduction," 193 nt 1.

More to the point here, while it is true that much ink has been spilled about (a) the theology of the Psalter and (b) the theology of CCM, little has been done to discuss the relationship between the two. How much does one influence the other?[5] To be specific, how much does CCM incorporate the theological motifs of *loyalty, salvation, identity, trust, refuge, wealth, kingship, holiness,* and *justice*?

LOYALTY

"Love" is a concept easily corrupted by contemporary interpreters and certainly one widely misunderstood by postmodern Westerners nurtured since birth on the medieval romance myth.[6] In the Bible, however, *ḥesed* has nothing to do with romantic "love," at least not as the term is popularly defined in contemporary literature, lyrics, and film. As pointed out above, *ḥesed* denotes "covenant *loyalty*," not romantic longing.[7] The former originates from a decision to trust in a covenant-making, covenant-keeping God, the latter in notions created by screenwriters and lyricists desperate to have their work submitted to film and record companies for that all-important "green light."[8] The first refers to a clearly-established relationship between a master and his servant; the second bobs fitfully on the cultural winds and waves.[9] Were the first to be truly championed in CCM one would hear much less adolescent talk about "God's precious *love*" and "how much *I love* the Lord."[10] Instead there would be more talk about "keeping the faith," "taking up the cross" and "counting the cost."[11] The psalmists praise Yhwh for his loyalty (*ḥesed*), not just his "love" (*'ahava*), and if CCM wants to help worshipers (re)discover what this means, it must decide whether or not to conform more intentionally to categories congruent with the biblical notion of *ḥesed*.[12]

---

5. Attempting to address this question via quantitative analysis, Porter ("Music," 83) studies the lyrics of 22 CCM songs, discovering that nine allude in some way to Christ's pain and suffering, while the other thirteen focus "more overtly" on "*our* pain and suffering."

6. Lewis (*Allegory*, 1–53) observes that the myth of romantic love is a Western invention, a fatalistic obsession relentlessly championed as the "key to all happiness."

7. Cf. the discussion in Moore, *Reconciliation*, 99–112.

8. Cf. Warner, *Greenlight*; Bethke, *Production*, 27.

9. Jas 1:6.

10. Following Swidler (*Love*, 129), Paris ("Love," 44–45) is justifiably critical of CCM's redefinition of "love" through lenses tainted by the "American romantic ideal."

11. Luke 14:28. Cf. Bonhoeffer, *Discipleship*, 57–78.

12. Paris ("Love," 52–53) makes three suggestions for improvement: "(a) increase

SALVATION

Another motif frequently watered down today is "salvation." The question "are you saved?" is in some churches little more than a sloganeering litmus test for "membership in the Christ Club." This is inappropriate, of course, but CCM, in what is doubtless a good-faith attempt to avoid such sloganeering, often pushes the pendulum too far to the other extreme, rarely even *mentioning* salvation, much less holistically defining it. Many worship leaders seem to cower before the question "are you saved?" because they fear it might raise another from their "audience";[13] viz., "saved from what?"[14] What needs to be clearly understood, however, is that the glaring absence of holistic "salvation" language in congregational worship today is almost certainly indicative of a passive-aggressive determination to resist Christ's call for *repentance*. Mature believers know that salvation is impossible without repentance, yet the fatalistic unwillingness even to *countenance* change[15] ("If God truly loves me, he'll accept me as I am"), much less champion it, must be recognized for what it is—a patent rejection of the Gospel. After all, Jesus minces no words when he tells the religious Pharisee Nicodemus that "unless you are born again you cannot see the kingdom of God."[16] Sadly, as Westermann sadly observes, the aftermath of World War II creates an environment where the need to *lament* is stifled,[17] but now the perception is that there is really no need to *repent* of sin.[18] Thus Jeremiah's prophecy is fulfilled: "I did not send your prophets, yet they ran. I did not speak to them, yet they prophesied. But if they had stood in my council, then they would have proclaimed my words to my people, and they would have *turned them*

---

reliance on scripture in song lyrics; (b) broaden the language of love beyond the romantic; and (c) expand the role of humans beyond passivity, weakness, and sinfulness."

13. Performing before an audience is not the same as "speaking to one another."

14. Reardon (*Psalms*, 215) thinks that contemporary worshipers "are far too disposed" to substitute for the Psalms their own "personal sentiments and spontaneous feelings." Often the last thing worship leaders want to do is make the "mistake" of making churchgoers, especially visitors, feel "uncomfortable."

15. Responding to the fatalistic ideology that one is predeterminedly born with a static "sexual orientation," Gallagher (*Eros*, 256–57) observes that "two hundred years ago ... homosexuality did not exist. There was sodomy, of course, and buggery, and fornication and adultery and other sexual sins, but none of these forbidden acts fundamentally altered the sexual landscape. A man who committed sodomy may have lost his soul, but he did not lose his gender. He did not become a homosexual, a third sex. That was the invention of the 19th century imagination."

16. John 3:3.

17. Porter ("Music," 77) pointedly defines *lament* as "something more substantial than just a 'whistling in the dark' that superficially props up our courage."

18. "Unless you repent, you will all likewise perish" (Luke 13:3, 5).

away from their evil will, and from the evil of their doings."[19] Paul underscores this truth to the Roman church with the question "do you not realize that God's kindness is meant to lead you to repentance?"[20] *Conclusion*: CCM too often appears to be squandering a golden opportunity to teach the whole gospel to the whole world. Is salvation possible without repentance? If not, then why is repentance not prioritized in contemporary worship?

IDENTITY

The Psalter focuses a good deal of attention on the Name because the psalmists are keenly aware of Israel's idolatrous history. To say "I believe in God" is a meaningless statement apart from a clear understanding of Yhwh's identity *vis-à-vis* other "gods." Psalm 106 reminds readers, for example, that Israel "worshiped a calf at Horeb," and that by so doing they embarrassingly "exchange the glory of God for the image of an ox that eats grass."[21] Afterwards they "yoke themselves to the Baʿal of Peor, eating sacrifices for the dead,"[22] mingling with the nations, sacrificing their children to demons, and worshiping the gods of Canaan.[23] Much of this polytheistic behavior is now confirmed by archaeological discovery. On an inscription from the NE Sinai village of Kuntillet ʿAjrud, for example, Yhwh is "blessed" as a male deity accompanied by a female deity (Asherah).[24] To be sure, such primitive, blatant idolatry may not seem problematic today, but Yhwh's identity continues to be grossly misunderstood. He may not be idolatrously sexualized as a male deity accompanied by female consorts, but the fact that "gender justice" is even *considered* to be more important than *loyalty* or *salvation* or *kingship* or *holiness* is problematic, to say the least.[25] The prophet Ezekiel warns of what happens when the Name is profaned:

---

19. Jer 23:21-22.

20. Rom 2:4. In v. 5 Paul warns that "the inflexible and impenitent heart" (τὴν σκληρότητά σου καὶ ἀμετανόητον καρδίαν) stores up wrath to be released on the Day (cf. Moore, *Babbler*, 45–57).

21. Ps 106:19-20. The Egyptian goddess Hathor is represented as a cow.

22. Ps 106:28. The Baʿal Peor cult remains swathed in mystery. Some believe it to be an orgiastic cult built around "Lord of Fire" gods from Anatolia (Mendenhall, *Tenth*, 109). Others doubt whether it has anything to do with sex at all, much less Anatolian religion (Levine, *Numbers* 2.294–97).

23. Ps 106:35-38.

24. This pithos jar inscription reads *brkt ʿtkm lyhwh šmrn wlʾšrth*, "I bless you by Yhwh of Samaria and by his Asherah" (cf. Meshel et al., *Kuntillet ʿAjrud*; Chase, "Inscription," 63; Wyatt, "Asherah," 99–105).

25. Elizabeth Achtemeier sensitively addresses this problem in her now-famous *CT*

> I will scatter them among the nations . . . And when they come to the nations . . . they will continue to desecrate my holy Name. So it will be said of them, "These are Yhwh's people, but they had to leave his land."[26]

TRUST

Trust is another motif easily distorted. Paul has to spell out to the Roman church what it means and does not mean; i.e., that those who *say* they trust in God are not justified, only those who actually *do* put their trust in him.[27] James's *Letter to the Diaspora* says much the same thing: "Be doers of the word, and not merely hearers who deceive themselves."[28] Faith has at least three stages—birth, adolescence, and maturity—and while God is active at each stage,[29] the lament psalms make it clear that moving from stage to stage involves the difficult process of learning how to deal with pain—betrayal, invasion, sickness, shame, persecution, enemies, exile, abandonment, and so forth.[30] Yet how many of the songs sung in church today even *recognize* these concerns, much less teach worshipers how to deal with them?[31] Reading the Psalms shows that it does not take long to realize (a) that trust in God always involves a serious commitment to his covenant; and (b) that apart from this commitment trust is not just elusive or challenging but unattainable.

---

article, "Why God Is Not Mother."

26. Ezek 36:18–20.

27. "It's not the hearers of the law, but the doers of the law who will be justified" (Rom 2:13). Psalm 56:4 reads, "In God I trust."

28. Jas 1:22. Paul's *Letter to the Romans* and James's *Letter to the Diaspora* have a lot in common, regardless of how often they are pitted against one another by Enlightenment theologians.

29. Cf. Fowler (*Stages*) and Haunz ("Development," 640–55).

30. A study of the stories in 1–2 Kings reveals nine types of pressure constantly challenging the faithful: *injustice, subversion, prophecy, famine, frailty, foreigners, reform, Yhwh,* and *violence* (cf. Moore, *Faith,* 343–50).

31. Is worship about "*teaching and admonishing* one another . . . with psalms" (Col 3:16), or is Lester Ruth ("Music," 29) correct that "churches are perhaps satisfied with worship that does not reach for a full vision because a consumerist culture leads us to believe that the most critical thing is that worship be true to us."

KINGSHIP

CCM often sings about Christ as King, yet how many postmodern Westerners truly understand what it means to be subject to a king? For most 21st-century worshipers the very *idea* of submission—even *mutual* submission[32]—is a repugnant notion deeply scarred by contemporary language about "patriarchy" and "oppression." Is this why it's never sung about? Is this why the equation *woman > man > Christ > God* is never even mentioned, much less celebrated?[33] Are worship leaders *that* afraid to offend people, even mature Christian sisters and brothers who understand what it means to be subject to Christ? Or has the Western church as a whole simply forgotten "thy kingdom come"?

The simple truth is this. The kingdom of heaven is not a democracy, nor is it a republic or confederation or association or organization or country club. Christ does not constantly teach his disciples that "the Republic of Heaven is at hand," or that "the Christ Club is now open for potential new members." Paul does not tell the Philippians that Christ's coming will make everyone happy. No, he tells them that every knee will *bow* and every tongue will *confess* that Jesus Christ is Lord. Peter's Pentecost sermon is clear: "Let all the house of Israel fully understand that God has made this Jesus whom you crucified both Lord and Christ."[34] When the Son of Man separates the sheep from the goats on the last day, he will not, in the name of "grace," suddenly create new hybrid categories of "geeps" and "shoats." No, the king will receive the sheep on his right hand and dismiss the goats on his left.[35] The royal psalms are clear: "Yhwh is king, robed in majesty! His throne sits upon the Flood before the beginning of time. He crushes the head of every leviathan and every dragon. He judges all the peoples of the earth impartially. Yhwh is a great God, a great king above all gods."[36]

WEALTH

Would it not be great to see worshipers from the richest country in history come together for worship on Sunday to sing about how "more blessed

---

32. "*Submitting* (ὑποτασσόμενοι) *to one another* (ἀλλήλοις) out of reverence for Christ" (Eph 5:21).
33. 1 Cor 11:3.
34. Acts 2:36.
35. Matt 25:31–46.
36. Pss 93:1; 74:12–14; 29:10; 96:10; 95:3.

it is to give than receive?"[37] That there is nothing approximating this lyric in the contemporary worship canon is an astonishingly sad state of affairs. Even though it is the Lord himself who pronounces this blessing, why are there no songs regularly sung about this radiant blessing, never mind darker songs about the dangers of "robbing temples?"[38] So many psalms focus on the poverty-wealth polarity, it's nothing less than astonishing to witness this lightless black hole. Psalm 52 surfaces this astonishment in a pointed rebuke of Doeg the Edomite, Saul's mercenary henchman responsible for murdering dozens of Yhwh's priests:[39]

> "Why do you boast, O arrogant man, of the trouble you plan to inflict upon the godly? Every day all you think about is hurting others. Your tongue is like a sharp razor, you worker of treachery. You love evil more than good. You love lies more than truth. You love only words that devour, not build up. Yet God will eventually tear you out, you deceitful tongue. He will snatch you up and cast you away from your tent. He will uproot you from the land of the living. The righteous will see all this and laugh, saying, 'Look at the man who chooses not to take refuge in God, but instead *chooses to invest his faith in riches and wealth!*'"[40]

HOLINESS

Thankfully, songs about divine "holiness" are relatively abundant in the CCM canon. Standing firmly in the shadow of Reginald Heber's "Holy, Holy, Holy," for example, Chris Tomlin's "Holy Forever" reverently celebrates Isaiah's *seraphim* vision:[41]

> And the angels cry, 'Holy'
> All creation cries, 'Holy'
> You are lifted high, 'Holy.'"[42]

---

37. Acts 20:35.

38. Rom 2:22. "Temple-robbing" (ἱεροσυλέω) is a terrible crime in the ancient world (cf. Plato, *Resp.* 575b; Moore, "Associations," 149–55), but perhaps its closest contemporary equivalent comes from "believers" refusing to recognize and affirm the blessedness of giving.

39. The actions of Doeg are reported in 1 Sam 21:7—22:22.

40. Ps 52:1–7. For more on the poverty-wealth polarity cf. Moore, *WealthWatch*, *WealthWarn*, and *WealthWise*.

41. Published posthumously after Heber's death in 1826.

42. Tomlin, "Holy Forever," track 4 on the album *Always* (released July 15, 2022). The heavenly scene in Rev 4:1–7 is itself an echo of the scene in Isa 6:1–4.

The Psalter is not unclear: Yhwh is indeed the "Holy One of Israel." The question remains, however, whether the psalmists merely *replicate* Isaiah's vision or *enhance* it. *Seraphim* never appear in the Psalter, of course, but the psalmists do weave the holiness motif into several contexts, often melding it to other theological motifs in ingenious ways. Thus "holiness" radiates from the deity toward his "holy hill," his "holy mountain," his "holy temple," his "holy Name," his "holy throne," his "holy oil," his "holy arm," his "holy ones," "his holy word," and of course, his "holy spirit."[43] The last of these, unfortunately, is over-interpreted in some churches and under-interpreted in others. In his first letter to the Corinthians, Paul deals with the first of these extremes by systematically defining what the Holy Spirit does and does not do,[44] and the apostle John warns his readers that though they are anointed by the Holy One, they still need to "test the spirits to see whether they come from God."[45] In his Thesssalonian correspondence, however, Paul deals with the second problem by urging readers to "test everything," but not so strictly that they "quench the spirit."[46]

REFUGE

"Refuge" is another motif frequently sung about today. The song "Refuge," for example, is not just emotionally powerful but theologically faithful to the refuge motif blanketing the Psalter, particularly in Pss 7, 11, 14, 17 and 52. But again, it's important to recognize that the psalmists meld the refuge motif to other theological motifs in order to create quilted lyrics far more interesting and effective than simplistic one-to-one conversations in the first person. Seeking refuge is not just about pain relief, the theological equivalent of taking a Tylenol or swallowing an aspirin. Much more is at stake. Often the Psalter contrasts Yhwh's "refuge," for example, with the "refuge" falsely dangled by other would-be "protectors" like Pharaoh,[47] and often they thank Yhwh for "refuge" from specific enemies like Cush the Benjaminite,[48] or contrast the Savior's offer of refuge with "hiding out in the mountains."[49] Note, for example, how Luther reconfigures the challenges in

---

43. Pss 2:6; 48:1; 5:7; 47:8; 30:4; 22:3; 16:3; 89:20; 98:1; 105:42; and 51:11.
44. 1 Cor 11–14.
45. 1 John 2:20; 3:10; 4:1.
46. 1 Thess 5:19–21.
47. Ps 135:9; 136:15.
48. Ps 7:1.
49. Ps 11:1.

Ps 46 to specify several of his own challenges in his classic hymn, "A Mighty Fortress is Our God":

> A mighty fortress is our God
> A bulwark never failing
> Our helper he amidst the flood
> Of mortal ills prevailing
> For still our ancient Foe
> Doth seek to work us woe
> His craft and pow'r are great
> And armed with cruel hate
> On earth is not his equal.[50]

Granted, Luther writes this hymn in the midst of terrible persecution perpetrated by an idolatrous religious masquerade,[51] but the point here is to notice how deliberately he names names, using colorful phrases like "ancient foe," "no earthly equal," "crafty and powerful," all prefaced by the vivid metaphor, "flood of mortal ills."[52] What Luther understands is what the psalmists understand; viz., that "refuge" is not fully defined until that from which such refuge is sought is clearly, succinctly, and confidently specified.

JUSTICE

In light of the clear linkage between worship and justice in the prophetic texts,[53] Richard Foster concludes (a) that "social justice is a divine mandate," and (b) that "liturgical life can never be divorced from it." But Jay Howard, after investigating how often the words "just" or "justice" appear in

---

50. Words and music by Martin Luther, 1528.

51. Cf. Bainton, *Reformation*, 3–21. Some think that Luther writes this hymn as a tribute to his Wittenburg student Leonhard Kaiser, who on August 16, 1527, is burned at the stake for heresy.

52. Succeeding verses even more explicitly name names.

53. Isa 1:15–17 reads, "When you stretch out your hands, I will hide my eyes from you; even though you pray many prayers, I will not listen; your hands are full of blood. Wash yourselves; make yourselves clean; remove the evil of your doings from before my eyes; cease to do evil, learn to do good; seek 'justice' (משפט), rescue the oppressed, defend the orphan, plead for the widow." Isa 58:4–6 reads, "You fast only to quarrel and fight and punch with wicked fists. 'Fasting' like this will not make your voice heard on high. Is this the fast that I choose" or "is *this* the fast that I choose—to untie the bonds of wickedness, to undo the thongs of the yoke, to let the oppressed go free, and to break apart every yoke?" Amos 5:23–24 reads, "Take away from me the noise of your songs! I will not listen to the sound of your stringed instruments. But let 'justice' (משפט) roll down like waters, and 'righteousness' (צדקה) like an ever-flowing stream."

seventy-seven contemporary worship songs,[54] finds it deeply disappointing that only one of these songs—"Great Is the Lord"[55]—even *mentions* the word "just," and further, that the noun "justice" does not appear in *any* of them.[56] Trying to make sense of this drought, he considers several explanations:

First, CCM artists like Terry Scott Taylor have been singing about social justice for years, but "the rock and new wave performance style of his songs probably eliminate them from consideration as worship music in most churches."[57] *Second*, the "lack of participation by historic Anabaptist and peace churches (Church of the Brethren, Mennonite, Quaker) may account, in part, for their lack of voice" with regard to "righteousness and justice in contemporary worship music."[58] *Third*, following Mark Noll,[59] he observes that the rise of fundamentalism in the 1930s shifted the focus of Western worshipers away from social justice to personal piety, and "this, coupled with what Noll calls a 'docetic tendency' among evangelicals to see the world as hopelessly polluted and on a downward spiral, may contribute to a viewpoint that because 'this world is not my home' the structures of society that contribute to injustice are unworthy of Christians' attention."[60]

Doubtless there are other factors to consider, but the bottom line is that Westerners worshiping in the wealthiest churches on earth are not singing about Yhwh's justice in congregational worship.[61] Psalm 10 speaks to this drought in plain language:

> "Why do the wicked renounce God, and say in their hearts, 'You will not call us to account?' But you do see! Indeed, you note trouble and grief, that you may take it into your hands. The helpless commit themselves to you; you are the helper of the orphan. Break the arm of the wicked and evildoers. Seek out their wickedness until you find none. Yhwh is king forever and ever, and the nations shall perish from his land. O Yhwh, listen to the desires of the meek, strengthen their hearts, and incline

---

54. The seventy-seven songs analyzed by Howard are those reported in CCLI as most popular between the years 1989–2005.
55. Body Songs, 1985 (Steve McEwan).
56. Howard, "Music," 69–71.
57. Howard, "Music," 72.
58. Howard, "Music," 73.
59. Noll, *Scandal*, 165.
60. Howard, "Music," 74.
61. To cite the Nazarene prophet, "Woe to you, scribes and Pharisees, hypocrites! For you tithe mint, dill, and cummin, and have neglected the weightier matters of the law: *justice*, mercy, and faith" (Matt. 23:23).

your ear to do justice for the orphan and the oppressed, so that those from earth may strike terror no more."[62]

---

62. Ps 10:13–18.

5

Concluding Remarks

CONTEMPORARY WORSHIP IS NOT where it needs to be theologically, and this state of affairs is at least partially due to the fact that worship leaders are not biblically, theologically, and/or pastorally trained. The usual expectation in most churches is simply that they be competent musicians who can sing and/or play a musical instrument. Of course, there are exceptions to this rule. More and more schools are attracting more and more worship leaders to the training they know they need if they are to serve the Church faithfully. But underneath this problem lies another one. *Question*: "Which comes first, *education* or *worship*?" Doubtless most worship leaders think (a) that worship comes first ("of course"), then education ("if necessary"),[1] or (b) that both are equally necessary, or (c) that the sequencing is irrelevant. The Queen of Sheba story challenges all three of these mindsets because the queen does not worship until she learns which deity *deserves* her worship.[2] Her development is clearly reported:

- The queen hears rumors about King Solomon's wisdom
- She decides to journey to Jerusalem to investigate these rumors
- Upon arrival she enrolls in "Wisdom 101," asking her teacher (Solomon) "hard questions" in order to obtain the information she "desires"
- She learns that Solomon's God is the source of all wisdom
- She *then* decides to become a Yhwh worshiper.[3]

1. I cannot recall the last time I saw a worship team member attending a Bible class.
2. 1 Kgs 10:1–13.
3. Cf. Moore, *Babbler*, 156–65. Whereas the Sabean queen's encounter helps her

There's no need to be rigidly linear about this sequence, but Emanuel Lévinas is right to presume that responsibility to the Other always precedes "the objective search for truth,"[4] and Tessa Rajak voices the opinion of many that the Psalter is "the richest of all biblical sources for liturgical texts, for private spiritual expression, and for reflection," a resource "capable of conveying an intimate connection to a gamut of human experience," proving it to be "the prime literary source for the performance of religion in Judaism and Christianity."[5] The word *performance*, however, is a two-edged sword. Like the word "love" it can mean different things to different people. On the one hand it merely denotes "activity" (as Prof. Rajak uses it), but in light of the contemporary celebrity culture climate its primary significance has to do with "image" over "substance."[6] Whether the musicians on stage on a given Sunday morning engage in *praise* or *performance* is impossible to ascertain, but in the words of Jesus, "Wisdom is justified by her works,"[7] and "You shall know them by their fruits."[8] The hope here is that the foregoing pages can help worshipers—and worship leaders—accomplish two things: (a) become "wise" to the ways of the world, especially its determination to prioritize "image" over "substance" by substituting *performance* for genuine *praise*; and (b) to pass the "fruit test" with such flying colors, even "the world itself cannot contain" the fruit produced.[9]

---

discover the *temporal* dimension, the Samaritan woman's encounter helps her discover the *spatial* dimension of worship ("neither in Jerusalem nor upon this mountain, but in spirit and truth," John 4:21).

4. Lévinas, *Totality*, 150.

5. Rajak, "Introduction," 3.

6. N.B. the theological drought in CCM with regard to the motifs of *wealth* and *justice*.

7. Matt 11:19.

8. Matt 7:16. Not just the "fruit" produced in the hearts of those standing on-stage, but also the "fruit" produced in the hearts of those sitting off-stage.

9. Cf. John 21:25.

Bibliography

Abernethy, Andrew. "The Shape and Shaping of Isaiah and the Psalms as Books in the Zion Tradition." *CBQ* 86 (2024) 659–80.
Achtemeier, Elizabeth. "Why God Is Not Mother: A Response to Feminist God-Talk in the Church." *CT* 37/9 (1993) 16–20, 20–23.
Ahn, John J. "Psalm 137: Complex Communal Laments." *JBL* 127 (2008) 267–89.
Allen, Leslie. *Psalms 101–150*. WBC 21. Grand Rapids: Zondervan, 2002.
Alroey, Gur. *Zionism Without Zion: The Jewish Territorial Organization and Its Conflict with the Zionist Organization*. Detroit: Wayne State University Press, 2016.
Alter, Robert. *The Book of Psalms: A Translation with Commentary*. New York: W. W. Norton and Company, 2007.
Ambrose. *Explanatio Psalmorum*. In *CSEL* 64.4–7.
Amzallag, G. Nissim. *Psalm 29: A Canaanite Hymn to Yhwh in the Psalter*. Leuven: Peeters, 2021.
Anderson, Arnold A. *The Book of Psalms: Vol. 1, Psalms 1–72, 1972*. NCBC. Grand Rapids: Eerdmans, 1981.
Anderson, Bernhard W. *Out of the Depths: The Psalms Speak for Us Today*. Louisville: Westminster John Knox, 2000.
Anderson, Gary A. "King David and Psalms of Imprecation." *ProEccl* 15 (2006) 267–80.
Anderson, George W. "Israel's Creed: Sung, Not Signed." *SJT* 16 (1963) 277–85.
Anderson, Romola, and Anderson, Roger Charles. *A Short History of the Sailing Ship*. Mineola, NY: Dover Publications, 2003.
Argyle, Aubrey W. "Philo and the Fourth Gospel." *ExpTim* 63 (1951–52) 385–86.
Arneth, Martin. *"Sonne der Gerechtigkeit": Studien zur Solarisierung der Jahwe-Religion im Lichte von Psalm 72*. BZABR 1. Wiesbaden: Harrassowitz, 2000.
Asencio, Felix. *Misericordia et Veritas, el Ḥesed y 'Emet divinos, su influjo religioso-social en la Historia de Israel*. AG 48.3.19. Rome: Apud Aedes Universitatis Gregorianae, 1949.
Assmann, Jan. *Herrschafft und Heil; Politische Theologie in Altägyptischen, Israel, und Europa*. Frankfort: Fisher-Taschenbusch Verlag, 2002.

Athanasius. "The Letter of St. Athanasius to Marcellinus on the Interpretation of the Psalms." In *On the Incarnation: The Treatise "De incarnatione Verbi Dei,"* 97–119. Crestwood, NY: St. Vladimir's Seminary, 1996.

Atwood, Joel. "Poetry and Emotion in Psalm 22 (Part 1)." *JESOT* 7 (2021) 1–26.

Auffret, Pierre. "Selon la Grandeur de ton Bras: Nouvelle Étude Structurelle du Psaume 79." *OTE* 26 (2013) 57–69.

Augustine. "Exposition on Ps 150." In *Expositions on the Book of Psalms, Vol. 6*, translated by J. H. Parker, 449–56. London: F. & J. Rivington, 1857.

Auwers, Jean-Marie. *La composition littéraire du Psautier. Un état de la question*. CRB 46. Paris: Gabalda, 2000.

Bail, Ulrike. *Gegen das Schwegen klagen: Eine intertextuelle Studie zu den Klagepsalmen Ps 6 und Ps 55 und der Erzählung von der Vergewaltigung Tamars*. Gütersloh: Chr. Kaiser/Gütersloher Verlaugshaus, 1998.

Bainton, Roland H. *The Reformation of the Sixteenth Century*. 2nd Ed. Boston: Beacon, 1985.

Balentine, Samuel E. *Prayer in the Hebrew Bible: The Drama of Divine-Human Dialogue*. OBT. Minneapolis: Fortress, 1993.

Barbiero, Gianni, et al., eds. *The Formation of the Hebrew Psalter*. FAT 151. Tübingen: Mohr Siebeck, 2021.

Barna, George. *Music and the Church: Relevance in Changing Culture*. Waco: Baylor University, 2002.

Barnes, Robin D. *Outrageous Invasions: Celebrities' Private Lives, Media, and the Law*. Oxford: Oxford University Press, 2010.

Baron, Anne-Marie. *The Shoah on Screen: Representing Crimes Against Humanity*. Strasbourg: Council of Europe, 2006.

Barron, Lee. *Celebrity Cultures: An Introduction*. London: Sage, 2015.

Barth, Karl. *Die Christliche Dogmatik im Entwurf*. Zürich: Theologischer Verlag, 1982.

Bartlett, John Robert. "Edom." In *AYBD* 2.287–95.

Barton, Casey. "On the Willows We Hung Up Our Harps: Preaching the Lament and Hope of Psalm 137." *JEHS* 22 (2022) 83–101.

Basson, Alec. "'Only Ruins Remain': Psalm 74 as a Test Case of *Mundus Inversus*." *OTE* 20 (2007) 128–37.

Beaty, Katelyn. *Celebrities for Jesus: How Personas, Platforms, and Profits Are Hurting the Church*. Grand Rapids: Brazos, 2022.

Beaucamp, Evode. *Le Psautier*, 2 Vols. Paris: Gabalda, 1979.

Becker, Joachim. *Wege der Psalmenexegese*. SBS 78. Stuttgart: Verlag Katholisches Bibelwerk, 1975.

Beckett, Joshua. "Lament in Three Movements: The Implications of Psalm 13 for Justice and Reconciliation." *JSFSC* 9 (2016) 207–18.

Begrich, Joachim. "Der Priesterliche Tora." *ZAW* 66 (1936) 81–92.

Bellinger, William H. "The Psalms as a Place to Begin for Old Testament Theology." In *Psalms and Practice: Worship, Virtue, and Authority*, edited by S. B. Reid, 28–39. Collegeville, MN: Liturgical, 2001.

Belnap, Daniel. "A Comparison of the Communal Lament Psalms and the Treaty-Covenant Formula." *SBAnt* 1 (2009) 1–34.

Beresford, James. *The Ancient Sailing Season*. Leiden: Brill, 2013.

Bethke, Erik. *Game Development and Production*. Plano, TX: Wordware, 2002.

Beyerlin, Walter. *Werden und Wesen des 107. Psalms*. BZAW 153. Berlin: de Gruyter, 1979.

Bidmead, Julye. *The Akītu Festival: Religious Continuity and Royal Legitimation in Mesopotamia*. Piscataway, NJ: Gorgias, 2004.

Blenkinsopp, Joseph. *Creation, Uncreation, Recreation: A Discursive Commentary on Genesis 1–11*. London: T & T Clark, 2011.

Bloom, Allan. *The Closing of the American Mind*. New York: Simon and Schuster, 1987.

Bond, Douglas. "Biblical Poetry in a Postbiblical, Postpoetry World." In *Forgotten Songs: Reclaiming the Psalms for Christian Worship*, edited by C. R. Wells and R. van Neste, 65- 79. Nashville: B&H Academic, 2012.

Bonhoeffer, Dietrich. *The Cost of Discipleship*. Translated by R. H. Fuller. London: SCM, 1959.

———. *Psalms: The Prayerbook of the Bible*. Translated by J. H. Burtness. Minneapolis: Augsburg Fortress, 1970.

Botha, Phil J. "'Wealth and Riches Are in His House' (Ps 112:3): Acrostic Wisdom Psalms and the Development of Anti-Materialism." In *The Shape and Shaping of the Book of Psalms: The Current State of Scholarship*, edited by N. deClaissé-Walford, 105-28. AIL 20. Atlanta: SBL, 2014.

Boyle, Geoffrey R. "The Imprecatory Psalms as Means of Mercy and Wellness." *CTQ* 86 (2022) 193–214.

Brennan, Joseph P. "Psalms 1–8: Some Hidden Harmonies. *BTB* 10 (1980) 25–29.

Brettler, Marc. "Psalm 136 as an Interpretive Text." *HeBAI* 2 (2013) 373–95.

Brian, Rustin E. *Covering Up Luther: How Barth's Christology Challenged the* Deus Absconditus *that Haunts Modernity*. Eugene, OR: Cascade, 2013.

Brichto, Herbert C. "Kin, Cult, Land, and Afterlife: A Biblical Complex." *HUCA* 44 (1973) 1–54.

Briggs, Charles A. *A Critical and Exegetical Commentary on the Psalms*. ICC. Edinburgh: T & T Clark, 1906.

Bringsjord, Selmer, and David A. Ferucci. *Artificial Intelligence and Literary Creativity: Inside the Mind of BRUTUS, A Storytelling Machine*. Mahwah, NJ: Lawrence Erlbaum Associates, 2000.

Brown, Cheryl A. "Judges." In *Joshua, Judges, Ruth*, 123–289. NIBC 5. Peabody, MA: Hendrickson, 2000. Reprint in UBCS. Grand Rapids: Baker, 2012.

Brown, William P. *Seeing the Psalms: A Theology of Metaphor*. Louisville: Westminster John Knox, 2002.

Broyles, Craig C. *Psalms*, 1999. UBCS. Grand Rapids: Eerdmans, 2012.

Brueggemann, Walter. *Abiding Astonishment: Psalms, Modernity, and the Making of History*. LCBI. Louisville: Westminster John Knox, 1991.

———. "The Costly Loss of Lament." *JSOT* 36 (1986) 57–71.

———. "Foreword." In *Psalms of Lament*, by Ann B. Weems, ix-xiv. Louisville: Westminster John Knox, 1995.

———. *The Message of the Psalms: A Theological Commentary*. Minneapolis: Augsburg, 1984.

Buber, Martin. *I and Thou*. Translated by R. G. Smith. London: Continuum, 2004.

Buckley, William K. "The Good, the Bad, and the Ugly in Amerika's Akadêmia." In *Beyond Cheering and Bashing: New Perspectives on the Closing of the American Mind*, edited by J. Seaton & W. K. Buckley, 37–48. Bowling Green, OH: Bowling Green State University Popular Press, 1992.

Buggle, Franz. *Denn sie wissen nicht, was sie glauben*. Hamburg: Reinbek, 1992.

Bultmann, Rudolph. "Welchen Sinn hat es von Gott zu Reden?" *TBl* 4 (1925) 129–35.

Burke, Peter. "The Rise of Literal-Mindedness." *Common Knowledge* 2 (1993) 108–21.

Burnett, Joel S. *Where Is God? Divine Absence in the Hebrew Bible.* Minneapolis: Fortress, 2010.

Busch, Eberhard. "The Barmen Theological Declaration in 1934: Its Formulation and Significance." In *The Legacy of the Barmen Declaration: Politics and the Kingdom,* edited by F. Dallmayr, 25–38. New York: Lexington Books, 2019.

Byars, Ronald P. *The Future of Protestant Worship: Beyond the Worship Wars.* Louisville: Westminster John Knox, 2002.

Calvin, John. *Commentary on the Book of Psalms.* 3 vols. Translated by J. Anderson. Grand Rapids: Eerdmans, 1963.

Camenga, Johnmark. *Unearth the Church: Exposing Foundations and Exorcising Selfishness.* Eugene, OR: Wipf & Stock, 2024.

Campbell, Caleb. *Disarming Leviathan: Loving Your Christian Nationalist Neighbor.* Downers Grove, IL: InterVarsity, 2024.

Cartledge, Tony W. "Conditional Vows in the Psalms of Lament: A New Approach to an Old Problem." In *The Listening Heart: Essays in Wisdom and the Psalms in Honor of Roland H. Murphy,* edited by K. G. Hoglund et al., 77–94. JSOTSup 58. Sheffield: JSOT, 1987.

Cashmore, Ellis. *Celebrity/Culture.* New York: Routledge, 2006.

Charaoui, Philipp, Chat-GPT2, and DALL-E. *AI-Generated Literature: An Example of Artificial Art Creation.* Ahrensburg, Germany: Tradition GmbH, Dept. "Imprint Service," 2023.

Charlesworth, James H. *The Earliest Christian Hymnbook: The Odes of Solomon.* Eugene, OR: Cascade, 2009.

Charney, Davida. "Maintaining Innocence Before a Divine Hearer: Deliberative Rhetoric in Psalm 22, Psalm 17, and Psalm 7." *BI* 21 (2013) 33–63.

Charnock, Stephen. *Discourses upon the Existence and Attributes of God.* New York: Robert Carter and Brothers, 1874.

Charry, Ellen T. "Seeking the Tropological Import of Psalm 35." In *Psychology and Spiritual Formation in Dialogue: Moral and Spiritual Change in Christian Perspective,* edited by T. M. Crisp et al., 123–32. Downers Grove, IL: InterVarsity, 2019.

Chase, Debra. "A Note on an Inscription from Kuntillet ʿAjrūd." *BASOR* 246 (1982) 63–67.

Cheung, Simon Chi-Chung. *Wisdom Intoned: A Reappraisal of the Genre "Wisdom Psalms."* LHBOTS 613. New York: Bloomsbury, 2015.

Childs, Brevard. *Introduction to the Old Testament as Scripture.* Philadelphia: Fortress, 1979.

Chisholm, Robert B. "Suppressing Myth: Yhwh and the Sea in the Praise Psalms." In *The Psalms: Language for All Seasons of the Soul,* edited by A. J. Schmutzer and D. M. Howard, 75–84. Chicago: Moody, 2013.

Clark, Eric. *The Want Makers. The World of Advertising: How They Make You Buy.* London: Hodder and Stoughton, 1988.

Clifford, Richard C. "Towards a Precise Translation of Psalm 115:1." *BZ* 56 (2022) 293–301.

Clines, David J. A. *Job 1–20.* WBC 17. Dallas: Word, 1989.

Cohen, Mark E. *BALAĜ Compositions: Sumerian Lamentation Liturgies of the Second and First Millenium BCE.* SANE 1/2. Malibu, CA: Undena, 1974.

———. *Sumerian Hymnology: The ERŠEMMA.* HUCASup 2. Cincinnati: Hebrew Union College, 1981.

Collins, C. John. "Always Alleluia: Reclaiming the True Purpose of the Psalms in the Old Testament Context." In *Forgotten Songs: Reclaiming the Psalms for Christian Worship*, edited by C. R. Wells and R. van Neste, 17–34. Nashville: B&H Academic, 2012.
Cooper, Jerrold. *The Curse of Agade*. Baltimore: Johns Hopkins, 1983.
Cornell, Collin. *Divine Aggression in Psalms and Inscriptions: Vengeful Gods and Loyal Kings*. SOTSMS. Cambridge: Cambridge University Press, 2020.
Cottrill, Amy C. *Uncovering Violence: Reading Biblical Narratives as an Ethical Project*. Louisville: Westminster John Knox, 2021.
Coverdale, Miles. *Goostly Psalmes and Spirituall Songes Drawen out of the Holy Scripture*. London: Iohan Gough, 1535.
Craigie, Peter C. (and Marvin E. Tate). *Psalms 1–50*. WBC 19. Grand Rapids: Zondervan, 2004.
Creach, Jerome F. D. *Yhwh as Refuge and the Editing of the Hebrew Psalter*. JSOTSup 117. Sheffield: Academic, 1996.
Crenshaw, James. *Old Testament Wisdom: An Introduction*. Louisville: Westminster John Knox, 1998.
Crow, Loren D. *The Songs of Ascents (Psalms 120–34): Their Place in Israelite History and Religion*. SBLDS 148. Atlanta: Scholars, 1996.
Cumont, Franz. *The Oriental Religions in Roman Paganism*. Chicago: Open Court, 1911.
Dahlke, Benjamin. "Psalm 22 in der Passion Jesu: Zur neueren Auslegungsgeschichte." *ETL* 93 (2017) 199–237.
Dahood, Mitchell. *Psalms: A New Translation with Introduction and Commentary*. 3 vols. AYBC. New Haven: Yale University Press, 2007.
Daschbach, Edwin. *Not Everyone Calls Me Father: Explaining the Bible and the Faith in Appalachia*. Techny, IL: Society of the Divine Word, 2004.
Davage, David W. "A Canon of Psalms in the Dead Sea Scrolls? Revisiting the Qumran Psalms Hypothesis." *BTB* 51 (2021) 196–205.
Davis, Ellen F. "Exploding the Limits: Form and Function in Psalm 22." *JSOT* 53 (1992) 93–105.
Dawn, Marva J. *How Shall We Worship? Biblical Guidelines for the Worship Wars*. Carol Stream, IL: Tyndale House, 2003.
DeClaissé-Walford, Nancy L. "Human on Human Violence in the Psalter." *RevExp* 120 (2023) 213–20.
———. *Reading from the Beginning: The Shaping of the Hebrew Psalter*. Macon, GA: Mercer University Press, 1997.
DeGroat, Chuck. *When Narcissism Comes to Church: Healing Your Community from Emotional and Spiritual Abuse*. Downers Grove, IL: InterVarsity, 2020.
Delitzsch, Franz. *A Commentary on the Psalms*. Translated by D. Eaton. New York: Funk and Wagnalls, 1883.
Dell, Katherine J. "'I Will Solve My Riddle to the Music of the Lyre' (Psalm 49:4): A Cultic Setting for Wisdom Psalms?" *VT* 54 (2004) 445–58.
———. "The Use of Animal Imagery in the Psalms and Wisdom Literature of Ancient Israel." *SJT* 53 (2000) 275–91.
Deutschmann, Barbara. "The Woman of Tekoa and Bloodguilt: Layers of Meaning in 2 Sam 14:1–24." *ABR* 71 (2023) 55–69.
Dobbs-Allsopp, F. W. *Lamentations*. Interpretation. Louisville: John Knox, 2002.

Donne, John. "Sermon 66 on Ps 63:7, Preached at St. Paul's Cathedral Jan. 29, 1625." In *Works of John Donne*. 6 vols. London: John W. Parker West Strand, 1839.
Douglas, Mary. *Purity and Danger: An Analysis of Concepts of Pollution and Taboo*. London: Routledge & Kegan Paul, 1966.
Driver, Samuel Rolles. *An Introduction to the Literature of the Old Testament*. New York: Scribner's, 1891.
DuChene, Mary Kay, and Mark Sundby. *A Path to Belonging: Overcoming Clergy Loneliness*. Minneapolis: Fortress, 2022.
Duguid, Timothy. *Metrical Psalmody in Print and Practice: English 'Singing Psalms' and Scottish 'Psalm Buiks.'* London: Routledge, 2014.
Duhm, Bernhard. *Die Psalmen*. KHAT 14. Freiburg: J. C. B. Mohr, 1899.
Dumm, Thomas. *Loneliness as A Way of Life*. Cambridge: Harvard University Press, 2008.
Eaton, John H. *Kingship and the Psalms*. SBT 32. London: SCM, 1986.
Ebeling, Erich. *Die akkadische Gebetsserie "Handerhebung."* Berlin: Akademie-Verlag, 1953.
Eichrodt, Walther. *Theology of the Old Testament*, 1933. Translated by J. A. Baker. OTL. Philadelphia: Westminster, 1961.
Eliade, Mircea. *The Sacred and the Profane: The Nature of Religion*, 1957. Translated by W. R. Trask. New York: Harcourt, 1959.
Emanuel, David. *An Intertextual Commentary to the Psalter: Juxtaposition and Allusion in Book 1*. Eugene, OR: Pickwick, 2022.
Engle, Cynthia. "I Delight in Your Law: A Study of Psalm 119." PhD diss., Cambridge University, 2005.
Estes, Daniel J. "The Transformation of Pain into Praise in the Individual Lament Psalms." In *The Psalms: Language for All Seasons of the Soul*, edited by A. J. Schmutzer and D. M. Howard, 151–63. Chicago: Moody, 2013.
Farmer, Kathleen A. "Psalms." In *Women's Bible Commentary, Expanded Edition with Apocrypha*, edited by C. Newsom & S. Ringe, 145–60. Louisville: Westminster John Knox, 1998.
Ferris, Paul Wayne. *The Genre of Communal Lament in the Bible and the Ancient Near East*. SBLDS 127. Atlanta: Scholars, 1992.
———. "Lamentations 2: Ancient Near Eastern Background." In *DOTW* 410–13.
Finch, Janet. "Naming Names: Kinship, Individuality, and Personal Names." *Sociology* 42 (2008) 711.
Finstuen, Andrew S. *Original Sin and Everyday Protestants: The Theology of Reinhold Niebuhr, Billy Graham, and Paul Tillich in an Age of Anxiety*. Chapel Hill: University of North Carolina Press, 2009.
Fleischer, Robert. *Artemis von Ephesos und verwandte Kultstatuen aus Anatolien und Syrien*. EPRO 35. Leiden: Brill, 1973.
Flint, Peter W. *The Dead Sea Scrolls*. Nashville: Abingdon, 2013.
———. "The Psalters at Qumran and the Book of Psalms." PhD diss., University of Notre Dame, 1999.
Fohrer, Georg *Introduction to the Old Testament*. Translated by D. Green. Nashville: Abingdon, 1968.
Foster, Benjamin. *Before the Muses: An Anthology of Akkadian Literature*. Bethesda, MD: CDL, 2005.
Foster, Richard. *Celebration of Discipline: The Path to Spiritual Growth*. New York: HarperCollins, 1978.

Foster, Robert L. "*Topoi* of Praise in the Call to Praise Psalms: Toward a Theology of the Book of Psalms." In *"My Words Are Lovely": Studies in the Rhetoric of the Psalms*, edited by R. L. Foster and D. M. Howard, 75–88. LHBOTS 467. London: T & T Clark, 2008.

Fowler, James W. *Stages of Faith: The Psychology of Human Development and the Quest for Meaning*. San Francisco: Harper & Row, 1981.

Fox, Michael V. "Three Theses on Wisdom." In *Was There a Wisdom Tradition? New Prospects in Israelite Wisdom Studies*, edited by M. Sneed, 69–86. AIL 23. Atlanta: SBL, 2015.

Fretz, Mark J. "Weapons and Implements of Warfare." In *AYBD* 6.893–95.

Frow, John. *Genre: The New Critical Idiom*. London: Routledge, 2006.

Futato, Mark D. *Interpreting the Psalms: An Exegetical Handbook*. Grand Rapids: Kregel, 2007.

Gabriel, Joseph M. "Damage." In *Rethinking Therapeutic Culture*. Edited by T. Aubrey and T. Travis, 24–33. Chicago: University of Chicago Press, 2015.

Gallagher, Maggie. *Enemies of Eros: How the Sexual Revolution Is Killing Family, Marriage, and Sex, and What We Can Do About It*. Chicago: Bonus, 1989.

Galling, Kurt. "Die Ausrufung des Namens als Rechtsakt in Israel." *TLZ* 81 (1956) 65–70.

Gamberoni, Johann. "חסה." In *TDOT* 6.64–75.

Gammie, John G. *Holiness in Israel*. OBT. Minneapolis: Fortress, 1989.

García-Bachmann, Mercedes L. "Reading Silence(s) in Psalm 39." *WW* 42 (2022) 362–70.

Gerstenberger, Erhard S. "Delight in Torah: The Book of Psalms." *BN* 191 (2021) 3–29.

———. *Praise and Petition in the Old Testament: Essays on the Psalms, Vol. 2*. Edited by K. C. Hanson. Eugene, OR: Cascade Books, 2024.

———. "Der Psalter als Buch und als Sammlung." In *Neue Wege der Psalmenforschung: für Walter Beyerlin*, edited by K. Seybold and E. Zenger, 3–13. Freiburg: Herder, 1994.

———. *Theologies in the Old Testament*. Translated by J. Bowden. London: T & T Clark, 2002.

Gestermann, Louise. "Zorn und Gnade ägyptischer Götter." In *Divine Wrath and Divine Mercy in the World of Antiquity*, edited by R. Kratz and H. Spieckermann, 19–43. FAT 2/33. Tübingen: Mohr Siebeck, 2008.

Gibson, Jeffrey B. "Echoes of 'the Voice': Psalm 29 in the Fathers." In *Psalm 29 Through Time and Tradition*, edited by L. K. Handy, 25–36. Eugene, OR: Pickwick, 2009.

Gillingham, Susan. *Psalms Through the Centuries*. 3 vols. Hoboken, NJ: Wiley Blackwell, 2012–2022.

Girard, Marc. *Les Psaumes redécouverts—De la structure au sens II (51–100)*. Bellarmin: Saint Laurent, 1996.

Glueck, Nelson. *Das Wort ḥesed im alttestamentlichen Sprachgebrauche als mensliche und göttliche gemeinschaftgemässe Verhaltungsweise*. Giessen: Töpelmann, 1927.

Goldingay, John. "The Dynamic Cycle of Praise and Prayer in the Psalms." *JSOT* 6 (1981) 85–90.

———. *Psalms*. Grand Rapids: Baker, 2008.

Görg, Manfred. "שׁכן." In *TDOT* 14.691–702.

Goulder, Michael D. *The Psalms of the Return (Book V: Psalms 107–150)*. JSOTSup 258. Sheffield: Academic, 1998.

Grant, Jamie A. "The Psalms and the King." In *Interpreting the Psalms: Issue and Approaches*, edited by P. S. Johnston and D. G. Firth, 101–18. Leicester: Apollos, 2005

Gruenwald, Ithamar. תעשה: *Rituals and Ritual Theory in Ancient Israel*. Leiden: Brill, 2010.

Gunkel, Hermann. *Die Psalmen*. HAT. Göttingen: Vandenhoeck & Ruprecht, 1926.

———, and Joachim Begrich. *Einleitung in die Psalmen: Die Gattungen der religiösen Lyrik Israels*. Göttingen: Vandenhoeck & Ruprecht, 1933.

———, and Joachim Begrich. *Introduction to Psalms: The Genres of the Religious Lyric of Israel*. Translated by J. D. Nogalski. Macon, GA: Mercer University Press, 1998.

Gurney, Oliver R. *Hittite Prayers of Mursili II*. Oxford: Oxford University Press, 1940.

Gutmann, Ruth. *A Final Reckoning: A Hannover Family's Life and Death in the Shoah*. Tuscaloosa: University of Alabama Press, 2013.

Haberman, Joshua O. *Healing Psalms: The Dialogues with God That Help You Cope with Life*. New York: John Wiley and Sons, 2003.

Habermas, Jürgen. *Glauben und Wissen: Friedenspreis des Deutschen Buchhandels 2001*. Frankfurt am Main: Suhrkamp, 2001.

Hackett, JoAnn. *The Balaam Text from Deir ʿAllā*. HSM 31. Chico, CA: Scholars, 1980.

Hakham, Amos. ספר תהלים דעת מקרא. Jerusalem: Rav Kook, 1979.

Halpern, Baruch. "Kenites." In *AYBD* 4.17–22.

Hamilton, Nadine. "Praying the Imprecatory Psalms? Reflections on an Unresolved Theological Problem with Dietrich Bonhoeffer." *IJST* 24 (2022) 380-401.

Hankle, Dominick D. "The Therapeutic Implications of the Imprecatory Psalms in the Christian Counseling Setting." *JPT* 38 (2010) 275–80.

Hardin, Les. "Review of *Hurting with God: Learning to Lament with the Psalms* by Glenn Pemberton." *SCJ* 16 (2013) 188–89.

Harrichand, James J. S. "Recovering the Language of Lament for the Western Evangelical Church: A Survey of the Psalms of Lament and Their Appropriation Within Pastoral Theology." *MJTM* 16 (2014–15) 101–30.

Hart, Lowell D. *Contemporary Christian Music Exposed*. Oxford: Hart, 2016.

Hass, Aaron. *In the Shadow of the Holocaust: The Second Generation*. Cambridge: Cambridge University Press, 1990.

Haunz, Ruth A. "Development of Some Models of God and Suggested Relationships to James Fowler's Stages of Faith Development." *RelEd* 73 (1978) 644–50.

Hays, Christopher B. *A Covenant with Death: Death in the Iron Age II and Its Rhetorical Uses in Proto-Isaiah*. Grand Rapids: Eerdmans, 2015.

Healey, John F. "Mot." In *DDD*, 598–603.

Hege, Brent A. R. *Myth, History, and the Resurrection in German Protestant Theology*. Eugene, OR: Pickwick, 2017.

Heiler, Friedrich. *Prayer: A Study in the History and Psychology of Religion*. Translated by S. McComb. New York: Oxford University Press, 1932.

Herrmann, Wolfgang. "Rider on the Clouds." In *DDD*, 703–5.

Hills, Sidney. "The ḥesed of Man in the Old Testament, and the ḥesed of God in the Old Testament." Unpublished paper delivered to the Biblical Colloquium meeting in Pittsburgh, PA on Nov 29, 1957.

Ho, Patrick C. W. *The Design of the Psalter: A Macrostructural Analysis*. Eugene, OR: Pickwick, 2019.

Ho, Peter C. W. "The Successful Life: Comparisons between the Opening Chapters of the Psalms and the Qur'an." *SID* 33 (2023) 203–20.

Hoenn, Karl. *Artemis. Gestaltwandel einer Göttin*. Zürich: Artemis Verlag, 1946.
Hof, Eleonora D. "A Missiology of Lament." *Svensk missionstidskrift* 101 (2013) 321–38.
Holladay, William L. *The Psalms Through Three Thousand Years: Prayerbook of a Cloud of Witnesses*. Minneapolis: Augsburg Fortress, 1993.
Hoppe, Leslie J. "Vengeance and Forgiveness: The Two Faces of Psalm 79." In *Imagery and Imagination in Biblical Literature: Essays in Honor of Aloysius Fitzgerald*, edited by L. Boadt, 1–22. CBQMS 27. Washington, DC: The Catholic Biblical Association, 2021.
Hossfeld, Frank L. and Erich Zenger. *Psalms 2: A Commentary on Psalms 51–100*. Hermeneia. Minneapolis: Fortress, 2005.
———. *Psalms 3: A Commentary on Psalms 101–150*. Hermeneia. Minneapolis: Fortress, 2011.
Howard, David M. "Divine and Human Kingship as Organizing Motifs in the Psalter." In *The Psalms: Language for All Seasons of the Soul*, edited by A. J. Schmutzer & D. M. Howard, 197–207. Chicago: Moody Publishers, 2013.
———. *The Structure of Psalms 93–100*. BJSUCSD 5. Winona Lake, IN: Eisenbrauns, 1997.
Howard, Jay R. "Let the Weak Say I am Strong: Contemporary Worship Music and God's Concern for Righteousness and Social Justice." In *The Message in the Music*, edited by R. Woods & B. Walrath, 65-75. Nashville: Abingdon Press, 2007.
Howard, Jay R., and John M. Streck. *Apostles of Rock: The Splintered World of Contemporary Christian Music*. Lexington: University Press of Kentucky, 2004.
Huffmon, Herbert B. *Amorite Personal Names in the Mari Texts*. Baltimore: Johns Hopkins, 1965.
Human, Dirk J. "Human Suffering in Need of God's 'Face' and 'Eyes': Perspectives on Psalm 13." *OTE* 34 (2021) 268–84.
Jacobson, Rolf A. "Christian Theology of the Psalms." In *The Oxford Handbook of the Psalms*, edited by W. P. Brown, 499–512. New York: Oxford University Press, 2014.
———. "Psalm 39." In *The Book of Psalms*, edited by N. DeClaissé-Walford et al. NICOT. Grand Rapids: Eerdmans, 2014.
Jefferis, Jennifer. *Hamas: Terrorism, Governance, and Its Future in Middle East Politics*. Santa Barbara, CA: Praeger, 2016.
Jacobs, Alan. *The Book of Common Prayer: A Biography*. LGRB. Princeton: Princeton University Press, 2013.
Janowski, Bernd. *Arguing with God: A Theological Anthropology of the Psalms*, 2003. Translated by A. Siedlecki. Louisville: Westminster John Knox, 2013.
Johnson, Bo. "צדק." In *TDOT* 12.243–64.
Joosten, Jan. *People and Land in the Holiness Code: An Exegetical Study of the Ideational Framework of the Law in Leviticus 17–26*. VTSup 67. Leiden: Brill, 1996.
Kaiser, Walter C. "The Laments of Lamentations Compared to the Psalter." In *The Psalms: Language for All Seasons of the Soul*, edited by A. Schmutzer and D. Howard, 127–33. Chicago: Moody, 2013.
Kalman, Jason. "Righteousness Restored: The Place of *Midrash Iyov* in the History of the Jewish Exegesis of the Book of Job." *OTE* 19 (2006) 77–100.
Katz, Brent, and Josh Morgenthau. *I Am Code: An Artificial Intelligence Speaks: Poems by Code-Davinci-002*. Boston: Little, Brown and Co., 2023.
Kellermann, Ulrich. "Überwindung des Todesgeschicks in der alttestamentlichen Frommigkeit vor und neben dem Auferstehungsglauben." *ZTK* 73 (1976) 259–82.

Kelman, Ari Y. *Shout to the Lord: Making Worship Music in Evangelical America*. New York: NYU Press, 2018.

Kibbe, Michael. "'You Have Answered Me?': Situational Shift (or Not) in Psalm 22." *BBR* 34 (2024) 43–53.

Kim, Jinkyu. "The Strategic Arrangement of Royal Psalms in Books IV and V." *WTJ* 70 (2008) 143–57.

Kirkpatrick, Alexander Francis. *The Book of Psalms with Introduction and Notes: Books II and III (Psalms XLII-LXXXIX)*. Cambridge: Cambridge University Press, 1900.

Klunzinger, Marlene, and Michael S. Moore. "Codependency and Pastoral Care: A Report from the Trenches." *ResQ* 38 (1996) 159–74.

Knapp, Arthur B. *Seafaring and Seafarers in the Bronze Age Eastern Mediterranean*. Leiden: Sidestone, 2018.

Krašovic, Jože. "Justification of God in His Word in Ps 51:6 and Rom 3:4." *VT* 64 (2014) 416–33.

Kraus, Hans-Joachim. *Psalms 1–59: A Commentary*. Minneapolis: Augsburg, 1988.

———. *Psalms 60–150: A Commentary*. Minneapolis: Augsburg, 1989.

———. *Theology of the Psalms*, 1979. Translated by K. Crim. Minneapolis: Augsburg, 1986.

Krebernik, Manfred. "'Wo einer in Wut ist, kann kein anderer ihm raten': Zum göttlichen Zorn in Alten Orient." In *Divine Wrath and Divine Mercy in the World of Antiquity*, edited by R. G. Kratz and H. Spieckermann. FAT 2/33. Tübingen: Mohr Siebeck, 2008.

Krecher, Joachim. *Sumerische Kultlyrik*. Wiesbaden: Harrassowitz, 1966.

Kreider, Eleanor and Alan Kreider. *Worship and Mission After Christendom*. Scottdale, PA: Herald, 2011.

Kroeger, Catherine Clark, and Mary J. Evans, eds. *The IVP Women's Bible Commentary*. Downers Grove, IL: InterVarsity, 2002.

Kselman, John S. "Psalms." In *The New Oxford Annotated Bible: The New Revised Standard Version with the Apocrypha*. 3rd ed. Edited by M. D. Coogan et al., 775–903. New York: Oxford University Press, 2001.

———, and Michael L. Barré. "Psalm 55: Problems and Proposals." *CBQ* 60 (1998) 440–62.

Kuntz, J. Kenneth. "Review of *Wisdom Intoned* by Simon Cheung." *Bib* 98 (2017) 138–40.

———. "Review of *Yhwh as Refuge and the Editing of the Hebrew Psalter* by Jerome Creach." *CBQ* 61 (1999) 740–42.

Kynes, Will. *An Obituary for "Wisdom Literature": The Birth, Death, and Intertextual Reintegration of a Biblical Corpus*. New York: Oxford University Press, 2019.

———. *My Psalm Has Turned into Weeping: Job's Dialogue with the Psalms*. BZAW 437. Berlin: de Gruyter, 2012.

Laato, Antti. *The Origin of Israelite Zion Theology*. London: T & T Clark, 2018.

Lambert, Wilfrid G. *Babylonian Creation Myths*. MC 16. Winona Lake, IN: Eisenbrauns, 2013.

Landsberger, Benno. "Die Eigenbegrifflichkeit der babylonischen Welt." *Islamica* 2 (1926) 355–72.

Landy, Francis. "Threshing Floors and Cities." In *Memory and the City in Ancient Israel*, edited by D. V. Edelman and E. Ben-Zvi, 79–98. Winona Lake, IN: Eisenbrauns, 2014.

Lasater, Phillip M. "Law for What Ails the Heart: Moral Frailty in Psalm 86." *ZAW* 127 (2015) 652–68.
Lash, Nicholas. "Performing the Scriptures." In *Theology on the Way to Emmaus*, 37–46. London: SCM, 1986.
Lee, Nancy C. *The Singers of Lamentations: Cities Under Siege, from Ur to Jerusalem to Sarajevo*. BibInt 60. Leiden: Brill, 2002.
Lemley, David. *Becoming What We Sing: Formation Through Contemporary Worship Music*. Grand Rapids: Eerdmans, 2021.
Leonard, James M. "Review of *The Psalms as Christian Lament* by B. Waltke et al." *RBL* 3 (2016). https://www.sblcentral.org/API/Reviews/9891_10940.pdf.
Lepojärvi, Jason. "Worship, Veneration, and Idolatry: Observations from C. S. Lewis." *RelS* 51 (2015) 543–62.
Lévinas, Emmanuel. *Outside the Subject*. Translated by M. B. Smith. London: Athlone, 1993.
———. *Totality and Infinity: An Essay on Exteriority*. Translated by A. Lingis. Pittsburgh: Duquesne University Press, 1969.
Levine, Baruch A. *Numbers*. 2 Vols. AYBC. New York: Doubleday, 1993, 2000.
Lewis, C. S. *The Allegory of Love: A Study in Medieval Tradition*. Cambridge: Cambridge University Press, 2013.
———. *The Four Loves*. London: Geoffrey Bles, 1960.
———. *The Problem of Pain*. New York: HarperCollins, 2000.
———. *Reflections on the Psalms*. New York: Harper One, 1958.
———. *The Screwtape Letters*, 1942. New York: HarperCollins, 2001.
Lewis, Ted. "The Ancestral Estate (נחלת אלהים) in 2 Samuel 14:16." *JBL* 110 (1991) 597–612.
Liebreich, Leon. "The Songs of Ascents and the Priestly Blessing." *JBL* 74 (1955) 33–36.
Lieu, Judith M. "Justin Martyr and the Transformation of Psalm 22." In *Biblical Traditions in Transmission: Essays in Honour of Michael A. Knibb*, edited by C. Hempel and J. M. Lieu, 195–211. Leiden: Brill, 2006.
Lim, Timothy H. "Liar." In *EDSS*, 493–94.
———. "Wicked Priest." In *EDSS*, 973–76.
Limburg, James. "Psalms." In *AYBD* 5.522–36.
Loader, James A. "Psalm 30 Read Twice and Understood Two Times." *OTE* 16 (2003) 291–308.
Lohfink, Norbert. "ירשׁ." In *TDOT* 6.368–96.
Longman, Tremper. *The Fear of the Lord is Wisdom: A Theological Introduction to Wisdom in Israel*. Grand Rapids: Baker Academic, 2017.
———. "Psalms 2: Ancient Near Eastern Background." In *DOTW*, 594–605.
Lucarini, Dan. *Why I Left the Contemporary Christian Music Movement: Confessions of a Former Worship Leader*. Welwyn Garden City: Evangelical, 2002.
Luther, Martin. "Preface to the Psalter." In *LW* 35.254.
Lyons, Michael A. "Psalm 22 and the 'Servants' of Isaiah 54; 56–66." *CBQ* 77 (2015) 640–56.
MacLaren, Alexander. *The Life of David as Reflected in His Psalms*. Edinburgh: MacNiven and Wallace, 1880.
Mahlendorf, Ursula. *The Shame of Survival: Working Through a Nazi Childhood*. University Park, PA: Pennsylvania State University Press, 2009.
Marcus, Sharon. *The Drama of Celebrity*. Princeton: Princeton University Press, 2019.

Maré, Leonard P. "Psalm 22: To Pray Like Jesus Prayed." *OTE* 17 (2004) 443–54.
———. "Psalm 58: A Prayer for Vengeance." *OTE* 16 (2003) 322–31.
Margalit, Avishai. *On Betrayal*. Cambridge: Harvard University Press, 2017.
Markter, Florian. *Transformationen: Zur Anthropologie des Propheten Ezechiel unter besonderer Berücksichtigung des Motivs "Herz."* FB 127. Würzburg: Echter Verlag, 2013.
Masing, Uko. "Der Begriff Ḥesed im alttestamentlichen Sprachgebrauch." In *Charisteria Iohanni Kõpp: octogenario oblata*, Papers of the Estonian Theological Society in Exile, 27–63. Stockholm: Holmiae, 1954.
Matthews, Victor H. "Entrance Ways and Threshing Floors: Legally Significant Sites in the Ancient Near East." *FH* 19 (1987) 25–40.
May, Herbert G. "Some Cosmic Connotations of *Mayim Rabbim*, 'Many Waters.'" *JBL* 74 (1955) 9–21.
Mays, James L. "The Place of the Torah-Psalms in the Psalter." *JBL* 106 (1987) 3–12.
———. *Psalms*. Louisville: Westminster John Knox, 1994.
McAlpine, Thomas H. *Sleep, Divine and Human, in the Old Testament*. JSOTSup 38. Sheffield: Academic, 1987.
McCann, J. Clinton. *A Theological Introduction to the Book of Psalms: The Psalms as Torah*. Nashville: Abingdon, 1993.
———. "Review of *The Design of the Psalter: A Macrostructural Analysis* by Peter C. W. Ho." *RBL* 2020. https://www.sblcentral.org/API/Reviews/13437_15004.pdf.
McCarter. P. Kyle. "When the Gods Lose Their Temper: Divine Rage in Ugaritic Myth and the Hypostasis of Anger in Iron Age Religion." In *Divine Wrath and Divine Mercy in the World of Antiquity*, edited by R. Kratz and H. Spieckermann, 78–91. FAT 2/33. Tübingen: Mohr Siebeck, 2008.
McMahon, C. Matthew, Ed. *The Puritans on Exclusive Psalmody*. Coconut Creek, FL: Puritan, 2013.
Mendenhall, George E. "Covenant." In *AYBD* 1.1179–1202.
———. *The Tenth Generation*. Baltimore: Johns Hopkins, 1973.
Menn, Esther. "No Ordinary Lament: Relecture and the Identity of the Distressed in Psalm 22." *HTR* 93 (2000) 301–41.
Merton, Thomas. *Praying the Psalms*. Collegeville, MN: Liturgical, 1956.
Meshel, Ze'ev, et al. Kuntillet ʿAjrūd (Ḥorvat Teman*): An Iron Age II Religious Site on the Judah-Sinai Border*. Jerusalem: Israel Exploration Society, 2012.
Mettes, Susan. *The Loneliness Epidemic*. Grand Rapids: Brazos, 2021.
Michalowski, Piotr. *The Lamentation over the Destruction of Sumer and Ur*. Winona Lake, IN: Eisenbrauns, 1989.
Millar, J. Gary. *Calling on the Name of the Lord: A Biblical Theology of Prayer*. Downers Grove, IL: InterVarsity, 2016.
Miller, Patrick D. "Kingship, Torah Obedience, and Prayer." In *Neue Wege der Psalmenforschung*, edited by K. Seybold and E. Zenger, 127–42. HBS 1. Freiburg: Herder, 1995.
———. "*Yāpîaḥ* in Psalm 12:6." *VT* 29 (1979) 495–500.
Miskotte, Kornelis H. *When the Gods Are Silent*. Translated by K. W. Doberstein. New York: Harper and Row, 1967.
Mitchell, David C. *The Songs of Ascents*. Glasgow: Campbell Publishers, 2015.
Moore, Michael S. "America's Monocultural Heritage." *FH* 15 (1982) 39–53.

———. *The Balaam Traditions: Their Character and Development*. SBLDS 113. Atlanta: Scholars, 1988.
———. *Chaos or Covenant? A Short Theological Introduction to the Pentateuch*. Eugene, OR: Wipf and Stock, 2024.
———. "Civic and Voluntary Associations in the Greco-Roman World." In *The World of the New Testament*, edited by J. Green & L. M. McDonald, 149–55. Grand Rapids: Baker Academic, 2013.
———. "A Critical Profile of Choan-Seng Song's Theology." *Miss* 10 (1982) 461–70.
———. "Divine Presence." In *DOTPr*, 166–70.
———. *Faith Under Pressure: A Study of Biblical Leaders in Conflict*. Abilene, TX: ACU Press, 2003.
———. "Human Suffering in Lamentations." *RB* 90 (1983) 534–55.
———. *Reconciliation: A Study of Biblical Families in Conflict*. Joplin, MO: College, 1994.
———. *Retribution or Reality: A Short Theological Introduction to the Book of Job*. Eugene, OR: Pickwick, 2023.
———. "Review of *Disembodied Souls: The Nefesh in Israel and Kindred Spirits in the Ancient Near East, with an Appendix on the Katamuwa Inscription* by Richard C. Steiner." *RBL* (2016). https://www.sblcentral.org/API/Reviews/10306_11440.pdf.
———. "Review of '*Sonne der Gerichtigkeit*' by M. Arneth." *JBL* 120 (2001) 541–42.
———. "Ruth." In *Joshua, Judges, Ruth*, 293–373. NIBC 5. Peabody, MA: Hendrickson, 2000. Reprint in UBCS. Grand Rapids: Baker, 2012.
———. "A Short Note on Mitchell Dahood's Exegetical Methodology." *HS* 22 (1981) 35–38.
———. "Two Textual Anomalies in Ruth." *CBQ* 59 (1997) 234–43.
———. *WealthWarn: A Study of Socioeconomic Conflict in Hebrew Prophecy*. Eugene, OR: Pickwick, 2019.
———. *WealthWatch: A Study of Socioeconomic Conflict in the Bible*. Eugene, OR: Pickwick, 2011.
———. *WealthWise: A Study of Socioeconomic Conflict in Hebrew Wisdom*. Eugene, OR: Pickwick, 2021.
———. *What Is This Babbler Trying to Say? Essays on Biblical Interpretation*. Eugene, OR: Pickwick, 2016.
Morenz, Siegfried. *Egyptian Religion*. Translated by A. Keep. Ithaca, NY: Cornell University Press, 1973.
Morgenstern, Julius. "The *ḤᵃSÎDÎM*—Who Were They?" *HUCA* 38 (1967) 59–73.
Mouw, Richard J. "Foreword." In *The Message in the Music: Studying Contemporary Praise and Worship*, edited by R. Woods and B. Walrath, 5–6. Nashville: Abingdon, 2007.
Mowinckel, Sigmund. *Psalmenstudien*, 6 Vols. Later revised and abridged into 2 vols. Amsterdam: P. Schippers, 1966.
———. "Psalms and Wisdom." In *Wisdom in Israel and in the Ancient Near East: Presented to Professor Henry Harold Rowley in Celebration of His Sixty-Fifth Birthday*, edited by M. Noth and D. W. Thomas, 205–44. Leiden: Brill, 1955.
———. *The Psalms in Israel's Worship*. Translated by D. R. Ap-Thomas. Nashville: Abingdon, 1962.
Muck, Terry. "Psalm, *Bhajan*, and *Kirtan*: Songs of the Soul in Contemporary Perspective." In *Psalms and Practice*, edited by S. B. Reid, 7–27. Collegeville, MN: Liturgical, 2001.

Muilenberg, James. "Form Criticism and Beyond." *JBL* 88 (1969) 1–18.
Munn, Michael. *Hitler and the Nazi Cult of Celebrity*. Sun Lakes, AZ: Robson, 2012.
Murphy, Roland E. "A Consideration of the Classification 'Wisdom Psalms.'" *Congress Volume Bonn 1962* (VTSup 9; Leiden: Brill, 1962) 156–67.
———. "Reflections on Contextual Interpretation of the Psalms." In *The Shape and Shaping of the Psalter*, edited by J. C. McCann, 21–28. JSOTSup 159. Sheffield: Academic, 1993.
Nascimento, Analzira. *Evangelization or Colonization?* Minneapolis: Fortress, 2021.
Nasuti, Harry P. "The Interpretive Significance of Sequence and Selection in the Book of Psalms." In *The Book of Psalms: Composition and Reception*, edited by P. Flint and P. Miller, 311–39. Leiden: Brill, 2005.
———. *Tradition History and the Psalms of Asaph*. Atlanta: Scholars, 1988.
Naudé, Jacobus A. & Miller-Naudé, Cynthia L. "Alternative Revisions of the *American Standard Version* (1901) and Retranslations within the Tyndale–King James Version Tradition." *HTS Teologiese Studies/Theological Studies* 78 (2022) a7650. https://doi.org/10.4102/hts.v78i1.7650.
Newmeyer, Frederick J. *Language Form and Language Function*. Cambridge: MIT Press, 2000.
Niebuhr, Reinhold. *The Nature and Destiny of Man*. New York: Charles Scribner's Sons, 1946.
Noll, Mark. *The Scandal of the Evangelical Mind*. Grand Rapids: Eerdmans, 1995.
Noonan, Benjamin J. *Advances in the Study of Biblical Hebrew and Aramaic: New Insights for Reading the Old Testament*. Grand Rapids: Zondervan, 2020.
Nord, Elisabet. *Vindicating Vengeance and Violence: Commentary Approaches to Cursing Psalms and Their Relevance for Liturgy*. Minneapolis: Fortress Academic, 2023.
Olson, Roger E. *Against Liberal Theology: Putting the Brakes on Progressive Christianity*. Grand Rapids: Zondervan, 2022.
Olyan, Saul M. "Honor, Shame, and Covenant Relations within Ancient Israel and Its Environment." *JBL* 115 (1996) 201–18.
Otto, Rudolf. *The Idea of the Holy: An Inquiry into the Non-Rational Factor in the Idea of the Divine and its Relation to the Rational*. Translated by J. W. Harvey. London: Oxford University Press, 1950.
Pagden, Anthony. *The Enlightenment: And Why It Still Matters*. Oxford: Oxford University Press, 2013.
Pardee, Dennis, and Nancy Pardee. "Gods of Glory Ought to Thunder: The Canaanite Matrix of Psalm 29." In *Psalm 29 Through Time and Tradition*, edited by L. K. Handy, 115–25. PTMS 110. Eugene, OR: Pickwick Publications, 2009.
Paris, Jenell Williams. "I Could Sing of Your Love Forever: American Romance in Contemporary Christian Worship Music." In *The Message in the Music: Studying Contemporary Praise and Worship*, edited by R. Woods & B. Walrath, 43–53. Nashville: Abingdon, 2007.
Parkinson, Richard B. "The Tale of the Eloquent Peasant." In *The Tale of Sinuhe and Other Ancient Egyptian Poems, 1940–640 BC*, 58–75. OWC. Oxford: Oxford University Press, 1998.
Pemberton, Glenn. *After Lament: Psalms for Learning to Trust Again*. Abilene, TX: ACU Press, 2014.
———. *Hurting with God: Learning to Lament with the Psalms*. Abilene, TX: ACU Press, 2012.

Perdue, Leo. *Wisdom and Cult: A Critical Analysis of the Views of Cult in the Wisdom Literatures of Israel and the Ancient Near East*. Atlanta: Society of Biblical Literature, 1977.
Perrin, Nicholas. *The Kingdom of God: A Biblical Theology*. Grand Rapids: Zondervan, 2019.
Peterson, Eugene. *Answering God: The Psalms as Tools for Prayer*. San Francisco: Harper and Row, 1989.
Phillips, Christopher N. *The Hymnal: A Reading History*. Baltimore: Johns Hopkins University Press, 2018.
Pinson, J. Matthew, Ed. *Perspectives on Christian Worship: Five Views*. Nashville: Broadman and Holman, 2009.
Platt, David. *Radical: Taking Back Your Faith from the American Dream*. Colorado Springs: Multnomah Books, 2010.
Plekon, Michael. "Belonging to the Christian Community in the Twenty-First Century, When 'The Church has Left the Building.'" In *The Church Has Left the Building: Faith, Parish, and Ministry in the Twenty-First Century*, edited by M. Plekon et al., 1–16. Eugene, OR: Cascade Books, 2016.
Podella, Thomas. Ṣôm-*Fasten: Kollektive Trauer um den verborgenen Gott im Alten Testament*. AOAT 224. Neukirchen-Vluyn: Neukirchener, 1989.
Pope, Marvin H. *Job: A New Translation with Introduction and Commentary*. AYBC 15. New Haven: Yale University Press, 2021.
Porteous, Norman. "Soul." In *IDB* 4.428–29.
Porter, Wendy J. "Trading My Sorrows: Worshiping God in the Darkness—The Expression of Pain and Suffering in Contemporary Worship Music." In *The Message in the Music: Studying Contemporary Praise and Worship*, edited by R. Woods and B. Walrath, 76–91. Nashville: Abingdon, 2007.
Postman, Neil. *Amusing Ourselves to Death: Public Discourse in the Age of Show Business*. New York: Penguin Books, 1985.
———. *Technopoly: The Surrender of Culture to Technology*. New York: Knopf, 1992.
Price, Randall. *Secrets of the Dead Sea Scrolls*. Eugene, OR: Harvest House, 1996.
Prinsloo, Willem. "Psalms." In *Eerdmans Commentary on the Bible*, edited by J. D. G. Dunn & J. W. Rogerson, 364–436. Grand Rapids: Eerdmans, 2003.
Puech, Émile. "Hodayot." In *EDSS*, 365–69.
Puuko, Antti F. "Der Feind in den alttestamentlichen Psalmen." *OtSt* 8 (1950) 47–65.
Raabe, Paul R. *Psalm Structures: A Study of Psalms with Refrains*. JSOTSup 104. Sheffield: Academic, 1990.
Radau, Hugo. *Sumerian Hymns and Prayers to God Dumu-zi from the Temple Library at Nippur*. München: Rudolf Merkel, 1913.
Rajak, Tessa. "Introduction: New Approaches." In *The Power of Psalms in Post-Biblical Judaism: Liturgy, Ritual, and Community*, edited by C. Bergmann et al., 3–16. AJEC 118. Leiden: Brill, 2023.
Reardon, Patrick H. *Christ in the Psalms*. Chesterton, IN: Conciliar, 2000.
Reid, Stephen Breck "The Voice of Our Sister to the Frenemy Among Us: Psalm 55." *Int* 78 (2024) 131–39.
Reiner, Erica. "Die akkadische Literatur." In *Neues Handbuch der Literatur-Wissenschaft: Altorientalische Literaturen*, edited by Wolfgang Röllig, 1.151–210. Wiesbaden: Athenaion, 1978.
Reiterer, Friedrich V. "שם." In *TDOT* 15.128–74.

Reynolds, Kent A. *Torah as Teacher: The Exemplary Torah Student in Psalm 119.* VTSup 137. Leiden: Brill, 2010.

Richter, Sandra L. *Deuteronomistic History and the Name Theology:* לשכן שמו שם *in the Bible and the Ancient Near East.* BZAW 319. Berlin: de Gruyter, 2002.

Ridderbos, Nic H. *Die Psalmen. Stilistische Verfahren und Aufbau. Mit besonderer Berücksichtigung von Pss 1–41.* BZAW 117. Berlin: de Gruyter, 1972.

Rilke, Rainer Maria. *Letters of Rainer Maria Rilke.* Translated by J. B. Greene and M. D. H. Norton. New York: Norton, 1972.

Ringgren, Helmer. "חסיד." In *TDOT* 5.75–79.

———. "צדק." In *TDOT* 12.239–43.

Roberts, J. J. M. "Davidic Origin of the Zion Tradition." *JBL* 92 (1973) 329–44.

———. "Mowinckel's Enthronement Festival: A Review." In *The Book of Psalms: Composition and Reception,* edited by P. Flint and P. Miller, 97–115. Leiden: Brill, 2005.

Robertson, O. Palmer. *The Flow of the Psalms: Their Structure and Theology.* Phillipsburg, NJ: P & R, 2015.

Robinson, Henry Wheeler. *Inspiration and Revelation in the Old Testament.* Oxford: Clarendon, 1946.

Rojek, Chris. *Celebrity.* London: Reaktion Books, 2001.

Rosenzweig, Franz. *The Star of Redemption.* Translated by B. Galli. Madison: University of Wisconsin Press, 2005.

Ross, Allen P. *A Commentary on the Psalms, Vol. 1 (1–41).* KEL. Grand Rapids: Kregel, 2011.

———. "The 'Thou' Sections of Laments: The Bold and Earnest Prayers of the Psalmists." In *The Psalms: Language for All Seasons of the Soul,* edited by A. J. Schmutzer and D. M. Howard, 135–50. Chicago: Moody Publishers, 2013.

Ruth, Lester. "How Great Is Our God: The Trinity in Contemporary Christian Worship Music." In *The Message in the Music: Studying Contemporary Praise and Worship,* edited by R. Woods and B. Walrath, 29–42. Nashville: Abingdon, 2007.

Rutherford, Paul. *The Adman's Dilemma: From Barnum to Trump.* Toronto: University of Toronto Press, 2018.

Sakenfeld, Katharine D. *The Meaning of* ḥesed *in the Hebrew Bible: A New Inquiry.* Missoula, MT: Scholars, 1978.

Sanders, James A. *The Psalms Scroll of Qumran Cave 11 (11QPs^a).* DJD 4. Oxford: Clarendon, 1965.

Schaper, Joachim. "The Septuagint Psalter." In *The Oxford Handbook of the Psalms,* edited by W. P. Brown, 173–84. Oxford: Oxford University Press, 2014.

Scharbert, Josef. "ברך." in *TDOT* 2.279–308.

Schmidt, Werner H. "Gott und Mensch in Ps 8. Form- und überlieferungsgeschichtliche Erwägungen." *TZ* 25 (1969) 1–15.

Schmutzer, Andrew J. "Refuge, Protection, and Their Use in the New Testament." In *The Psalms: Language for All Seasons of the Soul,* edited by A. J. Schmutzer and D. M. Howard, 85–108. Chicago: Moody, 2013.

Schorch, Stefan. "The Pre-Eminence of the Hebrew Language and the Emerging Concept of the 'Ideal Text' in Late Second Temple Judaism." In *Studies in the Book of Ben Sira,* edited by G. Xeravitz and J. Zsengellér, 43–54. Leiden: Brill, 2008.

Schultze, Quentin J. *Televangelism and American Culture: The Business of Popular Religion.* Grand Rapids: Baker, 1991.

Scott, R. B. Y. *The Way of Wisdom.* New York: Macmillan, 1971.

Seerveld, Calvin. "Why We Need to Learn to Cry in Church: Reclaiming the Psalms of Lament." In *Forgotten Songs: Reclaiming the Psalms for Christian Worship*, edited by C. R. Wells and R. van Neste, 139-58. Nashville: B&H Publishing Group, 2012.
Seybold, Klaus. "גמל." In *TDOT* 3.23–33.
———. *Studien zur Psalmenauslegung*. Stuttgart: Kohlhammer, 1998.
———. *Die Wallfahrtpsalmen. Studien zur Entstehungsgeschichte von Psalm 120–34*. BTS 3. Neukirchen-Vluyn: Neukirchener Verlag, 1978.
Shepherd, David J. *King David, Innocent Blood, and Bloodguilt*. Oxford: Oxford University Press, 2023.
Sheppard, Gerald T. *Wisdom as a Hermeneutical Construct: A Study in the Sapientializing of the Old Testament*. BZAW 151. Berlin: de Gruyter, 1980.
Shipp, R. Mark. *Of Dead Kings and Dirges*. AcBib 11. Atlanta: Society of Biblical Literature, 2002.
Sider, Ronald J. *Rich Christians in an Age of Hunger: Moving from Affluence to Generosity*. Nashville: Thomas Nelson, 2015.
Simmons, Edward G. *Talking Back to the Bible: An Historian's Approach to Bible Study*. Pittsburgh: Dorrance, 2016.
Smelik, Klaas A. D. "Ma`at." In *DDD*, 534–35.
Smith, Janet K. *Psalm 49 and the Path to Redemption*. Eugene, OR: Resource, 2017.
Smith, Justin E. H. *Irrationality*. Princeton: Princeton University Press, 2019.
Smith, Mark S. *The Early History of God: Yhwh and the Other Deities in Ancient Israel*. 2nd ed. Grand Rapids: Eerdmans, 2002.
———. "Taking Inspiration: Authorship, Revelation, and the Book of Psalms." In *Psalms and Practice: Worship, Virtue, and Authority*, edited by S. B. Reid, 244–73. Collegeville, MN: Liturgical, 2001.
Snaith, Norman. *Distinctive Ideas of the Old Testament*. London: Epworth, 1944.
Snearly, Michael K. "The Return of the King: Book 5 as a Witness to Messianic Hope in the Psalter." In *The Psalms: Language for All Seasons of the Soul*, edited by A. J. Schmutzer and D. M. Howard, 209–17. Chicago: Moody, 2013.
Sneed, Mark R. "Methods, Muddles, and Modes of Literature: The Question of Influence Between Wisdom and Prophecy." In *Riddles and Revelations: Explorations into the Relationship Between Wisdom and Prophecy in the Hebrew Bible*, edited by M. J. Boda et al., 30–44. LHBOTS 634. London: T&T Clark, 2018.
Soll, Will. *Psalm 119: Matrix, Form, and Setting*. CBQMS 23. Washington, DC: Catholic Biblical Association of America, 1991.
Spencer, Michael E. "Grappling with Legacies of Pain, Shame, and Blame in Independent Schools: Reclaiming Lament and Refocusing Praise through Psalm 22." *ATR* 105 (2023) 305–21.
Stähli, Hans-Peter. *Solare Elemente im Jahweglauben des Alten Testaments*. OBO 66. Göttingen: Vandenhoeck & Ruprecht, 1985.
Starr, Charlie W. "So How Should We Teach English?" In *Contemporary Perspectives on C. S. Lewis's The Abolition of Man: History, Philosophy, Education, and Science*, edited by T. M. Mosteller and G. J. Anacker, 63–82. New York: Bloomsbury Academic, 2017.
Stearns, Peter N. *Consumerism in World History: The Global Transformation of Desire*. London: Routledge, 2001.
Steiner, Richard C. *Disembodied Souls: The Nefesh in Israel and Kindred Spirits in the Ancient Near East, with an Appendix on the Katumuwa Inscription*. ANEM 11. Atlanta: SBL, 2015.

Stepaniants, Marietta T. *Introduction to Eastern Thought.* Translated by R. Kohanovskya. Oxford: Roman & Littlefield, 2002.

Stoebe, Hans Joachim. "Die Bedeutung des Wortes Ḥäsäd im Alten Testament." *VT* 2 (1952) 244–54.

Stolz, Fritz. "Sea." In *DDD*, 737–42.

Suriano, Matthew J. "Foreword" to *A Covenant with Death* by C. Hays, xii-xiv. Grand Rapids: Eerdmans, 2015.

Surls, Austin D. Making Sense of the Divine Name in the Book of Exodus: From Etymology to Literary Ononmastics. PhD. diss., Wheaton College, 2015.

Swanson, Dwight D. "Qumran and the Psalms." In *Interpreting the Psalms: Issues and Approaches,* edited by D. Firth and P. S. Johnston, 247–62. Downers Grove, IL: InterVarsity, 2005.

Swidler, Ann. *Talk of Love: How Culture Matters.* Chicago: University of Chicago Press, 2003.

Sylva, Dennis D. "Precreation Discourse in Psalms 74 and 77: Struggling with Chaoskämpfe." *R&T* 18 (2011) 244–67.

Tanner, Beth LaNeel. "How Long, O Lord? Will Your People Suffer Forever?" In *Psalms and Practice: Worship, Virtue, and Authority,* edited by S. B. Reid, 143–52. Collegeville, MN: Liturgical, 2001.

Theodore of Mopsuestia. *Commentary on Psalms 1–81.* Translated by R. C. Hill. WGRW 5. Atlanta: SBL, 2006.

Thomas, David Winton. "Psalm 35:15f." *JTS* 12 (1961) 50–51.

Thomas, Derek. *Acts.* REC. Phillipsburg, NJ: P&R, 2011.

Thompson, Denys. *Voice of Civilization: An Enquiry into Advertising.* London: F. Muller, 1943.

Tournay, Raymond Jacques. "Le Psaume 8 et la doctrine biblique du Nom." *RB* 78 (1971) 18–30.

Tucker, W. Dennis. *Constructing and Deconstructing Power in Psalms 107–150.* AIL 19. Atlanta: Society of Biblical Literature, 2014.

———. "Psalms: Book Of." In *DOTW* 578–93.

Ulmer, Rivkah. "Psalm 22 in *Pesiqta Rabbati*: The Suffering of the Jewish Messiah and Jesus." In *The Jewish Jesus: Revelation, Reflection, Reclamation,* edited by Z. Garber, 106–28. SSJS. Lafayette, IN: Purdue University Press, 2011.

"US Teacher Charged with Using AI to Frame Principal with Racist Audio." *The Guardian,* Apr. 25, 2024. https://www.theguardian.com/us-news/2024/apr/25/maryland-teacher-ai-principal.

van der Horst, Pieter. "Evil Inclination." In *DDD,* 317–19.

VanderKam, James, and Peter Flint. *The Meaning of the Dead Sea Scrolls.* London: T&T Clark, 2002.

van der Ploeg. Johannes P. M. "Le Psaume 119 et la Sagesse." In *La Sagesse de l'Ancien Testament,* edited by H. Gossai, 82–87. Paris: Gembloux, 1979.

van der Toorn, Karel. *Family Religion in Babylonia, Ugarit, and Israel: Continuity and Change in the Forms of Religious Life.* SHANE 7. Leiden: Brill, 1996.

———. "In the Lions' Den: The Babylonian Background of a Biblical Motif." *CBQ* 60 (1988) 626–40.

van Rooy, Herrie F. "The Enemies in the Headings of the Psalms: A Comparison of Jewish and Christian Interpretation." In *Animosity, the Bible, and Us: Some European, North American, and South African Perspectives,* edited by J. T. Fitzgerald et al., 41–58. SBLGPBS 12. Atlanta: SBL, 2009.

van Wolde, Ellen J. "A Network of Conventional and Deliberate Metaphors in Psalm 22." *JSOT* 44 (2020) 642–66.
———. "A Prayer for Purification: Ps 51:12–14, a Pure Heart, and the Verb ברא." *VT* 70 (2020) 340–60.
Vaters, Karl. *De-Sizing the Church: How Church Growth Became a Science, Then an Obsession, and What's Next.* Chicago: Moody, 2024.
Vishanoff, David R. "Images of David in Several Muslim Rewritings of the Psalms." In *The Character of David in Judaism, Christianity and Islam: Warrior, Poet, Prophet and King*, edited by M. Zawanowska and M. Wilk, 273–98. Leiden: Brill, 2021.
von Rad, Gerhard. *Deuteronomium-Studien*. FRLANT 58. Göttingen: Vandenhoeck & Ruprecht, 1947.
Vos, Richard L. "Thoth." In *DDD*, 861–64.
Wächter, Ludwig. "Unterweltsvorstellungen und Unterweltsnamen in Babylonien, Israel, und Ugarit." *MIO* 15 (1969) 327–36.
Wagner, Andreas. *God's Body: The Anthropomorphic God in the Old Testament.* London: Bloomsbury Academic, 2019.
Wälchli, Stefan H. *Gottes Zorn in den Psalmen: Eine Studie zur Rede vom Zorn in den Psalmen im Kontext des Alten Testaments und des Alten Orients.* OBO 244. Göttingen: Vandenhoeck & Ruprecht, 2012.
Wallis, Gerhard. "אהב." In *TDOT* 1.101–18.
Walker, Christopher, and Michael Dick. *The Induction of the Cult Image in Ancient Mesopotamia: The Mesopotamian Mīs Pî Ritual.* SAALT 1. Helsinki: Helsinki University, 2001.
Waltke, Bruce K., et al. *The Psalms as Christian Lament: An Historical Commentary.* Grand Rapids: Eerdmans, 2014.
Wanke, Günter. *Die Zionstheologie der Korachiten in ihrem traditionsgeschichtlichen Zusammenhang.* BZAW 97. Berlin: de Gruyter, 1966.
Warner, Brooke. *Greenlight Your Book: How Writers Can Succeed in the New Era of Publishing.* New York: Simon & Schuster, 2016.
Washburn, Jennifer. *University, Inc.: The Corporate Corruption of American Higher Education.* New York: Basic, 2005.
Watson, John R. *The English Hymn: A Critical and Historical Study.* Oxford: Clarendon, 1999.
Watters, William R. *Formula Criticism and the Poetry of the Old Testament.* Berlin: de Gruyter, 1976.
Webber, Robert E. *Ancient-Future Worship: Proclaiming and Enacting God's Narrative.* Grand Rapids: Baker, 2008.
———. *Planning Blended Worship: The Creative Mixture of Old and New.* Nashville: Abingdon, 1998.
Weinfeld, Moshe. "Deuteronomy." In *AYBD* 2.168–83.
Weiser, Artur. *The Psalms: A Commentary.* Translated by H. Hartwell. OTL. Philadelphia: Westminster, 1962.
Wellhausen, Julius. *Prolegomena to the History of Israel.* Translated by J. S. Black and A. Menzies. Edinburgh: Adam and Charles Black, 1885.
Wells, C. Richard. "Conclusion." In *Forgotten Songs: Reclaiming the Psalms for Christian Worship*, edited by C. R. Wells and R. van Neste, 203–12. Nashville: B&H Academic, 2012.
Westermann, Claus. *Der Psalter.* Stuttgart: Calwer Verlag, 1967.

———. *Praise and Lament in the Psalms*, 1961. Translated by K. Crim. Atlanta: John Knox, 1965.

———. "The Role of the Lament in the Theology of the Old Testament." *Int* 28 (1974) 20–38.

———. "Struktur und Geschichte der Klage im Alten Testament." *ZAW* 66 (1954) 44–80.

White, James R. *The King James Only Controversy: Can You Trust Modern Translations?*, 1996. 2nd ed. Bloomington, MN: Bethany House, 2009.

Willis, Timothy M. "'So Great Is His Steadfast Love': A Rhetorical Analysis of Psalm 103." *Bib* 72 (1991) 525–37.

Wilson, Gerald H. *The Editing of the Hebrew Psalter*. SBLDS 76. Chico, CA: Scholars, 1985.

———. "The Structure of the Psalter." In *Interpreting the Psalms: Issues and Approaches*, edited by D. Firth and P. S. Johnston, 229–46. Downers Grove: InterVarsity, 2005.

———. "The Use of the Royal Psalms at the 'Seams' of the Hebrew Psalter." *JSOT* 35 (1986) 85–94.

Witvliet, John D. "Words to Grow Into: The Psalms as Formative Speech." In *Forgotten Songs: Reclaiming the Psalms for Christian Worship*, edited by C. R. Wells and R. van Neste, 7–16. Nashville: B&H Academic, 2012.

Wolff, Hans Walter. *Anthropology of the Old Testament*. Translated by M. Kohl. Philadelphia: Fortress, 1974.

Wood, William. *Blaise Pascal on Duplicity, Sin, and the Fall: The Secret Instinct*. Oxford: Oxford University Press, 2013.

Woods, Robert, and Brian Walrath. "Introduction." In *The Message in the Music: Studying Contemporary Praise and Worship*, edited by R. Woods and B. Walrath, 13–28. Nashville: Abingdon, 2007.

———, et al. "We Have Come Into His House: *Kerygma, Koinonia, Leitourgia*—CWM That Models the Purpose of the Church." In *The Message in the Music: Studying Contemporary Praise and Worship*, edited by R. Woods and B. Walrath, 92–105. Nashville: Abingdon, 2007.

Wray Beal, Lissa M. "Psalms 3: Interpretation." In *DOTW* 605–13.

Wright, Norman T. *The Case for the Psalms: Why They Are Essential*. New York: HarperCollins, 2016.

Wyatt, Nicolas. "Asherah." In *DDD*, 99–105.

———. "The Liturgical Context of Psalm 19 and Its Mythical and Ritual Origins." In *"There's Such Divinity Doth Hedge a King": Selected Essays of Nicolas Wyatt on Royal Ideology in Ugaritic and Old Testament Literature*, 2005. SOTSMS. London: Routledge, 2016.

———. *Religious Texts from Ugarit*, 2nd ed. Sheffield: Academic, 2002.

Young, Edward J. *Introduction to the Old Testament*. Grand Rapids: Eerdmans, 1964.

Zafirovsky, Milan. *The Enlightenment and Its Effects on Modern Society*. New York: Springer, 2011.

Zenger, Erich. *A God of Vengeance? Understanding the Psalms of Divine Wrath*. Translated by L. Maloney. Louisville: Westminster John Knox, 1996.

Zobel, Hans-Jürgen. "חסד." In *TDOT* 5.44–64.

Name Index

Aaron, 22, 82
Abernethy, A., 6
Abigail, 34
Abraham, 54
Achtemeier, E., 97
Ahn, J. J., 50
Allen, L., 58, 59, 67
Alroey, G., 50
Alter, R., 3
Ambrose, 2
Amos, 102
Amzallag, G., 66
Anat, 45
Anderson, A., 45, 67
Anderson, B., 5, 9
Anderson, G. A., 2, 6, 44
Anderson, G. W., 3
Anderson, R., 61
Andrew, S., 19
Argyle, A., 73
Arneth, M., 45, 72, 73
Asencio, F., 78
Assmann, J., 44
Asherah, 97
Astarte, 90
Athanasius, 2
Athirat, 33, 90
Atwood, J., 2
Auffret, P., 43
Augustine, 3, 6
Auwers, J.-M., 6

Ba`al, 5, 24, 30, 33, 35, 46, 54, 56, 57, 64, 66, 68, 70, 82, 88, 97

Bail, U., 37
Bainton, R. H., 102
Balaam, 49
Balentine, S., 18, 20
Barbiero, G., 10
Barna, G., 94
Barnes, R., 11
Baron, A.-M., 48
Barré, M., 36
Barron, L., 11
Barth, K., 17, 57
Bartlett, J., 51
Barton, C., 1, 44, 50
Basil, 65
Basson, A., 41
Bathsheba, 31
Beaty, K., 13
Beaucamp, E., 50
Becker, J., 56
Beckett, J., 19
Begrich, J., 21
Bellinger, W., 6
Belnap, D., 39
Beresford, J., 61
Bethke, E., 95
Beyerlin, W., 58
Bidmeade, J., 9
Blenkinsopp, J., 33
Bloom, A., 18
Boaz, 36
Bond, D., 12
Bonhoeffer, D., 1, 2, 4, 17, 18, 43, 95
Botha, P. J., 71
Boyle, G., 6, 44, 45

Brennan, J., 6
Brettler, M., 7
Brian, R., 57
Brichto, H. C., 41
Bringsjord, S., 12
Brown, C., 62
Brown, W., 84, 85
Broyles, C. C., 58
Brueggemann, W., 8, 9, 19, 21, 24, 64, 84
Buber, M., 18, 19, 40, 84
Buckley, W., 18
Buggle, F., 43
Bultmann, R., 18
Burke, P., 17
Burnett, J., 57
Busch, E., 17
Byars, R., 14

Calvin, J., 3, 18
Camenga, J., 13
Campbell, C., 17
Cartledge, T., 22
Cashmore, R., 11
Charaoui, P., 12
Charlesworth, J., 8
Charney, D., 27
Charnock, S., 55
Charry, E., 45, 50, 57
Chase, D., 97
Cheung, S., 71
Childs, B., 88
Chisholm, R. B., 65
Clark, E., 11
Clifford, R. C., 82
Clines, D. J. A., 63
Cohen, M. E., 39
Collins, C. J., 10
Cooper, J., 39
Cornell, C., 44
Cottrill, A., 37
Coverdale, M., 14
Craigie, P., 26, 56, 64, 66, 67, 70
Creach, J., 6, 9, 10, 72, 84, 89
Crenshaw, J., 67
Cross, F. M., 81
Cumont, F., 13
Cyrus, 60

Dahood, M., 8, 28, 29, 32, 36, 39, 41, 45, 46, 56, 58, 60, 66, 68, 70, 72, 73, 83
Dahlke, B., 23
Danel, 22, 33, 57
Daniel, 33
Daschbach, E., 57
Davage, D., 7
David, 31, 32, 34, 44, 50, 79, 82, 85
Davis, E., 10
Dawn, M., 12, 14
DeClaissé-Walford, N., 6, 37
DeGroat, C., 13
Delitzsch, F., 56
Dell, K. J., 25, 67
Deutschmann, B., 32
Dick, M., 90
Diodorus, 65
Donne, J., 3
Douglas, M., 91
Driver, S. R., 6
DuChene, M., 19
Duguid, T., 14
Duhm, B., 27
Dumm, T., 19

Eaton, J. H., 89
Eichrodt, W., 78, 84
Eliade, M., 90
Elijah, 24
Emanuel, D., 64
Engle, C., 67
Estes, D. J., 53
Esther, 23
Ezekiel, 34, 42, 97
Ezra, 42, 81

Farmer, K., 4
Ferris, P., 5, 39, 41, 58
Ferruci, D., 12
Finch, J., 80
Finstuen, A., 32
Fleischer, R., 14
Flint, P., 7, 56, 91
Fohrer, G., 56
Foster, B., 5
Foster, R., 4, 102
Foster, R. L., 7, 8, 10, 53

NAME INDEX 129

Fowler, J., 98
Fox, M., 5
Fretz, M., 47
Futato, M., 8

Gabriel, J., 12
Gallagher, M., 96
Galling, K., 66
Gamberoni, J., 83, 86
Gammie, J. G., 90
García-Bachmann, M., 74
Gerstenberger, E., 4, 6, 10, 24, 52, 53, 57
Gestermann, L., 44
Gibson, J. B., 65
Gilgamesh, 5, 59
Gillingham, S., 20
Girard, M., 43
Glueck, N., 78
Goldingay, J., 5, 51, 53, 54, 56, 59, 66, 71
Görg, M., 71
Grant, J. A., 89
Gruenwald, I., 8
Gunkel, H., 7, 8, 9, 10, 21, 54, 89
Gurney, O., 2
Gutmann, R., 48

Habakkuk, 5, 65
Hackett, J., 62
Haberman, J., 1
Habermas, J., 11, 18
Haggai, 34
Hakham, A., 89
Hamilton, N., 45
Hankle, D. D., 45
Hardin, L., 15
Harrichand, J., 1
Hart, L. D., 94
Hass, A., 17
Hathor, 97
Haunz, R., 98
Hays, C. B., 57
Healey, J., 35
Heber, R., 100
Hege, B., 18
Heiler, F., 22
Herrmann, W., 82
Herzl, T., 50
Hills, S., 78

Hippocrates, 3
Ho, Patrick, 6
Ho, Peter, 14
Hoenn, K., 14
Hof, E. D., 13
Holladay, W., 2
Homer, 5
Hosea, 27
Hossfeld, F., 36, 43, 50, 51
Howard, D., 6, 8, 89
Howard, J., 94, 102, 103
Huffmon, H. B., 88
Human, D., 21

Ilimilku, 5
Isaac, 54
Isaiah, 42, 85, 101
Israel, 3, 9, 10, 16, 17, 23, 24, 26, 27, 29, 41, 42, 47, 50, 51, 53, 54, 60, 62, 68, 72, 73, 80, 81, 84, 85, 90, 91, 97, 99, 101

Jacob, 24, 42, 54, 68, 81, 86
Jacobs, A., 1
Jacobson, R., 74, 77
Janowski, B., 2, 6, 17, 18
Jefferis, J., 17
Jeremiah, 4, 35, 60, 85, 96
Jezebel, 26, 48
Job, 25, 46, 67
Johnson, B., 91
Jonah, 62
Joosten, J., 71
Joseph, 57
Josiah, 41
Judah, 51, 57, 57, 68
Justin Martyr, 25

Kaiser, W., 8
Kalman, J., 81
Kato, A., 19
Katz, B., 12
Kellermann, U., 70
Kelman, A. Y., 94
Kibbe, M., 26
Kim, J., 62
Kirkpatrick, A., 37
Kirta, 27, 29, 47, 60

Klunzinger, M., 12, 15
Knapp. A. B., 61
Krašovic, J., 32
Kraus, H.-J., 22, 27, 45, 89
Krebernik, M., 56
Krecher, J., 39
Kreider, A., 11, 12
Kreider, E., 11, 12
Kroeger, C., 89
Kselman, J. , , 1, 36
Kuntz, J. K., 71, 84
Kynes, W., 5, 67

Laato, A., 34
Lambert, W. G., 8
Landsberger, B., 18
Landy, F., 59
Lasater, P., 30
Lash, N., 12
Lee, N. L., 38
Lemley, D., 94
Lenzi, A., 81
Leonard, J., 19
Lepojärvi, J., 12
Lévinas, E., 3, 106
Levine, B., 97
Lewis, C. S., 4, 7, 12, 43, 46, 72, 95
Lewis, T., 41
Lieu, J. M., 25
Lim, T. H., 40, 46
Limburg, J., 2
Loader, J. A., 57
Lohfink, N., 71
Longman, T., 67
Lucarini, D., 94
Luther, M., 3, 57, 102
Lyons, M., 27

MacLaren, A., 65
Mahlendorf, U., 17
Marcus, S., 11
Marduk, 8, 30, 56, 69
Maré, L. P., 45, 46
Margalit, A., 35
Markter, F., 30, 33, 34
Masing, U., 78
Matthews, V., 59
May, H. G., 65

Mays, J., 7, 64, 66, 67
McAlpine, T., 22
McCann, C., 6
McCarter, P. K., 44, 54, 56
McEwan, S., 103
McMahon, C. M., 14
Mendenhall, G., 78, 97
Menn, E., 23
Merton, T., 4
Mettes, S., 19
Michalowski, P., 58
Milcom, 88
Millar, J. G., 5, 6, 29
Miller, P. D., 89
Miller-Naudé, C. , 1
Miskotte, K. H., 57
Moore, M. S., 7, 8, 9, 12, 13, 14, 15, 16,
    22, 23, 26, 27, 29, 31, 32, 33, 34,
    35, 36, 37, 40, 41, 42, 43, 45, 47,
    48, 49, 51, 54, 56, 58, 59, 60, 63,
    66, 67, 68, 69, 70, 72, 75, 77, 78,
    79, 81, 83, 86, 87, 88, 91, 92, 95,
    97, 98, 100, 105
Morenz, S., 92
Morgenthau, J., 12
Morgenstern, J., 28
Moses, 21, 30, 31, 54, 81, 82, 90
Mowinckel, S., 8, 9, 10, 53, 67
Mouw, R., 94
Muck, T., 7
Muilenberg, J., 8
Munbaz, 69
Munn, M., 18
Murphy, R., 7, 20, 67

Naomi, 36, 80
Nascimento, A., 13
Nasuti, H., 10
Naudé, J. , 1
Newmeyer, F., 20
Nicodemus, 96
Niebuhr, R., 83
Niemöller, M., 17
Noll, M., 103
Noonan, B., 91

Olson, R. E., 43
Olyan, S., 47

NAME INDEX 131

Osiris, 30
Otto, R., 90

Pagden, A., 17
Pardee, D., 66
Pardee, N., 66
Paris, J. W., 95
Pascal, 38
Paul, 13, 14, 67, 73, 79, 97, 98, 99, 101
Pemberton, G., 5, 15
Perdue, L., 7, 67
Perrin, N., 27
Peter, 99
Peterson, E., 3, 14, 18
Phillips, C., 2
Pinson, J. M., 14
Plato, 100
Platt, D., 12
Plekon, M., 13
Podella, T., 57
Polybius, 3
Pope, M., 32
Porteous, N., 22
Porter, W. J., 53, 95, 96
Postman, N., 10
Price, R., 33
Prinsloo, W., 7, 68
Puech, É., 64
Puuko, A., 28

Raabe, P. R., 58
Radau, H., 2
Rajak, T., 106
Reardon, P., 12, 96
Reid, S. B., 36
Reiner, E., 5
Reiner, R., 10
Reiterer, F., 81
Reynolds, K., 67
Richter, S. L., 81
Ridderbos, N., 56
Rilke, R., 3
Ringgren, H., 29, 92
Roberts, J. J. M., 8, 9, 34
Robinson, H. W., 3, 78
Rojek, C., 11
Rosenzweig, F., 70
Ross, A., 2, 21, 72

Ruth, 36, 77, 80, 88
Ruth, L., 98
Rutherford, P., 11

Sakenfeld, K., 78, 79
Samuel, 82
Sanders, J., 7
Saul, , 44, 100
Schaper, J., 2
Scharbert, J., 53
Schmidt, W. H., 66
Schmutzer, A. J., 85
Schneider, P., 17
Schorch, S., 17
Schultze, Q., 12
Scott, R. B. Y., 67
Seerveld, C., 16, 25, 43, 74, 91
Seybold, K., 53, 56
Sheba, 105
Shepherd, D., 34
Sheppard, G., 67
Shipp, R. M., 39, 69
Sider, R., 87
Simmons, E. G., 21, 37, 52
Sîn-lēqi-unninī, 5
Sirach, 72
Smelik, K. A. D., 92
Smith, J. E. H., 17
Smith, J. K., 69
Smith, M. S., 5, 35
Snaith, N., 78
Snearly, M., 89
Sneed, M., 5
Soll, W., 67
Solomon, 29, 105
Spencer, M., 20
Stähli, H.-P., 73
Starr, C., 20
Stearns, P., 11
Steiner, R., 22, 28
Stepaniants, M., 52
Sternheimer, K., 11
Stoebe, H. J., 78
Stolz, F., 60
Streck, J. M., 94
Sukenik, E., 56
Sundby, M., 19
Suriano, M., 20

Surls, A. D., 81
Swanson, D., 7
Swidler, A., 95
Sylva, D., 41

Tammuz, 88
Tanner, B. L., 12
Taylor, T. S., 103
Theodore of Mopsuestia, 36, 65
Theodoret, 65
Thomas, D., 2, 48
Thompson, D., 11
Tobit, 41
Tomlin, C., 100
Tournay, R. J., 66
Tucker, W., 3, 58

Ulmer, R., 25
Uriah, 34

van der Horst, P., 55
VanderKam, J., 56
van der Ploeg, J., 68
van der Toorn, K., 35, 65
von Rad, G., 81
van Wolde, E., , 25, 33
Vaters, K., 13
Vergil, 5
Vishanoff, D., 31
Vos, R. L., 33

Wächter, L., 30
Wagner, A., 28
Wälchli, S., 43
Walker, C., 90

Wallis, G., 78
Walrath, B., 94
Waltke, B., 19
Warner, B., 95
Weiser, A., 8, 54
Wanke, G., 34
Washburn, J., 18
Watson, J. R., 64
Watters, W., 78
Webber, R., 13, 94
Weinfeld, M., 81
Wellhausen, J., 31
Wells, C. R., 12
Westermann, C., 1, 8, 9, 16, 18, 19, 20,
      21, 52, 56, 64, 66, 96
White, J., 1
Willis, T., 53
Wilson, G., 6, 9, 20, 58, 88, 89
Witvliet, J., 12
Wolff, H. W., 20, 28
Wood, W., 38
Woods, R., 2, 94
Wray Beal, L. M., 10
Wright, N. T., 2
Wyatt, N., 72, 97

Young, E., 8

Zadok, 90
Zafirovsky, M., 17
Zedekiah, 59
Zenger, E., 36, 40, 43, 44, 50, 51
Zephaniah, 36
Zobel, H.-J., 22, 29, 77,

Scripture Index

Genesis
6:4	90
11:1–9	36
25:26	35
28:17	61
37:26	57

Exodus
1:1	16
1:6–22	16
3:7–9	16
3:7	60
3:10	16
3:14	81
3:20	30, 54
15	64
15:1–21	16
15:1	22
15:3	47
15:18	88
23:20	47
34:6	81

Leviticus
23:28	42
23:34	84

Numbers
22:31	47
36:13	16

Deuteronomy
12:1–11	81
12:5	26
13:3	46
21:23	41
26:5	16
26:6	16
26:7a	16
26:7b–9	16
26:10–15	16
32:35	43

Joshua
24:1–26	8

Ruth
1:2	88
1:20	80
3:2	36
4:5–10	80

1 Samuel
21:7	100
22:16–20	87
25:31	34
26:9	44
28:13	28

2 Samuel
14:16	41
16:5	85

1 Kings

10:1–13	105
11:5	88
21:10	48

2 Kings

9:35–37	26
17:7–8	60
23:8	41
23:11	45

Ezra

5:12	42

Isaiah

1:15–17	102
6:1–4	100
6:3	57
7:17	42
9:11	42
14:32	85
27:10	63
30:1	85
30:2–3	85
31:1	80
45:1–2	60
45:15	57
47:11	48
58:4–6	102
66:2	34

Jeremiah

2:13	4
20:7	35
23:18	60
23:21–22	97
44:17	85, 88

Ezekiel

3:12	42
3:23	42
8:4	42
8:14	88
9:3	42
10:4	42
28:3	33
36:18–20	98
47:1–12	63

Daniel

6:4–15	35

Hosea

4:10	27

Joel

2:17	42

Amos

1:11	51
4:1–3	25
5:23–24	102
6:1–6	12

Jonah

1:4–5	62
1:15	62

Habakkuk

2:5	40
3:1	65

Zephaniah

3:1	36

Haggai

2:10–14	34

Zechariah

9:9	89

Malachi

2:10	37

SCRIPTURE INDEX 135

Job

1:9	47
2:31	47
3:1–3	24
3:10	25
3:10–12	24
3:16	24
3:17	25
3:26	25
6:4	75, 83
6:24	74
7:1	83
7:17–18	63, 67
12	63
12:21	63
12:24	63
13;15	74
13:19	74
24:12	61
25:5–6	67
33:31	74
33:33	74
34:10–12	81
42:10–12	87

Psalms

1–41	9
1	7, 58, 89
1:1	88
1:3	68
2	7, 89
2:1	68
2:2–6	89
2:6	34, 101
2:12	88, 89
3	5
3:8	22
4	5
4:5	79
5	5
5:2	89
5:7	101
5:11	26
6	5, 83
6:3	2
6:5	83
7	85, 92, 101
7:1	5, 83, 85, 101
7:2–3	37
7:5	2, 22
7:6–8	92
7:17	26
8	7, 63, 66, 67
8:1	26, 42, 66
8:2	22
8:3	66
8:4–5	67
8:4	75
8:5–8	67
8:5	42
8:9	26
9–10	7
9	7, 92
9:2	28
9:10	26, 79
9:13	61
9:14	61
9:16	92
10	87, 89, 103
10:2–10	87
10:6	56
10:13–18	104
10:15–18	89
10:16	89
11	85, 101
11:1	85, 101
12	7, 39
12:1	39
12:2	39, 77
12:3	39, 40
12:4	40
12:5	40, 87
12:7	40
12:8	40
13	7, 21
13:1	21, 41
13:2	2, 21, 22, 28
13:3	22
13:4	22
13:5	22, 56, 77
13:6	22
14	7, 85, 101
14:6–7	85
14:6	87
14:7	34

Psalms (*cont.*)

16:1	5, 85
16:3	101
16:8	56
16:9	2
17	5, 101
17:7–8	85
17:7	83
17:11–12	37
18	85
18:1–2	85
18:5	30
18:17	22
18:30	85
18:49	26
18:50	89
19	7, 72, 73, 74
19:1–6	7, 72
19:1	42, 72, 73
19:2–4	73
19:2	73
19:3	73, 74
19:4	73, 74
19:6	73
19:7–9	73
19:7	2
19:7–14	7
19:12	74
19:14	74
20	7, 81
20:1	25, 26
20:2	82
20:5	26, 82
20:7	26, 82
20:9	89
21	89
21:7–10	89
22	7, 25, 45, 82, 83, 87
22:1–21	27
22:1	23
22:2	23
22:3	23, 90, 101
22:4–5	24
22:5	23
22:6	24
22:8	23, 24
22:9	24
22:10	24
22:11	25
22:12	25
22:13	23
22:14	25
22:15	25
22:16	25, 26
22:17	26
22:18	26
22:20	2, 23, 26
22:21	26, 83
22:22–31	27
22:22	26, 82
22:23	26, 30
22:24	24, 26, 27
22:25	27
22:26	26, 27, 87
22:27–28	27
22:27	27
22:29	28
22:31	28
23:1	69
23:3	2
23:4	59
24	89
24:7–10	42, 89
24:7	88
24:8	88
25	7, 85
25:1	2
25:2	79
25:10	77
25:20	86
25:22	83
26	7
27:5	25
27:6	14
28	7, 83
28:8	83
29	7, 64, 65, 66, 89, 91
29:1–10	90
29:1	64
29:2–9	91
29:2	42, 64, 90
29:3	42, 61, 65
29:8	65, 90
29:9	42, 65

SCRIPTURE INDEX 137

29:10	65, 89, 99	35:18	26, 49
29:11	66	35:21	49
30	5, 7, 56	35:23	47
30:1	56	35:24	49
30:3	2, 30, 56	35:25	49
30:4–5	57	35:26	49
30:4	56, 77, 101	35:27	50
30:5	56	36:7	86
30:6–12	57	36:86	86
30:6–7	57	37	7, 71, 86, 92
30:6	56	37:3–5	80
30:7	23, 57	37:3	71
30:9	56, 57	37:7	45, 71
30:10	56	37:9	71
30:11	25, 57	37:10	71
30:12	2	37:11	71
31	7, 83, 86	37:14	71, 72, 87
31:1	83, 86	37:16	72
31:3	83, 84	37:21	72, 87
31:4	86	37:22	72
31:5	84	37:26–30	92
31:6–14	79	37:28	72, 93
31:15	83	37:29	72
31:16	84	37:34	71, 72
31:17	30	37:39–40	86
31:19	86	38	83
31:21	84	39	74
32	5, 7, 83	39:1–2	34
32:1–2	7	39:1	74
32:3–7	7	39:2	34, 74
32:8–11	7	39:3	75
32:10	79	39:4	75
33	7	39:5–6	75
33:5	77	39:5	75
33:17	83	39:6	75
34	7	39:7	75
35	7, 46, 50	39:9	34, 74, 75
35:1	46	39:10	75
35:2	47	39:11	76
35:3	47	39:12	29
35:6	47	39:13	76
35:7–8	37	40	7
35:7	47	40:3–4	79
35:8	48	40:5	79
35:10	48	41	5, 35, 87
35:13	48	41:1	87
35:15	48	41:9	35, 43
35:17	26, 49	41:11	22

Psalms (*cont.*)

41:14	25
42	5
42:5	58
42:9	22
42:11	58
42–43	7
42–72	9
43	86
43:2	22, 86
43:5	58
44	7, 80, 82
44:4	89
44:5	82
44:6	80
44:12	70
44:16	22
44:20	82
45	5
46	4, 5, 86, 91, 102
46:1	83, 86
46:2–4	91
46:7	4, 86
46:12	86
47	7, 89
47:2–8	89
47:2	89
47:6–7	89
47:8	89, 101
48	7
48:1	101
48:2	89
49	68, 69, 87
49:1	29, 68
49:2	68
49:3	68
49:4	68
49:5–6	87
49:6	68, 80
49:7–9	87
49:7	69
49:8	69
49:9	69
49:11	69
49:12	69
49:13	69
49:14–15	30
49:14	30, 68, 69
49:15	30, 70
49:16–17	87
49:16	70
49:17	70
49:18	70
49:19	70
49:20	69
49:21	68
50	7
50:15	25
50:21	74
51	7, 31, 32, 80, 83
51:1	22, 31, 32, 101
51:2–3	32
51:2	32
51:3	32
51:4	32
51:5	32
51:6	32, 33
51:10	33
51:11	33, 77, 90
51:12	33
51:13	33
51:14–15	34
51:14	34
51:15	34
51:17	34
51:18	34
51:19	34
52	7, 86, 87, 100, 101
52:7	80, 86, 87
52:8–9	80
53	7
54	7
54:1	82
55	35, 80
55:1	29
55:3	22, 35, 36
55:6	36
55:9–11	36
55:9	36
55:11–23	80
55:12	36
55:13–15	36
55:13	36, 37
55:14	36
55:15	37
55:18	37

SCRIPTURE INDEX

55:19	37	68:24–29	89
55:20–21	37	68:24	89
55:20	37	69	7, 43, 84
55:21	37	69:1	84
55:22	38	69:14	84
55:23	38	69:35	84
56–60	5	71	7, 84, 86
56	36, 80	71:2	84
56:1	36	71:3	86
56:3–4	80	71:5	79
56:4	98	71:7	86
56:7	46	71:12	83
56:11	80	72:4	87
57–59	7, 43	72:5	73
57	44, 84	72:7	71
57:1	86	72:17	73
57:3	84	73–89	9
58	44	73	86
58:1	45	73:28	86
58:2	45	74	7, 41, 82
58:3	45	74:3	22
58:4	46	74:7	81
58:6	46	74:10	22
58:8	46	74:12–15	90, 99
58:9	46	74:12	89
58:10	46	74:18	22
58:11	46	74:19	87
59:2	83, 84	74:21	82
60	7	75	7
61:3–4	86	75:1	81
61:3	22	76	84
61:6	89	76:7	46
61:8	77	76:9	84
62:3	56	77	7
62:7	56	77:3	25
62:8	80	78	5, 7, 80
62:10–12	79	78:18–22	80
62:13	78	78:40	59
63:11	89	78:68	34
64:1	22	79	7, 41, 82, 91
65	7, 91	79:1–6	43
65:3–4	91	79:1–3	91
65:6	79	79:1	41, 90
66	7	79:2	41, 77
67	7	79:5	41
68	82	79:6	42, 82
68:2	25	79:7	42, 43
68:4	82	79:8–13	43

Psalms (*cont.*)

Reference	Pages
79:8	42
79:9	42
79:10	42, 82
79:11	43
79:12	43
79:13	43
80	7
81:2–3	5, 84
82:1	45
83	7
84	7, 89
84:1–3	89
84:1	89
84:3	89
85	7
85:5	41
85:11	77
86	5, 7, 31, 82
86:1	29
86:2	29, 56, 63, 77, 83
86:4	29
86:5	29, 77, 78
86:6	29
86:7	25, 29, 83
86:8–10	28
86:8	29, 30
86:9	30, 82
86:11	30, 82
86:12	30, 82
86:13–15	79
86:13	30, 77
86:14	30
86:15	31, 77
86:16	31
86:17	31
87	7
88	7, 21
89:2–4	79
89:3	77
89:15	77, 78, 79
89:17–18	89
89:18	89
89:20	101
89:22	22
89:35	37
89:48	30
90–106	9
90	58
91	85, 86
91:6	85
92	62
93	7
93:1	8, 88, 89, 99
93:3–4	90
93:4	65
94	7
94:1	9
95	7
95:3	89, 99
95:5	90
95:7–11	7
96	7, 64, 89
96:3–10	89
96:8	82
96:10	8, 9, 88, 89, 99
97	7
97:1–7	89
97:1	9, 89
97:12	82
98	7
98:1	8, 88, 101
98:6	89
99	7, 82, 92
98:1–9	89
99:1	8, 88, 89
99:4	89, 93
99:6	82
100	7
101:1	78
102	7, 82, 83
102:8	82
102:12	82
102:15	82
102:21	34, 43, 82
103	53, 91
103:1–5	53, 91
103:1	53, 90
103:2	53
103:3–4	54
103:4	54, 77, 79
103:5	54
103:6–9	53
103:6	54
103:7	54
103:8–10	79

103:8	77	107:30	62
103:9	54	107:31	30, 77
103:10–14	53	107:32	26
103:10	53	107:33–34	62, 63
103:11	77	107:35–38	62, 63
103:12	54	107:39–43	63
103:14–16	55	107:39–40	62
103:14	55	107:40	63
103:15–18	53	107:41–42	62
103:17–18	55	107:43	63, 77
103:17	77	109	7, 43
103:19–22	53	109:5–6	37
103:19	55	109:12	77
103:20–22	55	109:13	80
104:29	57	109:26	83
105	7, 24, 84	111	7
105:42	101	112	7
106	7, 24, 84, 97	113	87
106:10	22	113:7	87
106:14	59	115	82
106:19–20	97	115:1	82
106:21	83	115:2	42
106:28	97	115:4–8	90
106:35–38	97	115:8–11	80
106:43	84	116:3	30
106:47	58, 84	116:4	83
107–50	9	118	86
107	7, 58, 62	118:8–9	86
107:1–5	59	118:19–29	7
107:1	58, 77	119	7, 67, 92
107:2–9	58	119:64	81
107:3	58	119:84	92
107:4	59	120–34	7
107:4–32	58	120	7
107:7	59, 62	121	92
107:8	30, 77	123	7
107:10–16	57	125	80
107:12	60, 61	125:1	80
107:13	60	128:5	34
107:15	30, 77	129:5	34
107:16	60	130	7, 83
107:17–22	58	132:13	34
107:17	61	132:15	87
107:18	61	135:9	101
107:20–32	58	135:21	34
107:21	30, 77	136	7
107:23	61	136:15	101
107:25–27	62	137	7, 43, 50

Psalms (cont.)

137:1–4	50
137:1	50
137:2	50, 68
137:3	50
137:5–6	50, 51
137:6	51
137:7–9	50, 51
137:7	51
137:8	51
137:9	51
138	7
139	7, 43
141:5	78
142	5, 7
142:7	83
143	83
143:3	22
143:9	83
145	7
145:1	5, 89
145:8	77
146:10	34
149	7, 43
149:1	89
149:2	89
151	7

Proverbs

11:12	74
11:28	69
15:16	72
17:28	74
23:5	71
26:23	40

Qohelet

1:2	75
1:14	75
2;1	75
2:15	75
2:17	75
2:19	75
2:21	75
2:26	75

Tobit

1:17–19	41
13:6	27

Sirach

4:27—5:8	70
50:1–29	81

1 Maccabees

2:24	28
7:13	28

Matthew

5:5	71
6:26	89
7:13	38
7:16	106
7:24	63
8:11	54
10:28	80
11:19	106
26:25	35
27:3	35
25:31–46	84, 99
27:46	23

Mark

3:19	35
4:39	62
15:35–36	24

Luke

2:16	80
13:3	96
13:5	96
14:28	95
20:42	1
22:48	35
23:23	103
23:46	84

John

1:1–14	73
1:14	43

3:3	96
3:8	55
4:20–22	81
4:21	106
6:71	35
9:1–3	60
12:4	35
13:2	35
18:2	35
18:5	35
21:25	106

Acts

1:16	35
1:20	1
2:36	99
19:24–28	14
20:35	100

Romans

1:19–20	73
2:4	97
2:5	97
2:13	98
2:22	100
3:4	32
11:29	79
12:19	43
15:11	41

1 Corinthians

10–14	14, 101
11:3	99
15:27–28	67

2 Corinthians

8–9	33

Ephesians

2:1	13
5:18–19	14
5:18	13
5:19	14
5:21	99

Colossians

3:16	13, 98

1 Thessalonians

5:19–21	101

Hebrews

2:6–7	67
2:9	67

James

1:6	95
1:22	98
3:5	69

1 John

2:20	101
3:10	101
4:1	101

Revelation

4:1–7	100
4:6	65

www.ingramcontent.com/pod-product-compliance
Lightning Source LLC
Chambersburg PA
CBHW070908160426
43193CB00011B/1403